FOX

FOX

THE LIFE OF
CHARLES JAMES FOX

STANLEY AYLING

JOHN MURRAY

First published in 1991
by John Murray (Publishers) Ltd
50 Albemarle Street, London W1X 4BD

British Library Cataloguing in Publication Data

Ayling, Stanley
  Fox: The life of Charles James Fox.
  I. Title
  941.07092

ISBN 0-7195-4720-2

Typeset in 11/13pt Palatino
Printed and set in Great Britain by
Butler & Tanner Ltd, Frome
and London

*You know I have a natural propensity to
what some people call rebels.*

Charles Fox to Mrs Armistead, 1789

Let him do what he will, I must love the dog.

Edward Gibbon to Lord Sheffield, 1793

CONTENTS

ILLUSTRATIONS

The author and publisher would like to thank the following for permission to reproduce illustrations: 1, 2, 14 Private Collection; 3, 4, 6, 7, 10, 12, 16, 18 National Portrait Gallery; 5 Her Majesty the Queen; 9 National Gallery of Ireland; 11 Yale Center for British Art, Paul Mellon Collection. The cartoons on pp. 28, 94, 184 and 222 are by James Gillray.

FOXES AND LENNOXES

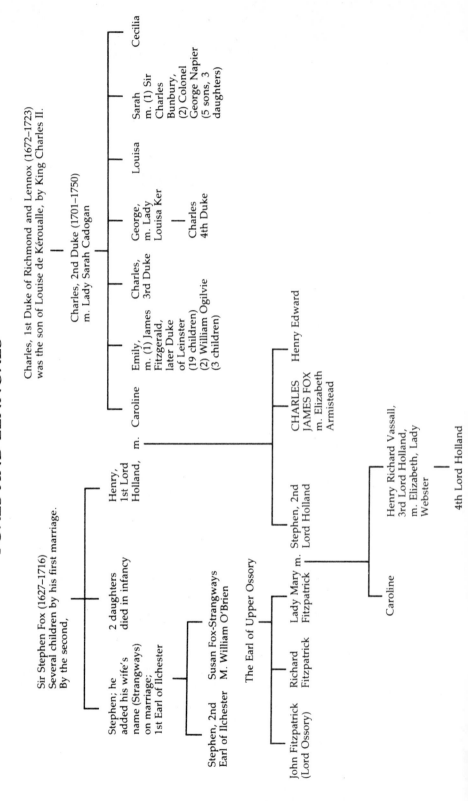

Charles, 1st Duke of Richmond and Lennox (1672–1723) was the son of Louise de Kéroualle, by King Charles II.

Charles, 2nd Duke (1701–1750) m. Lady Sarah Cadogan

Caroline   Emily, m. (1) James Fitzgerald, later Duke of Leinster (19 children) (2) William Ogilvie (3 children)   Charles, 3rd Duke   George, m. Lady Louisa Ker   Louisa   Sarah m. (1) Sir Charles Bunbury, (2) Colonel George Napier (5 sons, 3 daughters)   Cecilia

Charles 4th Duke

Sir Stephen Fox (1627–1716) Several children by his first marriage. By the second,

Henry, 1st Lord Holland,

2 daughters died in infancy

Stephen; he added his name (Strangways) on marriage; 1st Earl of Ilchester

Susan Fox-Strangways M. William O'Brien

Stephen, 2nd Earl of Ilchester

The Earl of Upper Ossory

John Fitzpatrick (Lord Ossory)   Richard Fitzpatrick   Lady Mary m. Stephen, 2nd Fitzpatrick   Lord Holland

m. CHARLES JAMES FOX m. Elizabeth Armistead   Henry Edward

Caroline

Henry Richard Vassall, 3rd Lord Holland, m. Elizabeth, Lady Webster

4th Lord Holland

1

ORIGINS AND
BEGINNINGS

On both sides of his parentage, Charles Fox's antecedents relate directly to Charles II. His mother was that monarch's great-granddaughter (by his Breton mistress Louise de Kéroualle, Duchess of Portsmouth); and Sir Stephen Fox, his father's father, had risen from the humblest origins to extremes of wealth by long and meritorious service to Charles II from the earliest days of his exile, after Cromwell had apparently extinguished for ever the Stuart cause by his victory at Worcester in 1651.

Sir Stephen Fox (1627–1716), the founder of the Fox fortunes, was the remarkable man who, by a little luck and a great deal of talent and enterprise, rose to become by the end of Charles II's reign the wealthiest commoner in the entire country, and this – again remarkable, surely – without losing his reputation for amiability and straight dealing. He was born the seventh of a large family in Farley, near Salisbury, the same little village in whose church – a fine new building of his own donation – he chose later to be buried. His parents were cottagers, not poverty-stricken but poor enough, nevertheless claiming small gentlefolk as relatives, and locally allowed much respect for the manner in which they reared their children.[1] At the age of 6 Stephen Fox was sent to stay with his great-uncle, who lived in Salisbury's cathedral close, and he attended the choir school there until he was 13. Then he was off to join his elder brother, who had already gained employment as chapel-keeper and organist in the Court at Richmond. Thus began a career which was to last sixty-two years, not ending until his retirement at the beginning of Anne's reign. In all he was to serve five monarchs, six if we are to include Queen Anne, at whose coronation he assisted by leading the procession of commoners.

During the decade of the civil wars, he was employed as page-boy by various members of the royalist nobility, sometimes in company with this same brother. After spells in the Netherlands, France, and Jersey with Queen Henrietta and Prince Charles, he returned briefly to spend one happy winter at Farley; married; and then, with his wife, elected to return to France, after the final royalist defeat at Worcester, to join the service of the by that time exiled Charles. This former assistant choir-keeper, successively then 'gentleman of the horses', 'clerk of the stables', and 'clerk of the kitchen', now found himself suddenly promoted to be Charles's *'maître d'hotel'* – effectively manager of the chaotic finances of the King in exile – having it seems been recommended for this post by his fellow-Wiltshireman Sir Edward Hyde, the future Chancellor and historian Lord Clarendon. Fox, so Clarendon wrote in his *History of the Rebellion*, was 'a young man ... very well qualified with languages, and all other parts of clerkship, honesty, and discretion'. Further qualities which Clarendon singled out were his industry and modesty. Most importantly of all, as Lord Ormond reminded the still exiled King six years later, 'Mr Fox knows to a stiver what money you can depend on'.[2]

At the Restoration in 1660, Fox was rewarded for his services; first, with an appointment to the Board of Green Cloth, which handled the financial administration of the royal Household, and then to the pay-mastership of the King's Guards. A standing army, small though it was, was still a great and potentially alarming novelty; an *unpaid* army would present acute political danger; and Charles II's Treasury, inheriting an obsolescent structure of taxation, lacked the money to pay. What Fox, therefore, now undertook was to raise that money. 'Undertook', very precisely: Fox assumed for Charles II what came to be known as the 'Great Undertaking' for the payment, first, of the Foot Guards and, eventually, of all the royal Guards and Garrisons. He was given the right to take 5 per cent for himself of that part of the pay which came from the public purse; but the remainder he was to raise by his own enterprise. To that extent the army's finances were thus 'privatized'. As Undertaker (Paymaster) for the Forces, Fox showed himself to be a brilliantly successful entrepreneur, while performing at the same time an indispensable public service. To his lucrative paymastership he then proceeded to add the cashiership of that vital branch of tax collection, the Excise. Not only did he raise very large sums of money for the state (for which he had to pledge his own credit as collateral security), but his wealth soon becoming immense, he was able also to lend money privately at very profitable, though never exorbitant, rates of interest, a good deal of it to the highest in the land in need of ready cash; much too to the Treasury itself, which like all government treasuries was similarly and perpetually in need.

He lent, he borrowed, he invested; and, of course, like everyone else of that day seeking status, he put a large proportion of his investment into houses and lands. Conveniently near to his handsome official apartments in Whitehall, he took a large country house at Chiswick, which he later demolished, rebuilding during 1683 within the same grounds a new and grander house handsomely furnished and embellished (by among others Antonio Verrio and Grinling Gibbons) costing him a little over £7,000. By Evelyn's account he did it to please his wife. When Evelyn dined with Fox at this time, he was impressed both by the house and by the 'sweete' man himself: both 'vertuous and very religious', he proclaimed him.[3] And as for his wealth, Evelyn thought that Fox must be worth perhaps £200,000, a very large sum indeed then, and all of it 'honestly gotten and unenvied, which is next to a miracle'. Pepys too writes of dining once with that 'fine gentleman' Sir Stephen Fox, 'and his lady, a fine woman, and seven of the prettiest children … that ever I saw'. 'A very genteel dinner', records Pepys, 'and in great state and fashion, and excellent discourse'.[4]

Fox also built himself a second country mansion at Redlynch (near Bruton, in Somerset) on a manor which he had earlier acquired for £8,700. In fact by the mid-1680s he had bought or leased some thirty country properties in Wiltshire and just beyond into Somersetshire, including one large Wiltshire estate at Water Eaton which cost him £20,000. He purchased also Hungerford Market (in London, roughly the site of the modern Charing Cross Station), a dozen or so more manors, lands, farms, and advowsons, mostly in Wiltshire but some further afield. One of the manors was his home village of Farley, where eventually he was to found a 'hospital' (or almshouse) and a charity school, as well as build the new church.*

A better-known monument to Fox's memory is Chelsea Hospital, the famous retreat for soldiers too infirm for further service. The building itself was to the designs of Wren, but the idea for this most necessary humanitarian project, which was to save many old soldiers from beggary,

---

* The fine Wren-style church, with its Fox family tombs and memorial tablets, including one to Charles James Fox himself, has as its close neighbour the quietly dignified old almshouse, still actively functioning. The charity school failed to survive long.

came from King Charles himself – *not* Nell Gwyn, despite the persistent legend – while the financing and supervision of it, with the expenditure of a good deal of his own time and money, came from Fox. In this he took justifiable pride. 'The King was pleased to say', he wrote, 'the Thursday before his sickness (that carryd him off) that Fox and hee had done this great work, upon wch I made modest answere, whereupon he was pleased to turne to the company that attended him, and told them that I was the person that had performed that work without any charge out of the Treasury.'[5]

Most of his building of houses and purchase of estates came to a close by the 1680s, when he was in his fifties, and by then he had ceased to be Paymaster. But his parliamentary and administrative career continued throughout the reigns of James II and of William and Mary. For twenty-three years, with only two short breaks, he was a Lord Commissioner of the Treasury, being once, briefly, in 1696–7, the First Lord. In parliament, he represented at different times Salisbury, Cricklade, and Westminster.

It would be surprising if a man of such standing, such longevity, and from so large a family were found not to have secured positions and benefits for several of his kin; and this of course he did. Charles, the only one of his seven sons who passed the age of 20, was for instance Paymaster for a time; and other less close relations found in Sir Stephen a useful influence. One of them, a great nephew (in all, quite close relatives could then be numbered by the dozen) actually stood, by the time of Sir Stephen's retirement, to become the chief beneficiary of his will, though the daughters and sons-in-law and their families had by no means been forgotten. This great nephew's apparent good fortune was to be another *Stephen Fox*, and Sir Stephen was powerfully minded to see his own name perpetuated in proper style.

However, after seven years as a widower, he married a second wife, his bride being a lady of 'a strict rule of piety' who had recently been entertaining the 'spare hours' of his retirement by reading to him. 'I thought her conversation would bee usefull to my olde age' Fox wrote, ' ... being advanced in my 77 yeares.'[6] It did prove so indeed, and not only her conversation. The following year she bore him a son – Stephen again, of course – and then the year after, twins: a boy, Henry (Charles Fox's father) and a girl who died in infancy from a fall out of a window. A fourth child, another daughter who eventually married into the Digby family, was born during Fox's eightieth year.

As it turned out, he still had another decade of life in him, but the birth of a son bearing his own name occasioned a radical rewriting of his testamentary intentions. Under the terms of his new will, this latest Stephen was to inherit most of his father's property, including the new mansion at Redlynch, which was afterwards to become for a time his principal seat. Half a century later he would add a second barrel to his Fox surname. Marrying the 13-year-old Elizabeth Strangways-Horner, he later under the terms of her mother's will adopted the extra surname of Strangways, and gained thereby the extensive Strangways estates to add to the already far from meagre property inherited from Sir Stephen. By that time he was 54 and ennobled, the uncle of our Charles Fox (then aged 9): Stephen Fox-Strangways, first Earl of Ilchester, one of the great landowners of south-western England, his rich realm centred no longer upon his father's Redlynch but on the Strangways mansion of Melbury in neighbouring Dorset.

Sir Stephen's other son by his felicitous second marriage, Charles Fox's father Henry, came off, if less affluently, at least satisfactorily enough, inheriting an allowance until he reached the age of 21, a useful sinecure (the South Wales Receivership), leasehold property at Lambeth Wick to the south of the Thames, and an annuity of £70. This gave him in all an annual income of between £600 and £700, advanced after his mother's death in 1719 to some £900 – hardly great wealth by the standards of the Georgian aristocracy, but still a gentlemanly competence.

The two brothers were together at Eton and Oxford. Then, Henry, so it always used to be said, wasted his patrimony in riotous living during his twenties. Among his notable contemporaries it was for instance Lord Chesterfield who wrote of his enjoying 'the common vices of youth, gaming included', and biographers in general afterwards have tended to follow Chesterfield. Yet evidence of this wastrel behaviour is lacking, and Chesterfield's word, he being admittedly hostile, is in any case suspect. However, Fox did, like his brother and most of his well-heeled young contemporaries, spend time touring abroad, where his days and nights were hardly likely to have been altogether devoid of some expensive pleasures. What is demonstrable, from his brother's very full sporting diary,[7] is that at home he followed the usual pursuits of the Georgian country gentleman, often for instance joining the shooting parties (Stephen was a crack shot and brought damage over many years to the partridge and pheasant population of Wiltshire) with such companions as Charles Hanbury Williams and Thomas Winnington. It was partly through Winnington, a follower of Sir Robert Walpole, that Henry Fox first entered politics, becoming in 1735, at the age of 30, member of parliament for Hindon in Wiltshire, at just the time when his future rival and enemy, William Pitt, was being returned for Hindon's close neighbour, Old Sarum.

Henry Fox, like Winnington, was to remain a steady Walpole man and has therefore to be accounted a Whig, though since both government and much of the opposition, 'ins' and 'outs', were similarly 'Whigs', the description carries limited significance. What is clear is that Fox's industry, shrewdness, and managerial talent soon impressed Walpole, whose administration and those of his immediate successors Fox was to serve for over six years as Surveyor General of Works. In 1743, after Sir Robert Walpole's political day was at last over and he was advising the next prospective prime minister, Pelham, on the formation of his government, his recommendation was terse but decisive: 'Fox you cannot be without'. That year Henry Fox was appointed a Lord of the Treasury.

In the following year he married; and whereas his political progress had been sheltered from the general gaze, his marriage was to create a considerable public sensation. During 1743 he fell in love with the Duke of Richmond's eldest daughter Caroline, who warmly returned his affection. The Duke and his Duchess, however, the Duchess particularly, would not hear of the match, and Fox's protestations took no effect. In March 1774 he was writing, not for the first time, to the Duke:

> The Dss of Richmond told me I should thank her [for the refusal] six months hence. What makes her Grace think so I don't know, unless it is that I am so little known to her. But do's her Grace or you believe the same of Lady Caroline too? ... Do's your Grace think she could take a fancy lightly? Or that she can ever alter? Indeed, my Lord, she will not ...[8]

And she did not. Two months later, Fox (then 39) and Caroline (21) were secretly married, the Duke of Marlborough and Charles Hanbury Williams (who allowed them to use his house in Privy Gardens) being the only others present at the ceremony apart from the clergyman, who asked no unnecessary questions and according to Fox did not even know whom it was he was marrying. The fury of the bride's parents was made immediately and publicly manifest, and remained long unassuaged. If the Duke and Duchess had been outraged, London society was enjoyably scandalized. If the King's daughter (another Caroline) had been stolen, so Horace Walpole gossiped away to Horace Mann, 'there could not have been much more noise'; and seeing shock on the face of Secretary of State the Duke of Newcastle, his fellow Secretary Carteret concluded that at least 'our fleet or our army was beat, or Mons betrayed into the hands of the French'.[9]

Lady Caroline Lennox, now Lady Caroline Fox, if not quite King George's daughter, *was* not only the Duke of Richmond's daughter but King Charles II's great granddaughter too, and thus for Henry Fox no mean catch socially – politically too perhaps in the long term. His marriage link with the Lennox family would indeed have ramifications, political as well as personal, both for him and later for his son Charles. The elder of Lady Caroline's brothers, the third Duke of Richmond, would for many years play an important if often maverick role in the Whig politics of George III's reign. Her sister Lady Emily Lennox was soon to marry into one of the wealthiest and most powerful families of the Irish Protestant ascendancy, her first husband* being James Fitzgerald, who would become Duke of Leinster (the only duke in all Ireland). Another very much younger sister, Lady Sarah Lennox, would one day so take the fancy of the newly acceded young George III that for a heady few months Henry Fox would even be able to convince himself that he might soon become brother-in-law to the Queen of England. But Lady Caroline herself was not just royally descended and influentially related. She proved to be a woman of shrewd judgement and cultivated intelligence; she read widely and critically in English and French; was a loving mother to those three of Henry Fox's sons who survived; and remained a staunch support when in his disappointed and embittered latter days he convinced himself that the entire world, from the King downwards, was leagued against him. Indeed Lady Caroline's judgement of character was frequently sounder than her husband's. Thus she came to have a strong dislike for some of those members of parliament with whom he closely associated, the regimental agent John Calcraft, for instance, or Welbore Ellis, or Richard Rigby – particularly Rigby of the Bedford group of Whigs. As she wrote to her sister in Ireland:

> I am not partial to that sort of people, I own they don't improve upon acquaintance ... indeed I don't like any of them in private life, I'm sure ... Mr Fox with all his good sense does not know people's characters at all, and ... admires people too much for being good company and clever, which after all is nothing valuable unless it's attended with as much good nature as he has with it.[10]

---

* She had two husbands and by them twenty-two children. One of her sons was Lord Edward Fitzgerald, the Irish rebel who died in prison during the Irish troubles of 1798.

Good-natured Henry Fox undoubtedly was. If as a politician he always thought in terms of place, patronage, and profit, and if his ready humour usually carried with it a strong flavour of cynicism, he was (as Horace Walpole conceded), however 'dark and troubled', nevertheless 'an agreeable man'.* Unfortunately for his reputation he could sometimes make even his kindness sound cynical.[11]

He was Secretary at War between 1746 and 1755. During that phase in his career, however, the matter with which he became most closely and contentiously involved concerned nothing military or even primarily political. When in 1753 Lord Chancellor Hardwicke's bill to outlaw clandestine marriages was being debated, it was Fox who led the Commons opposition (without success) and incurred much resentment by the extravagant hostility of his attacks, sometimes pointedly personal, upon the movers of the bill. Hardwicke himself, the chief target, became and remained a powerful enemy. Hardwicke's Marriage Act was not without one serious shortcoming: it failed to allow for the objection of many Dissenters and Catholics to being married according to the Anglican ritual. This however was not the ground upon which Fox attacked it. For him it was an affront to his own romance. His fierce dislike of this (on the whole necessary) measure is easily understandable in the light of his own clandestine marriage and its notably happy outcome, but politically it did him no good. It did however set up a mast to which future Foxes would nail their colours. Twice in the next generation, in 1772 and again in 1781, Charles Fox's filial loyalty would lead him to attempt the overturning of Hardwicke's Act, and in the following generation the 3rd Lord Holland would try again, and of course fail again like his uncle Charles and grandfather Henry.

The Foxes were always a close-knit family, and it is therefore to be expected that Henry, as Secretary at War, would have done what he could for his brother Stephen, Lord Ilchester. It must surely have been Henry's influence, and his keen nose for the spoils that went with influence, that secured for Ilchester, from the secret service fund, a salary for a Joint Comptrollership of Army Accounts. For nearly thirty years (1747–76) Ilchester could continue to receive income from this office, although evidence for any work he performed for it does not appear. Ilchester also managed to draw another £400 a year as 'additional salary', though it has

---

* The part played later by Fox in savaging the Whig opposition in 1762 evoked from Walpole a very different verdict: Fox was 'cruel, revengeful, daring, subtle'.

been suggested that this may have been a sort of 'retaining fee' for his interest at the parliamentary borough of Shaftesbury, in his home county of Dorset.[12]

On Pelham's death in 1754, and after the period of protracted negotiation and intrigue which ensued, Fox found himself without real power in the next administration: Secretary of State indeed, but with no share in the distribution of patronage, those vital 'loaves and fishes'. Eventually, at the formation of the Newcastle-Pitt ministry in 1757, on the threshold of Pitt's years of glory, Fox was content to accept the Paymastership, the office his father had held all those years before. 'The Pay Office', wrote Lady Caroline to her sister in Ireland, 'is all his ambition as well as mine' – which Fox's own words corroborate: 'the situation of all others I like best'.[13]

He had good reason to. He had obtained a post of no influence but great potential profit. Officially it was worth an annual £3,000, but the Paymaster was traditionally permitted to invest for his private enrichment any balances held while payment was pending: and even to 'play the market' with them. Thereby, it has been estimated, Fox's unofficial profits during the coming seventeen years amounted to about £400,000, a prodigious sum then. Fox's appetite for the nation's riches would always bear a strong resemblance to his animal namesake's for the chicken run, though he contended that the suddenness of his rise to such an extreme of affluence was to a degree fortuitous. In a *Memoir* written immediately after the end of his political career in 1763, he claimed:

> The sudden and great rise of stocks has made me richer than ever I intended or desir'd to be. Obloquy generally attends money so got, but with how much reason in all cases let this simple account of my gains show. The Government borrows money at 20 per cent discount, I am not consulted or concern'd in making the bargain. I have as Pay Master great sums in my hands, which ... must either lye dead in the Bank, or be employ'd by me. I lend this to the Government in 1761. A peace is thought certain ... My very bad opinion of Mr Pitt makes me think it will not be concluded. I sell out, and gain greatly. In 1772 I lend again; a peace comes ... I gain greatly ...[14]

What somewhat marred his satisfaction at netting these not entirely 'unintended' gains was his failure for a long time to obtain the peerage which he yearned for and thought he merited. After he had been in his office four or five years, with a new monarch by then on the throne, Lady Caroline was telling her sister, 'Mr Fox wants nothing but the peerage'.[15] But the most that he could manage at that time to win from the young

George III (who powerfully disliked him)* was a peerage *for his wife*. Lady Caroline became Baroness Holland in 1762.

By that time, her three surviving sons Stephen (Ste), Charles, and Henry (Harry) were aged 17, 13, and 7 respectively. Lady Holland's newly won title derived from the romantic old mansion, just west of Kensington Palace, which Fox first leased in the mid-1740s. But Charles Fox had not been born there. His father is reported in 1748 as 'daily improving' his new property, and even at the beginning of 1749 the house was still so beset by builders and decorators, that Charles was born (on 24 January, new style), not at home but at Conduit Street, three miles away, then in London's western suburbs. He did however spend most of his childhood at Holland House. It had been built during the reign of James I; had once been the seat of the Earls of Warwick; but had then declined in dignity, becoming a set of 'apartments'; and was, by the time Henry Fox acquired it, standing neglected and empty. He proceeded to spend much money upon it and, according to an early tourists' guide of 1748, 'restored it, repaired and beautified it, embellished the gardens, enclosed the park, and made a coach road into Acton Road and a coach-way through his own grounds from the turnpike to the house'.[16]

A lifetime later, Sir Walter Scott was lamenting that so fine a place would not last for ever. It would be a sad day, he thought, 'when this ancient house must come down,† and give way to rows and crescents. One is chiefly affected by the air of seclusion which is spread around the domain'.[17] Horace Walpole, too, thought it 'a brave old house'. Fox at first did not buy it outright, preferring to rent it until 1767 when he finally became its owner − and then made it over immediately to his wife. He paid 'a great deal more' for it, he said, than anything but her 'extreme fondness for it could make it worth'. This was at the very time when his beckoning fancies and extravagances were in fact drawing him away from Kensington to Kent − to Kingsgate on the North Foreland coast, 'another name for Paradise', he claimed − where, in his sixties by then and chronically unwell, he would soon be engaged in building a second great mansion for his days of proposed retirement. This was to be an ambitious Doric-

---

*This dislike − hatred even − dated from his days as Prince of Wales, when Fox was under the patronage of 'Butcher' Cumberland, George's 'wicked uncle', who was regarded by George and his mother the Dowager Princess of Wales as posing a possible danger to his undisputed accession to the throne.

† Holland House finally 'came down' as a result of air bombardment during the Second World War. Its park is now public ground.

porticoed affair inspired allegedly by Cicero's Formian villa, housing a rich collection of statues and objects of *virtu* imported from Italy; with its own landing stage and row of cannons on the terrace facing the sea, its 'conventual' quarters for guests, complete with 'cloisters', and the then almost obligatory 'ruined castle' in the grounds (conveniently housing Fox's stables).

That dream of a luxury retreat was not yet. At the mid-century he was far from any thoughts of retreating at all, in these his thrusting Holland House years. And already, even before he had won the gold-mine of the Paymastership, the Fox finances, despite the heavy expenditure on Holland House improvements, were prospering, being at this time further buttressed by family bequests to Lady Caroline worth £15,000 and by her husband winning £10,000 in a lottery.

A boy had been born to them in 1745 and, being a Fox son and heir, was of course named Stephen. He was very delicate from the outset, and his chances of survival were not viewed with any confidence. Indeed he was destined never to see his thirtieth birthday, and throughout his life was to remain an ever-renewable source of worry, to his mother especially. Latterly, during his twenties, the worst of her anxieties for him would stem from his ungovernable passion for gaming; before that, from the ill health, and particularly the nervous affliction of *chorea*, or St Vitus's dance, which seldom left him for long. Once, when Richard Rigby, who was then a parliamentary ally of Fox's, visited him at Holland House in 1753, when Stephen was 8, he wrote:

> I dined at Holland House, where, though I drank claret with the master of it from dinner till two o'clock in the morning, I could not wash away the sorrow he is in at the shocking condition his eldest son is in, a distemper they call *Sanvitoss dance* (I believe I spell it damnably) but it is a convulsion that I think must kill him.[18]

Then in January 1759, when Stephen was 13, Lady Caroline was writing:

> Dear Sister, ... I came here [to Eton] Tuesday with Ste, for whose state of health I am at present under the most cruel anxiety, as he has a return of St Vitus's dance ... enough to alarm me very much and fill me with a thousand melancholy ideas. I believe the fox-hunting at Goodwood brought it on.[19]

And two months later: 'Ste is very bad again, falls away most excessively, and is so alter'd; indeed ... when I exert my spirits for a time I feel more unhappy than I can express afterwards'. And when after some weeks he was 'a great deal better thank God', she was still afraid that 'to those who have not seen him before he would appear very bad'.[20]

2

A LIBERTARIAN
EDUCATION

The Foxes' second surviving son, Charles James, was also at first thought delicate, but very soon was thriving, and showing moreover the liveliest evidences of precocity. It is a little too simple to say (as has usually been said) that Stephen became his mother's favourite child and Charles his father's. But certainly, and naturally enough because of Stephen's extreme vulnerability, Lady Caroline had him always first in her thoughts, while her husband was soon almost lost for words to express his delight at having fathered a child of such quick intelligence and amiable disposition as little Charles. This said, they were both good parents, and good to all three of their sons. The youngest, Harry, was not born until 1755 – he was ten years younger than Stephen – and when he was 4, by which time his two elder brothers (together with their two Irish cousins) were at Eton, Lady Caroline was writing: 'Our [four] Etonians keep well I hear, God send they may! My Charles is a sweet boy, and so is Harry in his way, but I don't yet feel about him as I [do] about Ste and Charles. I suppose I shall.'[1] She clearly thought that she ought to.

Charles, when still very young indeed, was already impressing – and charming – all who saw him, as he would be doing for the rest of his life; and impressing his father most of all. 'I dined at home today *tête-à-tête* with Charles', Fox wrote when Charles was barely 3 years old. 'I grow immoderately fond of him.' He was so sharp, so 'pert', so 'argumentative', yet so sunny-natured and 'sensible'. 'I will not deny', the adult Charles Fox once admitted, 'that I *was* a very clever little boy. What I heard made an impression on me and was of use to me afterwards'.[2] By the age of 7 he was reading omnivorously and was already stage-struck; the passion for amateur theatricals would be long-lasting. Did he occasionally show an over-hasty temper? Never mind, said his father, 'he is a very sensible little fellow, and will learn to cure himself'.

It was Henry's considered judgement that repression and good education did not go together. 'Let nothing be done to break his spirit', he said; 'the world will do that soon enough'. There are plenty of tales of his over-indulgence of his children, and especially of Charles, at Holland House – many and perhaps most of them retailed or improved upon by one or other of Fox's many enemies, further to discredit him. But undoubtedly Charles was brought up under the most libertarian of domestic regimes. If young Charles was proposing to do something wanton or destructive, Henry Fox's attitude was 'Well, if you must, I suppose you must'. And he regarded as most important that one should never break any promise, however casually made, to a child. Here the best known of the relevant anecdotes, possibly apocryphal, possibly not, tells how his father had promised Charles that he should be present to see one of the brick walls at Holland House demolished, and had it rebuilt and demolished a second time because Charles had missed the original spectacle. To what extent this early upbringing – a combination of being seen as a charming prodigy and being allowed freedom to the point of licence – affected Charles Fox's adult character must remain guesswork. If it supplied defects, perhaps it also produced the virtues of the defects. If it is fair to describe Henry Fox as belonging to the educational avant-garde of his day, his wife too seems at least to have flirted with it. 'I have just finished Rousseau's *Emile, où de l'Education*', she writes in 1762; 'there are more paradoxes, more absurdities, and more striking pretty thoughts in it than any book I ever read ... Indeed by what I can judge it don't deserve being so violently abused and the character of the author being so run down as it is ...'* A few weeks later, she continues,

> Dear little Harry [her youngest] is a pleasant child ... he really works very hard all day out of doors, which is very wholesome and quite according to Monsr Rousseau's system; he eats quantities of fish, and is so happy and so pleased all day. At night we depart a little from Monsr Rousseau's plan, for he reads fairy-tales and learns geography on the Beaumont wooden maps; he is vastly quick at learning that or anything else.[3]

---

*Five years later she decided 'upon reflection' that his writings were 'so very dangerous, so very destructive of all principles ... both moral and religious that I hate to think I could be drawn in for a time to admire him'.

At least there seems poor evidence to support the elder William Pitt's sour comment that Henry Fox 'educated his children without the least regard to morality, and with such extravagant vulgar indulgence, that the great change which has taken place among our youth has been dated from the time of his sons going to Eton'.

Charles Fox was not at Eton until he had reached the age of 9. Before that, he had been at the fashionable little school of Monsieur Pampelonne at Wandsworth in Surrey, in company with his two Fitzgerald cousins William and George. 'I beg to know', his father had written when Charles was still only 7, 'what disposition Charles comes up in, and which you would have me encourage; his going immediately to Wandsworth, or staying till he can go to Eton'; and, a little later, 'I was going to dine *tête-à-tête* with Charles, and then I was sent for to the House of Commons. It proved a false alarm, and only prevented me dining with him, but not playing at picket with him ... He is infinitely engaging, and clever, and pretty. He coughs a little ... Would it not be best to persuade him to go to Wandsworth for his health?' No persuasion was needed. 'Charles determines to go to Wandsworth', his father declared.[4] And Lady Caroline wrote:

> I pity you, dear siss, from my heart, being obliged to part with [her two boys, the Fitzgerald cousins], but I do think Wandsworth School is the best nursery for delicate children in the world. I pity you, for I can hardly accustom myself to the absence of my two boys (Ste indeed I live in continual fears about), but sweet Charles I miss vastly.[5]

Charles had gone to Wandsworth ahead of his cousins, and a letter to his brother Ste, already at Eton, tells us:

> ... Harry sends his love and a kiss. I chose to come to school before the Fitzgeralds, and I am very glad of it ... I see my mama as often and oftener than they do, for I come home every Saturday and I shall be able to go to Eton before them. Pray send Fitzgerald's cricket bat as soon as you can.[6]

Soon after he had arrived at Eton, and still aged 9, he was commissioning his mother to deliver a 'message' to his cousin Lord Offaly (George Fitzgerald). He 'begged' that George would 'make himself exceedingly perfect in the Greek grammar', since it was 'of more consequence towards making learning there [at Eton] than can be imagined'. Lady Caroline complied, and continued, 'I fancy Ophaly loves riding so much he will be a great rider of horses at Eton; it's much the fashion there. Charles don't love it at all, but Ste is most passionately fond of it and it certainly does him good . . .'

During his years at Eton, Charles made precocious advance on several fronts. He rapidly acquired an all-round proficiency, but especially in the classical languages and literatures, in mathematics, and in French, to which he soon added Italian. It was no hardship for one so gifted, so in love with learning, to work hard, and this he did. Lord John Russell, in his biography of Fox, tut-tutted very censoriously about 'desultory habits of study' and – 'what was much worse' – a 'fondness for the pleasures of unbridled youth', having in mind the latter years at Eton (when Fox was 14 or 15) and then his time at Oxford as an undergraduate. However, these mid-Victorian tongue-clickings are not to be taken too solemnly.[7] Fox's youthful pleasures, at least in his earlier Etonian years, read innocently enough, even when it indeed becomes clear that in affairs of the heart, as in matters of the mind, he was away to a very prompt start. It seems, for instance, that by $12\frac{1}{2}$ he was much enamoured of his pretty cousin Lady Susan Strangways (Lord Ilchester's daughter) and writing love poetry in Latin to prove it. 'Oh Lord, only think, I had almost forgot the most important thing', wrote Charles's aunt Lady Sarah Lennox,* in October 1761: 'Charles Fox has made some lattin verses . . . the purpose of them is to desire a pigeon to fly to his love Susan, and carry her a letter from him, and that if it makes haste, it will please both Venus its mistress and him. There now, are you not proud, to have your name wrote in a Scholar's exercise?' A 'pretty' translation made specially for Lady Susan followed later.[8] At this stage, at least, Fox seems hardly to be plumbing even the shallows of depravity.

During the Eton holidays, Lady Susan, Lady Sarah and Charles saw much of one another, sharing as they did an enthusiasm for the private theatricals which were then fashionable in the great houses of the aristocracy, several of which, like Holland House itself, had their own theatre. When he had only just reached the age of 12, for instance, Charles was in the cast of the Holland House production of Rowe's *Jane Shore*, the performance in which Lady Sarah's beauty so dazzled the visiting Horace Walpole. For such occasions professional players, sometimes the finest and the highest-paid, would be hired to flesh out the bones of the amateur

---

* Lady Sarah Lennox was twenty-two years younger than her sister Lady Caroline. Although she was Charles Fox's aunt, she was less than four years his senior. A few months previously, the young George III had shown every sign of wanting to marry her, but his prime minister, his prudence, and his sense of duty combined to direct him instead towards Charlotte of Mecklenburg.

cast; such enterprises would be undertaken with the utmost seriousness, alike by the performers and their select audiences, consisting in the main usually of relatives and friends.

In this year 1761, it happened that Lady Susan was not among the cast rehearsing at Christmas for the Holland House play, which appears to have caused an already love-sick Charles, just short of 13, a degree of disgruntlement. He was to play Zanga, in Edward Young's *The Revenge*. A few months later this 'tragedy of ungoverned passion' was given at Holland House on three nights in April 1762, when 'Charles really play'd most astonishingly well' (at least by his mother's account); 'there never was a play better acted'. Yet back at Christmas-time Lady Sarah had been complaining to Lady Susan, 'Charles is as disagreeable ... as he can be ... He won't learn his part perfect, won't rehearse, and, in short, shews plainly that your not being here is the reason he won't enter into it'.[9] A letter from Lady Caroline a few months later confirms the state of her son's emotions: 'Lady Sue is his passion'. However, Lady Susan, to the chagrin of her parents and the shock of respectable society, at length eloped with one of the hired professional actors, the handsome William O'Brien; and when they were both old ladies, more than half a century later, Lady Sarah and Lady Susan recalled to one another young Charles's anguished cry of affront: 'She liked him better than me! Why did she like him better than me?'

By the time of the elopement, Charles was just 15. There would be no shortage of other goddesses for him to bow down before. At Christmas-tide 1764, Lady Sarah, now married to Sir Charles Bunbury, was writing to her 'disgraced' friend Lady Susan, who with her husband had emigrated (with Henry Fox's help) to America:

> Charles is in town, and is violently in love with the Duchess of Hamilton [who had been Elizabeth Gunning, one of the most celebrated beauties of her day]; think of his riding out to see her. You know how he hates it; he is all humbleness and respect and never leaves her. I am vastly glad to see him improve so much, he is now quite manly, and is very much liked, I think, in the world; he is a sweet boy ...[10]

Lady Sarah herself, no mean beauty, was not averse to being worshipped a little, or as she put it 'toad-eaten'. Her married state by no means forbade flirting with men other than her (as so many thought) less than attentive husband. One such was the young Earl of Carlisle, a close friend of Fox's. He was the 'most agreeable young man I ever saw', declared Lady Sarah;

and for a time, too, she was proclaiming that she had 'grown very thick' with Ste Fox. 'Charles is mad as a dog', she wrote, 'and takes it very ill of me'. A little later there is mention of another inamorata-at-a-distance, her name being mysteriously rendered by Lady Sarah as 'Mrs Burrer'd'. Fox tried to be 'presented' to her, with no success. 'Poor soul, he is in a piteous taking.'[11]

When Charles was 10 years old, his mother had been remarking fondly but sagely upon the way his character was shaping, and contrasting it with that of 14-year-old Stephen, who was, alas, still looking '*abattu* and languid':

> Tho' I love Ste better, I could with much more ease part with his company for some time, and Harry's too, than Charles's; you can have no idea how companionable a child he is, nor how infinitely engaging to us he is. If Mr Fox and I are alone, either of us, or only us two, he never leaves one, enters into any conversation going forwards, takes his book if we are reading, is vastly amused with any work going on out of doors or indoors ... will sit and read by me when my stomach is bad and I lie down between sleeping and waking, and is in every respect the most agreeable companion. I know you'll make allowances for my partiality, for these same qualities so pleasing to us often make him troublesome to other people. He will know everything, watches one if one wants to speak to anybody, and is too apt to give his opinion about everything, which tho' generally a very sensible one, makes him appear pert to other people ...[12]

Poor Ste, having to be 'idle at home', was at

> an awkward age; he can't amuse himself as Charles can with reading five or six hours together, nor with seeing the [building and gardening] works go on here, which Charles can also do ... Do you know that Charles never leaves his Papa when there are any of the lawyers ... with him, and is *au fait* of it all as much as anybody but the law people are. Is this not an odd turn at his age?[13]

Fox's years at Eton coincided approximately with the duration of the Seven Years War, the latest (and at the time apparently decisive) phase in the protracted hostilities, military, naval, and above all colonial, which began with the wars against Louis XIV's France, when Sir Stephen Fox was Lord of the Treasury to William III, and did not end until the Battle of Waterloo, when Charles Fox had been nine years in the grave. Henry Fox's role in the Seven Years War – apart from amassing a fortune as Paymaster of the Forces – was to be the parliamentary instrument through which it was eventually ended. In achieving this, he touched briefly the highest point of his political power and, by exercising it, of his unpopularity.

George III had acceded; had married; and had chosen as his chief minister his old tutor and admired friend, Lord Bute. The war had been essentially won – in the Channel, the Atlantic, and the Mediterranean; in North America, and the West Indies; in India. Preliminaries of peace had been agreed, but there remained the task of persuading a possibly reluctant parliament, gorged with victories, to ratify the terms. The King and Bute were for the peace, but Bute sat in the House of Lords, and hence a Leader of the House of Commons was needed to force the matter through, by fair or if necessary rather less than fair means. The King disliked Fox, still regarding him as too closely connected to the Duke of Cumberland, of whom the old suspicions lingered. But both Bute and the King recognized in Fox a master of the arts of political management and, where required, of skulduggery, and the King had sufficient realism to accept that (as he put it) 'bad men' were sometimes necessary to effect desired results. There followed the parliamentary session of 1762–3, with Fox using all his tactical and manipulative skill, ruthlessly driving home his advantages, persuading the persuadable with the many thousands of money put at his disposal, securing the removal from their 'places' of many supporters of the Whig opposition. The King's purposes had been faithfully and efficiently served. And Fox was the best hated man in the Commons, as Bute was in the Lords.

It was generally assumed that Charles Fox, being so talented an offspring of so political an animal, would at no very distant day enter parliament. At much this time William Pitt, on a parallel assumption, was engaged in training *his* clever second son, still only a child, in the arts of oratory by standing him on a mounting-block in the grounds of his estate in Kent, and bidding him imagine that the surrounding trees were members of parliament to be declaimed to. Henry Fox's methods were different, but his ambition for his son's career was not. While still a schoolboy, Charles would be initiated into the atmosphere of the Commons by being occasionally taken there to listen to the debates and absorb the spirit of the place.

When Henry Fox first undertook the Leadership of the House in 1762 he had turned down the offer that he should accept with it the post of Secretary of State, on the grounds that the double responsibility would be too burdensome for his health. The Paymastership more than took care of his financial rewards; he had moreover already fallen in love with his vision of his new mansion at Kingsgate as he wished it to be; and he was looking forward impatiently to his seaside retirement. The one reward he did hunger after was a viscountcy or, if the King should prove grateful and generous, perhaps an earldom. (His brother had, several years previously, been moved up from the barony to the earldom of Ilchester). At first, as we have seen, all that was granted was a peerage for his wife, in April 1762.

Not for another twelve months would Lady Holland be able to have *Lord* Holland as husband, and even then the peerage so anxiously coveted – and, as he insisted, as good as promised – would be only a barony. For the last eleven years of his life, Charles Fox's father would be Baron Holland of Foxley in Wiltshire, a man in declining health harbouring a nagging resentment against his monarch, that monarch's ministers, and his own old political allies (Rigby, Calcraft, and Shelburne in particular; the antipathy to Shelburne was to be passed on to his son and would one day be politically significant). For the next three or four years he thought to blame Bute more than the King for the ingratitude and 'injustice' shown him, but after having finally been granted an audience at Court in 1767 he changed his mind:

> I saw obstinate, determined denial, without any reason given ... I have not been flattered even by a shuffling, promising answer, but told it would be very inconvenient to do it now, without being told why ...
> >   Of all Court service know the common lot,
> >   To-day 'tis done, to-morrow 'tis forgot.
> Don't ever, Charles, make any exception, or trust as I did. Well! I ... have nothing to do but to forget it. I trust I shall ... But my spirits are sometimes low.[14]

When the Earl of Bute, sick of the calumny and abuse constantly directed at him, decided in 1763 to retire from the premiership, he had recommended that the King should appoint Henry Fox as his successor. Overcoming an initial revulsion, George had come round (by March 1763, a month before the peerage was awarded) to the idea of accepting Fox, despite what he called 'his whole [corrupt] mode of government'. When he contemplated the political situation, he had decided that the possible alternatives to Fox – Newcastle, Devonshire, Hardwicke, Pitt, Grenville, Bedford, Legge, Halifax – were all as obnoxious or at best as unattractive. When it was suggested to him that Fox might actually reject the royal offer, George declared, 'He cannot refuse it'; but refuse Fox did. As his wife put it, he had reached 'a final determination' to be done with public life. 'Being a peer is not at all inconsistent', she wrote, 'with his keeping the Pay Office [which in fact he did, until 1765], indeed I feel happy at the thought of his being out of all other business.'[15]

Like a schoolboy released for the holidays after an unhappy term, he left for Kingsgate less than a week after he had become Lord Holland. From there he took his wife (travelling in her post-chaise on deck) and his sons Charles and Harry, via Calais – a four-hour 'tedious' crossing – to Spa. Even if the waters there should do him no good, the change of scene and the 'dissipation' might, so his wife hoped – the word's connotations were still largely innocent. As for herself, she had shrunk from leaving 'this lovely place', Holland House, in its springtime beauty, and had somewhat dreaded the journey; nevertheless she professed faith in the efficacy of the Spa waters for her chronic stomach ailment. And then, Charles? Were they wise to remove him, however temporarily, from Eton? They ran a risk; but 'if he returns to school very willingly, as he assures us he will in September next, I think no harm will be done, but rather good, as French will I hope have become easy to him. I have so high an opinion of his steadiness and understanding that I do flatter myself he will return to Eton and be the schoolboy again'.

Spa – Paris – Spa again, this time with Ste there too; the summer passed uneventfully. But Spa had gaming tables as well as 'Geronster waters'. In fact, gambling was 'the chief occupation' of the place – there was 'nothing else to be done'. Lady Holland herself took to playing *berlan*. And Ste, Ste especially, was so hooked on gambling that his mother could only express delight when he discovered an alternative attraction in making 'distant and humble love' first to Lord Spencer's wife,[16] and then to the 'vastly pretty' Miss Greville, later Mrs Crewe. Charles too was now being apprenticed to the vice which was to prove so irresistibly and damagingly attractive to him. His father misguidedly allowed him 5 guineas a night to gamble with. At the same time, his mother noted, 'he attach'd himself to every French coxcomb that came, admired and affected them'.[17]

Charles seems to have taken this continental 'coxcombry' back with him in September to Eton, where he is reported as affecting red-heeled shoes, Parisian velvet, and blue hair-powder – and to have earned himself, though for what offence we are not told, a flogging from Dr Barnard, the headmaster. But there is nothing to indicate that he failed to go on working hard. Lord Holland moreover was taking care that his son's political education suffered no neglect. When the furore over John Wilkes and

Number 45 of his *North Briton** reached the benches of the House of Commons, Holland made sure that his 14-year-old son was up in the Strangers' Gallery, listening and learning. He had himself just come back from Eton, where he had heard Charles in the public speaking exercises.

Charles wrote in mockery of himself as 'the *petit maître de Paris*', and he had enough common sense and self-criticism to see that education at Eton, however 'disagreeable' he said he was finding it, was going to be better for him than another jaunt to Paris at Christmas 1763. 'My mother will not be sorry to hear this', he wrote; and he told his father, 'I am resolved to stay [at Eton] until Christmas twelve month'; to be a good scholar 'is a glory you know I very much desire'. In the event he remained at Eton for only half that time, entering Hertford College, Oxford, as a gentleman commoner in October 1764. It had been promoted from Hart Hall to Hertford College only twenty-five years previously, by the reforming enterprise of Dr Newton, and its intellectual climate was perhaps not quite so torpid as that which Gibbon had found on going to Magdalen also as a gentleman commoner, some dozen years earlier. Certainly at Oxford Charles was to work strenuously, sometimes we are told up to ten hours a day, and to read omnivorously and voraciously 'as though', it was said, 'his bread depended on a fellowship'. All this was to the delight, and probably the initial astonishment, of his tutor William Newcome, who was later to become Archbishop of Armagh, and who was the writer of the often-quoted letter giving his approval to Charles' participating in another family expedition to France in 1765:

> Application like yours requires some intermission, and you are the only person with whom I have ever had connection to whom I could say this. I suspect that you will return with much keenness for Greek, and for lines and angles. As to trigonometry, it is a matter of entire indifference to the other geometricians ... whether they proceed to the other branches of mathematics immediately, or wait a term or two longer. You need not, therefore, interrupt your amusements by severe studies ... we shall stop until we have the pleasure of your company ...[18]

The study of mathematics was indeed one of Fox's chief pleasures at Oxford, partly as he said for its utility, but chiefly for its intrinsic interest.

---

* Wilkes, in the 45th issue of his *North Briton*, had accused George III's speech proroguing parliament of giving 'the sanction of his sacred name to the most odious measures' and in effect of *lying* when he declared the treaty under the Seven Years War to have been honourable to the Crown and beneficial to the people. The *North Briton*'s authors, printers and publishers were then arrested on a charge of seditious libel.

Classics of course lay at the educational centre, but history also engaged his always active mind. By his mother's account, Lord Holland considered that the history of France, in particular, was occupying too much of his son's time: 'Lord Holland says at Oxford he ought to study languages and things he can't so well study elsewhere'.

Although the attention paid in the old narratives to his youthful 'dissipation' seems disproportionate, he did of course waste a good deal of his father's money at the card table. For instance, 'I have been so foolish', he writes home, 'as to break all the good resolutions I had formed in regard to play, and have lost upwards of 80 guineas'. But this same 'dissipated' gambler – and of course before long he would be a very reckless gambler indeed – spent the greater part of one of his vacations with a contemporary and friend, Dickson, who later became Bishop of Down, and together

> they studied very hard, and their relaxation consisted in reading to one another, or by themselves, all the early dramatic poets of England; they spent their evenings for that purpose in the bookseller's shop, and I think I have heard Mr Fox say [it is his nephew writing] that there was no play extant, written, and published before the Restoration, that he had not read attentively.[19]

Fox and his friend Dickson were of the company for the next bout of theatricals, which were to be performed, not this time at Holland House, but on the estate of which Ste had just become the owner, at Winterslow in Wiltshire. This was only three miles away from the ancestral Fox village of Farley, and Lord Holland had bought it for his son and heir. Winterslow House and its amenities were still in the process of construction and 'improvement', and among the amenities, a hundred yards or so from the house, was 'a smart new play-house', where in August 1766 the Holland House young actors and actresses, with their friends and relations, were to present two plays, Dryden's *All for Love* (his version of *Antony and Cleopatra*), and *Rule a Wife and Have a Wife*. In the first, Fox was to play Antony to his aunt Sarah's Cleopatra; in the second, Ferez, the 'Copper Captain'. Ste, his wife, Lord Carlisle, and Harry Bunbury the artist and caricaturist were others in the cast. It was only a little while previously that Ste had married – indeed Winterslow House seems to have come as a wedding present. His wife had been Lady Mary Fitzpatrick, a daughter of the Earl of Upper Ossory. Cleopatra at this time was all admiration for her Antony: 'he improves every day, or rather the aimableness of his caracter appears every day, for 'tis all natural to him. You cannot imagine the comfort he is to both his father and his mother, and his constant attention to them is realy beyond what I can discribe.'[20]

In September 1766, the Hollands and their sons Charles and Harry left Kingsgate for Calais, and journeyed via Paris to Lyon, where they were joined by George Fitzgerald, Earl of Offaly, and later for a time by Ste Fox and his wife Mary. Ste was by this time dangerously addicted to high play; by now it was not so much his old nervous affliction or his asthma as his increasing deafness and compulsive gambling which gave occasion for worry. The greater part of the family tour, lasting in all eight months, was spent in Italy — Florence, Rome, Naples — and for much of the time the company split into two groups. In one, the more energetically inclined, there were Lord Holland and the boys. The profusion of servants and baggages and vehicles which the touring aristocracy employed in those days must have eased the rigours of travel, and Lord Holland was by now a somewhat sick man.* In the other and less adventurous group was Lady Holland. The Hollands returned home with Harry via Turin and Geneva in May 1767 leaving Charles abroad; but after a summer at Kingsgate they toured abroad again, mainly in the south of France, for a similar 8 months in 1767–8.

Fox's companions abroad during his first summer were the young Lord Fitzwilliam and an old Eton friend, Uvedale Price. Lord Carlisle was to have been one of the party, but his devotion to Lady Sarah, to whose beauty and encouraging flirtatiousness he was entirely in thrall, held him back. 'Tis a sweet pretty boy — he is Sarah's cicisbeo', explained her sister Lady Holland; and Sarah, she admitted, was never happier than when four love-sick gallants were competing for her attention. George Otto Trevelyan, citing Pope's *Dunciad*, gives us a sketch of the typical young English aristocrats of that day, amid the excitements and follies of their continental tour:

> Lads of eighteen and nineteen [he writes], who had been their own masters almost since they could remember; bearing names that were a passport to any circle; with unimpaired health, and a credit at their banker's which they were not yet old enough to have exhausted, made their grand tour after much the same fashion at all periods of the eighteenth century ... travelling with eight servants apiece; noticed by queens; treated as equals by ambassadors;

---

* Among the letters sent from abroad at this time by Lady Holland to her sister in Ireland is a revealing little postscript in her husband's hand: 'Your sister's kindness is proof against long journeys that she hates. No man was ever so happy as I am in my family. I feel infinitely oblig'd to them and particularly dear Caroline'. (Leinster, *Correspondence*, i. 470)

losing their hearts in one place and their money in another, and yet on the
whole getting into less mischief in high society than when left to their own
devices; they

> ... sauntered Europe round
> And gathered every vice on Christian ground ...[21]

Fox and, presumably, his friends certainly sampled the most traditional of
all the vices. On 22 September 1767 he writes to Ste's brother-in-law
Fitzpatrick, 'I have had one pox and one clap this summer. I believe I am
the most unlucky rascal in the universe'; and again to Fitzpatrick four
months later, a short time before setting out to join Carlisle in Italy:

> We live at a mile distance from the town of Nice, which is perhaps the dullest
> town in the world, and what is a terrible thing there are no whores. I am
> now quite well; my poxes and claps have weakened me a good deal, but by
> means of the cold bath I recover apace. *Je travaille toujours le matin*, and in the
> evening read, lounge, play at chess, at cards and talk.

At last Carlisle managed to tear himself away from dancing attendance on
Lady Sarah. In the company of Charles Fox's uncle, Lord Kildare, he crossed
the Alps in a chair carried by six men, and arrived in Italy to join Fox at
Genoa. They then proceeded to Piacenza, to Parma, to Bologna, to
Florence, to Rome. Fox may have found the supply of whores on the
Italian tour more satisfactory – we are not told. Even the dullness of Nice,
when he briefly returned there the following year, might be considerably
mitigated. 'There is a Mrs Holmes here', he wrote, 'an Irish woman, more
beautiful than words can express, and very agreeable into the bargain':

> This attraction draws me to Nice, which is about a mile distant from hence,
> every morning. Now it so happens that tho this woman is exquisite
> entertainment for *Charles*, yet, as she is chaste as she is fair, she does not
> altogether do for [his *alter ego*] *Carolino* so well. There is also at that same
> Nice a silversmith's wife, who is almost as fair as Mrs Holmes but not near
> so chaste, and she attracts me thither as regularly in the evening as the other
> does in the morning.[22]

Compare Lord Carlisle a few months later, writing from Venice to George
Selwyn in London: 'I was afraid I was going to have the gout the other
day. I had a pain in my foot that I could scarce walk, but it is gone off. I
believe I live too chaste; it is not a common fault with me'.[23]

If Fox was never likely to deny himself carnal pleasures, equally he
would never neglect the delights of the mind and the consolations of the
spirit. He worked continually at improving his Italian; he devoured Italian
poetry, and particularly Dante and Ariosto. 'For God's sake learn Italian

as fast as you can', he begs Fitzpatrick, 'if it be only to read Ariosto. There is more good poetry in Italian than in all other languages that I understand put together. In prose too it is a very fine language. Make haste and read all these things that you may be fit to talk to Christians.'[24] Italian drama, however, was inferior; it was imitation of the Greek, the Latin, the French. French actors he thought superior to English, but English *plays* were 'infinitely better'. Grand generalizations such as these still slipped easily off his young man's pen, and his youthful zest for the amateur stage was still strong. Perhaps this played as big a part as his schoolboy speech-training in the making of the accomplished public speaker he was soon to become. Why was Ste, he demanded, now apparently deserting dramatics? 'It will be very absurd if he has built a theatre for nothing', especially as his wife (than whom there was 'not another woman in England so capable of making my brother or indeed any man happy') had shown herself also to be an excellent actress. 'I hear the stage in England is worse than ever', he laments in a postcript to her brother, Richard Fitzpatrick. There is still barely a whisper from him concerning politics, though his father must already have been contemplating the purchase of some parliamentary borough which would suit this so faithfully filial, so rewardingly clever, son of his. (He was enormously proud of him: 'I wonder you never told me of your French verses', he wrote to him, 'as they are excessively good'.) Fox must surely have known that his father intended him for parliament; but, happy in Italy, he was very content to dismiss the subject from his mind: 'As for politics, I am very little curious about them, for almost everything I hear at this distance seems unintelligible.'[25] Even so, his distancing from politics was not quite total; he was more than willing to wish that every conceivable misfortune should overtake 'the Bedfords', the Whig group towards whom his father felt most bitterly of all.

By the summer of 1768 he was on his way home, via Turin and Geneva, being received *en route* by the 74-year-old Voltaire, as Ste also had been earlier. Uvedale Price was journeying with him, and left a brief account of their reception. Voltaire was very civil to them, writes Price, and gave them a list of some of his works which might open their minds 'and free them from any religious prejudices. He did not ask us to dine with him, but conversed a short time, walking backwards and forwards in his garden, gave us some chocolate, and dismissed us'.[26]

In Naples Fox had gambled quite heavily, and incurred substantial debts (it was reported, of £16,000) which it seems likely that Lord Holland had to honour. As usual, it was his mother rather than his father who seasoned her love and admiration with concern for what she called his 'indolence', by which surely she must have meant his self-indulgence in amusement and pleasure, and gaming particularly. Charles was the comfort of her life 'in every respect', she insisted, 'indeed an amiable boy as ever lived. I only fear his indolence will get the better of his superior genius, which won't satisfy my vanity. I shall not be content with his being only an amiable, sensible, agreeable man'.[27] And of course his father would not be content until his brilliant son was given the opportunity to astonish his elders from the benches of the House of Commons. Hence, in the spring of 1768, five or six months before Charles was due back home, his father and his uncle Lord Ilchester were clubbing together to buy their respective sons parliamentary seats.

It was Midhurst in Sussex that they agreed upon. This was one of the 'burgage' boroughs, where the right to vote went with certain cottages or parcels of land held under the centuries-old 'burgage tenure', a right commonly to be sold for cash, so that one or perhaps two or three rich men would come to 'own' a borough. Holland had been involved in complicated manoeuvres between competing interests to obtain control of Midhurst ever since 1761. Then in 1764 there had been a struggle between him and George Grenville, the prime minister, when Holland tried to secure the nomination of his protégé George Macartney but was defeated by Grenville, whose successful nominee was Bamber Gascoyne. The death in 1767 of Lord Montagu, who had by that time become effectively proprietor of the borough, enabled Holland to obtain from Montagu's son and successor the nomination to both the Midhurst seats.[28] To this end he had collaborated with his brother Lord Ilchester, so that they were together able to purchase the simultaneous return to parliament of their respective sons, Charles Fox, aged 19, and Ilchester's 21-year-old son and heir Lord Stavordale, brother to Charles's lost inamorata, Lady Susan. Such extreme youth in new members was not entirely unusual in Georgian parliaments, though it was less common than has been sometimes alleged; only about one in five among members of the lower house at that time were under 30.

At the same election Stephen Fox, aged 23, was returned for the borough of Salisbury. He at least had had to do some electioneering. In Salisbury it was membership of the city corporation which determined voting rights. This gave it an electorate of about 50, against the approximately 200 burgage-holders at Midhurst. At Salisbury, however, votes were *not* bought. It was a borough which preserved some electoral inde-

pendence and probity; where canvassing was discreet; and where the
electors' choice traditionally fell upon members of the local aristocracy or
gentry. Stephen Fox fitted the requirement well. His grandfather had been
a local man, schooled in Salisbury and later representing it in parliament;
and Stephen himself at his marriage only two years before had become a
major local landowner, when Holland made over his Wiltshire properties,
including the Winterslow estate which he had only just bought, to his
eldest son. The combined annual value of these gifts to Ste, and to his
wife if we include her jointure, came to at least £5,000, and perhaps
£6,000.[29]

3

WESTMINSTER AND ALMACK'S

Thus this young trio of Foxes were all comfortably established at Westminster in time for the climax of Act Two of the exciting Wilkes drama (Act One having been the *North Briton Number 45* affair and the spicy outrage of Wilkes's *Essay on Woman*).* The outlawed Wilkes, 'chieftain of riot and disturbance', returned daringly from exile; was within the space of a few months elected to parliament three times and three times expelled; and from the comfort – almost the luxury – of his prison quarters occasioned much mob uproar, many broken windows, and finally some lost lives in the quelling of riots by the King's troops.

This second protracted bout of 'Wilkes trouble' had begun with his original election for Middlesex in March 1768, several months before Fox left Italy. By August Fox was back at Kingsgate, where his father, sufficiently incommoded by asthma and a heart condition to be unable to contemplate another winter abroad, was still busying himself with embellishments to his paradise-by-the-sea. His latest folly *was* a folly, a tower built in honour of the current anti-Wilkite Lord Mayor of London, rather more he admitted 'for my private amusement than from public spirit. The truth is that I divert myself, but yet cannot help thinking that it were better it were all over.'[1] It was not, not yet; nor indeed was it to be for nearly another six years. And meanwhile his family – 'all here, and all well' – were round him, if he should take it into his head one day to die:

---

* A piece of bawdry mimicking Pope's *Essay on Man*, but sufficiently topical, lubricious, and venomous for the House of Lords to vote it a 'scandalous, impious, and obscene libel'.

'Lady Caroline, Lady Mary and my little granddaughter, and Ste, and Charles, and Harry'. He had even *nearly* become resigned to dying a mere baron. Now that his worst enemies the Bedfords had been included in the newly reconstructed government of the Duke of Grafton, it would hardly be realistic for him to expect an earldom any more.

It was a time when the Westminster air was full of noisy discord. Edmund Burke's cogent and influential *Thoughts on the Cause of the Present Discontents* reached the public in 1770, just after the main Wilkes furore; it was full of accusations of court conspiracy against what he presented as the blameless propriety of the Rockingham-Whig administration of a few years previously. In 1769 there had appeared the rapier-sharp *Letters of Junius*, a series of sensational anonymous attacks on the Duke of Grafton and his ministry, and even on the King himself. Petitions by the dozen were being organized by the parliamentary opposition, protesting against governmental corruption and alleging misuse of the royal prerogative. The Common Council of the City of London, anti-governmental as ever, was dispatching angry 'remonstrances' to the House of Commons in a quarrel which, like the Wilkes affair with which it was in part associated, provoked riots in London. Wilkes had led his agitation from Newgate Jail; in 1771 the Lord Mayor of London, Glynn Brass Crosby, and Alderman Oliver were briefly cooling their heels in the Tower of London. Wilkes himself had almost had his day as centre-stage hero of these protracted and furious alarums. He too became eventually Lord Mayor of London before dwindling into a conservative respectability. Received at last by the King at a levee, he protested amiably that though his friend Glynn had been a Wilkite, he, Wilkes had never been.

Charles and Stephen Fox took their seats in parliament in November 1768 when Charles was still two months short of 20. As a minor he was strictly ineligible. They were natural, even automatic, supporters of the government of the day, which meant until January 1770 the Duke of Grafton's ministry and, after that, Lord North's. Their father, reared politically during the 1730s and '40s in the school of Robert Walpole and Pelham, had always regarded himself not as a party man but as a servant of the Crown and of the King's administration. Often as he had had differences with various governments, he had never contemplated going into overt opposition. It was inevitable therefore that his sons, succeeding him at Westminster, should have become similarly administration-men, supporters of the King's government. To use terms such as Whig or Tory of Henry Fox, as at this stage of his son Charles, is widely misleading.

Until the accession of George III, Henry Fox served what have broadly to be called Whig administrations. Until the mid-century, 'Whig' could often mean little more than unequivocally Protestant, pro-Hanoverian, and therefore anti-Jacobite. But the government of Lord Bute (whose 'executioner of the Whigs' Henry Fox became in 1762) was undoubtedly of a different nature. That, however, did not make Henry Fox a Tory. Nor is it reasonable to describe Charles or Stephen Fox as Tories simply because they sat on the same side of the House as (from 1770) Lord North, who is often thought of as a Tory even though he himself would probably not have described himself so. The modern conception of two main well defined parties in the Commons, plus a number of numerically lesser parties, is quite anachronistic if it is applied to these mid-Georgian parliaments. Charles Fox went into parliament as his father's son (in truth, his nominee) and therefore as a supporter of the current administration.

It is instructive to compare one of his speeches in 1770, when he was 21, with a speech of his father's, made in 1742. Their stance, especially towards popular clamour, is strikingly similar. Charles was speaking against an opposition motion 'to enquire into ... the proceedings of the judges in Westminster Hall, particularly in cases relating to liberty of the press' — and even more particularly, it was made clear, into the conduct of Lord Chief Justice Mansfield. His strictures flowed eloquently against 'the miserable [anti-government] faction' whose voice emphatically ought *not* to be mistaken for 'the voice of the nation'. The confidence of members' constituents (just who these actually were at Midhurst surely involves some semantic niceties) would not be won

> by humouring, as foolish nurses humour great lubberly boys, the wayward whims of a misled multitude. The characteristic of this House should be a firm and manly steadiness, an unshaken perseverance in the pursuit of great and noble plans of general utility, and not a wavering inconstant fluctuation of councils regulated by the shifting of the popular breeze. If we are ... to be ever at the command of the vulgar and their capricious shouts and hisses, I cannot see what advantage the nation will reap from a representative body which they might not have reaped from a tumultuous assembly ... collected at random on Salisbury Plain or Runnymede ...[2]

Compare Henry Fox twenty-eight years before, just after the fall of Walpole:

> Our elections, thank God! do not depend on the giddy mob. They are generally governed by men of fortune and understanding ... Therefore, when we talk of people with regard to elections, we ought to think only of

those better sort, without comprehending the mob or the mere dregs of the people; for an election may be free and uncorrupted, though these appear against it, but would be very far from free if the electors were intimidated and compelled to vote as directed by a tumultuous mob of low people.[3]

The tutor was not to be disappointed in his pupil. One of Charles's earliest speeches, in April 1769, was made during the latest chapter in the long-drawn-out story of the House of Commons versus the electors of Middlesex, alias 'the People', and the motion before the House was to declare Wilkes's massive majority in a *fourth* election void, and his defeated opponent elected. Lord Holland wrote to a friend,

> I am told that few in parliament ever spoke better than Charles did on Tuesday – off-hand – with rapidity, with spirit, and such knowledge of what he was talking of as surprised everybody in so young a man. If you think this vanity, I am sure you will forgive it.

And, next month:

> I am told (and I willingly believe it) Charles Fox spoke extremely well. It was all off-hand, all argumentative in reply to Mr Burke and Mr Wedderburne, and excessively well indeed ... My son Ste spoke too ... very short and to the purpose.

Naturally Horace Walpole's account of these parliamentary occasions is considerably less partial, yet easily reconcilable. 'Stephen Fox indecently and indiscreetly said Wilkes had been chosen by the scum of the earth ... Charles Fox, with infinite superiority in parts, was not inferior to his brother in insolence'. And of the second occasion, 'Charles Fox, not yet 21, answered Burke with great quickness and parts, but with confidence equally premature'.[4] Nearly two years after this, in January 1771, the *Parliamentary History* was still thinking it worth reporting, 'The lad looked the image of his father'. In that same year 1771, Horace Walpole, in a passage of his *Memoirs* not included in the published version, was giving his impression of this brilliant young parliamentary newcomer:

> The faculties of his mind were genuine, strong, and mature. He conceived, digested, and replied at once. His reasoning and elocution were equally impetuous ... Such an amazing burst of parts ... produced ... in others admiration and envy, in himself excess of vanity and presumption, beyond what even flattery and intoxication could warrant. Bold, spirited, and confident, he behaved as if already in possession of all the triumphs he aspired to ... Thus at twenty-two he acted and was hated as a leader of a party; his arrogance, loquacity, and intemperance raising him the enemies of a minister before he had acquired the power of one.[5]

In the affair of Lord Mayor Crosby and Alderman Oliver, (the London magistrates confined to the Tower for presuming to set free two printers who had been arrested by order of parliament), Fox's speech of 25 March 1771 provides a model, indeed by Georgian criteria an impeccable defence of contemporary Whig constitutionalism. In it he praises the balanced polity finally achieved by the Revolution of 1688–9: the 'mixed monarchy' with its 'just prerogatives' which was 'the pride and envy of the universe'; the proper legal jurisdiction of the peers; the historical privileges of the Commons. There stood, so parliament was being told, Fox said, on the side of Crosby and Oliver (and of course by implication Wilkes), *the people.* 'Shall we then', he demanded 'do what is wrong because the people desire it?' Members of parliament were not to be regarded as 'slaves of the community', nor ought they to take 'dangerous instruction' from those advocating 'a democratical form of government'. 'We have sworn to maintain this constitution in its present form ... As we are chosen to defend order, I am for sending those magistrates to the Tower who have attempted to destroy it. I stand up for the constitution, not the people.' Burke himself could not have been more unequivocal. And not for another quarter-century would Fox be lifting his glass to toast 'our sovereign the people' – and having his name struck off the Privy Council for his pains. (Even then we need to enquire closely just which 'people' he really meant.)[6]

Fox's obvious abilities and well-practised skills in debate bringing him quickly to notice, and indeed prominence, in the Commons, Lord North wasted no time in promoting him to junior ministerial office. Soon after his twenty-first birthday, in February 1770, he was appointed a Lord of the Admiralty. After two years in the post, however, and despite being hailed by Horace Walpole, among others, as 'the phenomenon of the age', to the general puzzlement he resigned.

His explanations for what most observers of the political scene judged to be imprudence varied. To friends he complained of North's 'coolness' towards him, but without specifying grounds. It seems, however, that at least one ground must have been North's disapproval of his over-confident young colleague's personal initiative, taken in January 1772, to give notice of a motion for the repeal of Hardwicke's 1753 act outlawing clandestine marriages and requiring the preliminary reading of banns in church. This was the old Fox battlefield. Charles's mother had been a runaway bride; his father had vociferously led the opposition to Hardwicke's bill. Filial loyalty was strongly involved.

It happened also that, in the month following, the King sent parliament a 'message' by which he set much store. It was read to the Commons by North and received there with a mixture of outspoken opposition and glum resignation. And its subject matter was closely akin to that of Fox's intended motion to repeal Hardwicke's Marriage Act:

> His Majesty being desirous, from paternal affection ... and the honour and dignity of his crown, that the right of approving all marriages in the royal family (which has ever belonged to the kings of this realm ...) be made effectual, recommends to both Houses of Parliament to ... supply the defect in the laws now in being, and ... to guard the descendants of his late Majesty King George the Second ... from marrying without the approbation of his Majesty, his heirs or successors, first had and obtained.

It may be coincidence, but probably is not, that the date of North's reading of this message to the Commons is identical with that of Fox's resignation as a Lord of Admiralty: 20 February 1772. Indeed Fox himself wrote afterwards to Ste's father-in-law Lord Ossory, 'I should not have resigned at this moment merely on account of my complaints against Lord North if I had not determined to vote against the Royal Marriage Bill which, in place [i.e. in office] I should have been ashamed of doing'. Even so, he still had no intention, he assured his friends, of going into formal opposition.[7]

This very strong signal sent by the King to parliament – much more a requirement than a request – was occasioned by the sexual and matrimonial behaviour of his two surviving younger brothers, the Dukes of Gloucester and of Cumberland. This had caused him – although in his impressionable early twenties he had for a time undeniably dreamed of marrying Fox's charming young aunt Lady Sarah Lennox – to settle firmly for the conviction that the British Protestant blood royal ought in future to be commingled only with other Protestant blood royal (which in practice was to limit the field to Germans). George was honestly concerned for 'the honour and dignity' of his house, which he always equated to the honour and dignity of the nation itself.

He had long been concerned that the Duke of Gloucester was, as the world saw it, or as Lady Sarah herself put it, 'trotting about with' the very pretty young widow of Earl Waldegrave: a woman born not only a commoner but the natural child of Horace Walpole's brother Edward. What the world could not yet know was that, by the year 1772, Gloucester had been clandestinely married to Maria Waldegrave for more than five years. Worse, far worse, in the King's eyes, was brewing from his other brother Henry Duke of Cumberland. This lively little rake (he was as short of stature as of morality) had first 'gone rushing at once from the schoolroom to the stews';[8] then engaged himself in a passionate affair with Lady Grosvenor, which involved him to the delight of the scandal-greedy public in having to find £13,000 for 'criminal conspiracy', to be paid to the cuckolded Earl; and, at last, after a restorative interlude with a timber merchant's wife, had grossly flouted the King's wishes by marrying, in the words of Horace Walpole, 'a young widow of 24 ... very well made, with the most amorous eyes in the world, and eyelashes a yard long'. Naturally enough, Cumberland had gone to his brother for the £13,000; then George had inevitably been obliged to go to North for it; and North in turn had to apply to parliament.*

These were the antecedents of what was essentially George III's *own* bill, 'For the Better Regulating the Future Marriages of the Royal Family', which, broadly, was to enact that in future no descendant of George II, male or female, could marry without the monarch's consent — with the one safeguard that 'royals' aged over 25 persisting against the monarch's wishes and giving one year's notice to the Privy Council should be allowed to marry, provided that parliament itself did not forbid. This paternalistic and well-intentioned act — still on the statute book, though of very arguable applicability — was to bring troubles in its wake. During its author's reign alone, it was effectively to limit marital choice, for his sons, to German Protestant princesses; to bastardize the children of his son Augustus Duke of Sussex; to help persuade his son George Prince of Wales into his disastrous marriage; and so to limit the field for his daughters ('the Windsor nunnery') that they became obliged to choose between prolonged spinsterhood and desperate secret liaisons.

All that was some way into the future. George had reminded North that he expected his bill to be pushed through with 'becoming firmness'. It was *personal to himself*; hence, 'I have a right to expect hearty support from everyone in my service and shall remember defaulters'. When the second reading passed the Commons by only 200 votes to 164 (its final margin fell to 18), he stressed to North that 'every engine' must be employed, and asked to have a list of 'deserters' sent to him. By 24 March 1772 the bill was safely through all its stages. Fox had already resigned by then, but remained in general a government supporter and could hardly

---

* Seven years later, when the King agreed to be formally reconciled to his brothers, he still refused to grant social reprieve to their wives; and he continued to forbid the young Prince of Wales to visit his uncles' private houses 'either in town or the country'. However, time with its gift of irony had a word to add to the story. The King's fourth daughter, Mary, would one day (at 40) marry a son of Gloucester and his 'odious' Duchess, and thus herself become Duchess of Gloucester.

therefore avoid being classed among the defaulters and deserters, especially as his own attacks upon the King's measure had always (so Walpole judged) 'seized the just point of argument' and been thrust home 'with most amazing rapidity and clearness'.[9] *Rapidity* is perhaps especially worth notice here: Fox was to be a formidable debater, but never a great set-piece orator in the style, for example, of Burke. His words came tumbling forth, the next idea sometimes in its urgency tripping over its predecessor.

His own bill, for the repeal of Hardwicke's Marriage Act, came forward a mere fortnight after the final passage of the Royal Marriages Act, and was successful, by a single vote, 62–61, in its infant stage (gaining formal leave to be introduced) before being emphatically rejected, 92–34, at its first substantial division. Fox's handling of this abortive measure of his is revealing of both the best and the worst of him. When he first gave notice of his intention to move, he admitted that he had never read Hardwicke's Act. Then, when it came to the vital vote, he had been so involved with the racing at Newmarket and its allied pleasures that he managed to arrive back at Westminster only just in time to observe his motion's final obsequies. On the other hand, Walpole had been excitedly impressed by his earlier speech at the preliminary stage on 7 April. He wrote:

> Though I had never been in the House of Commons since I had quitted Parliament, the fame of Charles Fox raised my curiosity, and I went this day to hear him. He made his motion for leave to bring a bill to correct the old Marriage Bill, and he introduced it with ease, grace, and clearness, and without the prepared or elegant formality of a young speaker. Lord North opposed ... and spoke well. Burke made a long and fine oration against the motion ... Charles Fox, who had been running about the House talking to different persons and scarce listening to Burke, rose with amazing spirit and memory, answered both Lord North and Burke, ridiculed the arguments of the former and confuted those of the latter with a shrewdness that ... as much exceeded his father in embracing all the arguments of his antagonists as he did in his manner and delivery, and laboured only one forcible conclusion. Charles Fox had great facility of delivery; his words flowed rapidly ... He had nothing of Burke's variety of language or correctness, nor his method. Yet his arguments were far more shrewd ... He had that very morning returned from Newmarket, where he had lost some thousand pounds the preceding day. He had stopped at Hockerel, found company, had sat up drinking all night, and had not been in bed when he came to move the bill, which he had not even drawn up. This was genius – was almost inspiration.[10]

Fox remained out of North's administration at this time for only ten months. By December 1772 he found himself more than ready to be accepted back, this time as a junior Lord of the Treasury at £1,600 per annum – money not yet required quite to the point of desperation, but still welcome and extremely necessary. £1,600 was, in fact, not much more than small change to Fox, in these his wild early twenties, with his candle burning away merrily at both ends. At this time he was sharing rooms in Piccadilly with his nearest friend and fellow man-about-town, Ste's brother-in-law Fitzpatrick; but his London existence was centred essentially on Almack's club in St James's Street and, away from London, at Newmarket racecourse. Here, with Lord Foley, he set up a racing partnership which at one time owned a string of thirty horses, among them a famous runner called Pantaloon which almost, but unluckily not quite, won back for Fox money substantial enough to be set credibly against what he was currently losing on the tables at Almack's or White's. His fortunes at Newmarket did however prove much less disastrous than his losses at cards, and racing was for many years a source of passionate excitement for him. 'When his horse ran,' it was said, 'he was all eagerness and anxiety.'

> He placed himself where the animal was to make a push or where the race was to be most strongly contested. From this spot he eyed the horses advancing with the most immovable look; he breathed quicker as they accumulated their pace; and, when they came opposite to him, he rode in with them at full speed, whipping, spurring and blowing, as if he would have infused his whole soul into his favourite racer.[11]

Almack's club was a comparatively recent accession to the amenities of St James's. Indeed, clubs of its sort for men of fashion had themselves arrived only shortly before the mid-century, when they began to supplant the coffee-houses and chocolate-houses of earlier decades. High on the menu of these had been gossip and scandal, but also political news and argument. But the new clubs specialized in wagering and 'high play', and were in the most literal sense very exclusive. At White's, the first of them (originally White's Chocolate House), the habitués in 1736 formed a club specifically to exclude outsiders from their 'subscription rooms'; one blackball sufficed for a veto. Others followed: among them, Tom's in Covent Garden; the Cocoa Tree in Pall Mall; Boodles and Almack's in St James's Street.

The more expensive and extravagant of these clubs soon achieved notoriety. The citizens of London, said Horace Walpole, 'trudge to St James's Street in expectation of seeing judgements executed on White's, angels with flaming swords and devils flying away with dice-boxes'.

Almack's began as a rival to White's, on the opposite side of the street, its name representing a reversal of the name of its founder Macall. From its start it concentrated on 'high play', though its masquerades also attracted the cream, and doubtless along with it some of the froth, of London's *beau monde*. Walpole admitted being himself mildly infected by the craze for gambling which he saw as being one of the grand evils of the age. 'In less than two hours t'other night', he wrote, 'the Duke of Cumberland lost four hundred and fifty pounds at Loo, Miss Pelham won three hundred, and I the rest'. And on another occasion, at Lady Hertford's, he managed to lose 'fifty-six guineas before I could say an Ave Maria'. This however was child's play to the sort of gaming which provided the nightly amusement at White's or Almack's, and was 'worthy the decline of our Empire':

> The young men of the age lose five, ten, fifteen thousand pounds in an evening at White's. Lord Stavordale [Fox's cousin], not one and twenty, lost eleven thousand there last Tuesday, but recovered it by one great hand at hazard; he swore a great oath – Now, if I had been playing *deep*, I might have won millions.

Unhappily Fox was to prove habitually a loser, even to the extent, one might well think, of invalidating the law of averages. Or was it, as Fox and Fitzpatrick are held to have sometimes wondered, that some club members knew a trick or two of their own. These were the men Fox knew as *the hounds*, for whom gambling was less an amusement than a profession. Certainly it soon became common knowledge that Fox and the law of averages consorted ill together:

> If he touches a card, if he rattles a box,
> Away fly the guineas of this Mr Fox . . .
> No man can play deeper than this Mr Fox,
> And he always must lose, for the strongest of locks
> Cannot keep any money for this Mr Fox . . .

Over three consecutive nights in 1772, the year when he was mainly out of office and without income, he and his brother Ste succeeded in losing £32,000 – several or even many millions in modern money; for Ste too was again 'playing deep'. Gibbon reports that on another occasion Charles Fox sat playing at hazard for twenty-two hours on end, and thereby managed to lose £11,000. Although the brothers were able to borrow freely both from moneylenders and from their wealthy friends, the bottom line of their indebtedness was inevitably the huge fortune of their father, who repeatedly came to their rescue. It was of course knowledge of the existence of this horn of parental plenty that gave the professional, largely Jewish, moneylenders their security. Not only was Lord Holland known to support his sons, but there was the added reassurance that he was physically in serious decline, and would before long be leaving handsome fortunes to them.

If Lord Holland bore any resentment against Charles and his follies, he would not allow it to be mentioned to him. 'Never let Charles know', he begged Ste in this same year 1772, 'how excessively he afflicts me'.[12] Charles was still his ever-admirable genius of a son, his particular pride and glory. Since retrospection of his own political career left a sour taste in his mouth, anticipation of the favourite son's was all that remained to sweeten for him the flavour of the future. For Lady Holland it was harder than for her husband to forgive her sons, especially Ste, worries over whom had made up half her life. Now she upbraided him:

> You have played again, lost 3,000£. God knows how much more perhaps; for after this what dependence can be had on your resolution. You will, you must, inevitably be ruin'd. I'm hurt, I'm angry, and I will trust myself to say no more. Your own feelings will suggest to you all mine; but remember your promise. Let your name be scratch'd out of every club in London ... Oh! Ste, what misery you bring on, and will do to all you love.

Charles's attendance at race-meetings and his hectic follies at Almack's continued through most of the year 1773, though he was seldom guilty of omitting to attend to his parliamentary and ministerial duties on their account. Neither moreover did he fail to preserve that air of insouciant effrontery and devil-may-care, which even his, and his entire family's, year of nemesis (1773–4) would shake only very temporarily. For a while yet, he still had what he was pleased to call his Jerusalem chamber at Almack's, where the moneylenders habitually attended and did not yet judge the security inadequate. Fox's borrowing became ever more crazily reckless, and had by now involved several of his wealthy young friends, whose misplaced generosity at this stage is almost beyond belief. Lord Carlisle and John Crewe, for instance, actually saddled themselves with, respectively, annuities of £1,500 and £1,200 on his behalf. There were others too, for Charles was an excellent fellow and never short of friends.

He was a Lord of the Treasury; but in the public eye he was still, with his outrageousness of behaviour and attire, essentially one of 'the Macaronis'. Walpole for instance classes him among them and, just then, he thought, they were 'at their *ne plus ultra*'. The public prints and scandal-sheets of the day were happy to find in him a copious source of copy, and perhaps too a challenge to their own powers of invention. One of the best known stories relating to Fox at this the peak of his youthful follies may or may not be true, or perhaps may be half-true. Whichever, it tells what the public of the day were anxious to believe of him. And if we may judge from George Selwyn's correspondence with Lord Carlisle, where he refers with some circumstantial detail to 'that foolish business with Mrs Grieve', there must surely have been at least a fraction of truth in the story somewhere. It told how this 'Mrs Grieve', an adventuress and impostor, had undertaken for a consideration to find Fox a wife in the person of a West Indian heiress, an alleged but highly dubious 'Miss Phipps', worth £80,000 – and that Fox had let himself be duped. The frills to the story – that she preferred fair men to dark, and therefore, when he was introduced to her, would Fox kindly powder his eyebrows, etc. etc., – may perhaps be ignored. (But again, perhaps not; with Fox, at 23 or 24, the truth is seldom sober.) About now his father, failing fast, made nevertheless the still very Lord Hollandish remark that he hoped the rumour concerning Charles's marriage proved true, because that would mean he would have to go to bed at least once in his life.

What first began to threaten Fox's position, and bring a note of caution into the Jerusalem chamber, was the news that Ste's wife, Lady Mary, was pregnant. Ste's health had been so chronically bad and his expectation of life so poor that, so long as he had no son, Charles's prospects of coming into a substantial fortune and the barony of Holland had looked good. After seven years of marriage Lady Mary had had only one child, a daughter. But now disaster struck for Charles, when in the autumn of 1773 she was safely delivered of the son who would one day – and, as it was to happen, tragically soon – become the third Baron Holland. Disaster too, it appeared, for the moneylenders, as Charles's little joke suggested: Lady Mary, like her virgin namesake, had given birth to a Messiah, this latter-day one 'born for the destruction of the Jews'.

Soon all Grub Street as well as St James's Street, every politician and journalist and wit, had heard the story. One version of it came from the mock-heroic-poetical-satirical pen of William Mason, friend of Walpole and Gray:

> But hark, the voice of battle shouts from far.
> The Jews and Macaronis are at war.
> The Jews prevail, and thundering from the stocks,
> They seize, they bind, they circumcise Charles Fox.

For the Jews were not, of course, 'destroyed'. Nor was the family honour, though it was left to Lord and Lady Holland to save it. Lord Holland was by now very seriously ill, as also was his wife, and given only a few weeks more to live. (It became, in fact, more like six months.) Wasting no time, he started repairing such damage as was reparable. He began, first, the process of buying up his son's annuities. Haste was important, since necessary signings and authorizations had to win what promised to be a close race with death; to John Powell therefore, of the Pay Office, who acted as his agent, he gave immediate directions:

> to sell and dispose of my long annuitys, and of so much of my other stock, estates, and effects as will be sufficient to pay and discharge the debts of my son the Honble Charles James Fox, not exceeding the sum of one hundred thousand pounds ...[13]

In fact, that sum was in the end heavily exceeded. The estates of Lord and afterwards Lady Holland were eventually to pay about £140,000 to complete, after many delays, all the outstanding payments. Even that, moreover, marks by no means the end of the story. The massive indebtedness of Stephen Fox had by 1773 exceeded £100,000.[14] Some of this his father had already relieved, but much awaited final settlement. Mortally ill, and failing at times now mentally as well as physically, Holland remained capable of flashes of his ready, wry humour. An old friend had called to enquire after his health – George Selwyn, who had acquired a reputation, probably quite undeserved, for being unduly and eccentrically fascinated by death-scenes and public executions.* 'The next time Mr Selwyn calls', said Holland, 'show him up – if I am alive I shall be delighted to see him, and if I am dead, he will be glad to see me'.[15] Lady Holland's failing fires were not given to such lively flickerings. Her predicament was at least as bad as her husband's: she was dying of cancer. 'A good deal changed ... grown thin and looks ill', a visitor reported to Selwyn; 'the least trifle alarms her, and she often bursts into an involuntary effusion of tears'. In an undated letter, probably of early 1774, she wrote to Ste:

> Lord H. is much the same; better, I fear, I must never expect to see him. Oh! Ste this last attack ... I'm persuaded, is solely owing to the vexations of his mind ... Rigby, Calcraft [his political enemies], etc., etc., began ... Sarah

---

* Charles Fox, hearing that a namesake of his had been hanged at Tyburn, asked Selwyn if he had attended the execution. 'No', replied Selwyn, 'I make a point of never frequenting rehearsals'.

greatly contributed;* and Charles and you have put the finishing stroke. How painful this idea must be to you. Charles does not yet feel it, but he will severely one day; so he ought. And indeed, Ste, fondly as I once loved you both, I do not scruple distressing you by telling you how much you are in the wrong; indeed, indeed you ought to feel it, and let it be deeply imprinted on your mind.[17]

In the middle of the complicated operations to rescue the situation of the two brothers, Stephen Fox was to experience a new disaster. In January 1774 Winterslow House, the new with the old, was entirely destroyed by fire. Lord and Lady Holland had gone to Bath; but Charles Fox, Ste Fox, Ste's wife, and numerous guests were all at Winterslow when, at five in the morning, the flames took hold. A few hours before, the two Fox brothers had been putting on one of their dramatic evenings, with Mrs Hodges (Garrick's leading lady at that time) especially imported to head the cast. The company had enacted Nicholas Rowe's *The Fair Penitent*, with *High Life Below Stairs* for the customary light relief; and Charles, Stephen, and Lady Mary (although she 'had the toothache and was not in spirits') had as usual all played parts. The house was full of guests, driven or carried in from neighbouring houses, the Earl and Countess of Pembroke and the future Earl of Malmesbury among them. 'By seven', Malmesbury recounted, the house 'was consumed ... Mr [Stephen] Fox, Lady Mary, and their two children are gone to Wilton House; Thursday they go to Bath to Lord and Lady Holland. I fear they will not build on the same site again, so we shall lose a most agreeable neighbour'.[18] No lives had been lost.

It continued to be a year of disaster for the entire Fox family. Financial retribution had arrived in the autumn of 1773. Winterslow House was burned to a cinder in January 1774. In February Fox was dismissed from his Treasury post. In July, within about three weeks, first Lord and then Lady Holland died. (Lord Holland's will bequeathed the residue of his estate to Lady Holland. Hers in turn left everything to be divided among her three sons, priority being given to the settlement of their debts.) In November Stephen, latterly dropsical, followed his parents; he had been the second Lord Holland for a little over four months, and his successor to the title was a baby 1 year old. To round off the mournful tale, the

---

* Lady Sarah, her better reason (as she admitted) overwhelmed by her passion for Lord William Gordon, had, with her 20-year-old nephew Charles Fox as travelling escort, deserted her husband Sir Charles Bunbury, and made secret rendezvous with her lover, taking their new-born baby daughter with her. The Hollands, and Lady Holland particularly, felt the family disgrace keenly. Lady Sarah herself survived many years of social ostracism to make a notably happy and successful second marriage with Colonel George Napier.

baby's mother, 'the most amiable woman that ever was ... the best mother, the kindest friend, the most perfect example of merit', herself died less than four years later. 'Good God!' wrote Lady Sarah, 'what an ending to that once happy family! How it tears one's heart to think of it.'[19]

Fox loved what Burke called 'his darling popularity', and certainly he was a most likeable man. Certainly, too, there were always to be those around him for whom his excesses and improprieties were never excessive or improper; for whom he could do no wrong. But the reckless manner in which he had treated his friends' and his father's money as his own could hardly expect to escape condemnation – although there were some who, being convinced that his father's vast wealth had been the wages of monetary malversation, thought that the halving or quartering of it could be no bad thing. More telling were the opinions of some old and well-regarded friends of the family. George Selwyn was one of these. He clearly thought that Lord Carlisle (and no doubt Crewe and Lord Foley as well) had been foolish to make over to so rash a gambler such very large sums of money – in Carlisle's case £15,000 – and was now acting for Carlisle in the role of avuncular adviser in the business of getting as much as possible of it back. He reminded Carlisle of Fox's 'gratification of his pleasures and his determination never to put himself under the disagreeable restraint of one minute'.[20] Even such 'astonishing parts' as Fox possessed could not excuse the harm he had done to his closest friends:

> Charles ... was perhaps your first and warmest friend, who, I believe, now loves you, that is, as he loves Lord and Lady Holland, *à sa façon* [this was four months before their death]. I have lived, notwithstanding the disparity of our years, in great friendship and intimacy with him. His behaviour to me has been always kind and obliging ... Under these circumstances, it is not without much reluctance that I talk to you in the manner in which I do. But *amicus Plato, amicus Socrates, magis amica veritas.* [Plato is my friend, Socrates is my friend, but a greater friend is the truth].[21]

It appeared, said Selwyn, that a handful of the members of Almack's had 'imbibed such a belief of the necessity of Charles's being the first man of the country, that they cannot conceive there should be the least impediment to it'. This voices a complaint – repeated rather frequently over the decades, trenchantly for instance by Burke during the French Revolution debates of 1791 – a complaint concerning the existence of a band of Fox idolaters (Burke's 'little dogs and all') among each new generation of aristocratic young bloods at Almack's, or later at Brooks's. According to such people, wrote Selwyn:

> The Messrs Foxes must be indemnified, *coûte que coûte*. They were born for
> great stations, they were educated with great indulgence, and in extreme
> luxury. They have been imprudent, it is true, but they must not be now
> deprived of it. If they have had extravagances, they must have them paid
> for by others. If Jews won't pay for them, the Gentiles must. Charles is ... to
> be settled honourably in the world; he is to go into great employments, he is
> to be the dispenser of them. Ergo, he is now to be free of every incumbrance
> but that which honour has fettered him with, and these incumbrances may
> be greater or less according to your notions of honour.[22]

Selwyn did not cease being a friend and admirer, but his judgement of
Fox's character remained a long way short of idolatry,[23] even if less
bewildered and horrified than that of Mme du Deffand, at whose salon
and faro table Fox had been present, with Fitzpatrick, shortly before the
final crash. (They were both there again in the summer of 1776.) She, who
half a century before had been mistress to the Regent of France, was now
an old lady in her late seventies, but her perceptions were still clear and
penetrating. On the subject of *le Fox* and *le Fitzpatrick* she commented to
her now regular correspondent Horace Walpole:

> This strange feeling of security raises them, so they imagine, above the rest
> of mankind. They must be very dangerous to other young men ... Where
> they get the money I do not understand ... I should never have believed it,
> if I had not seen for myself that there could be such madness ... I declare it
> disgusts me; I do not know what to make of such fools ...
>   No doubt [Fox] has plenty of spirit, and above all great talents. But I am
> not sure that he is right in the head ... He seems to me to live in a sort of
> intoxication ... I declare it horrifies me; his future seems to me frightful ...
> At twenty-four to have lost everything, to owe more than one could ever
> pay, and not even to care about it: nothing is more extraordinary ... It is
> such a pity: he has so much intelligence, goodness, and truthfulness, but that
> does not prevent him being detestable ...[24]

More than once in parliament during 1772 and 1773 the question had
arisen of relief for Protestant Dissenters. Indeed, over the next half-century
and more, this would remain a constantly recurring parliamentary theme
until the final repeal in the 1820s of the anti-Dissenter legislation of Charles
II's reign. At the Revolution of 1688 it had been laid down that only those
dissenting ministers of religion who were willing to subscribe to those of
the Thirty-Nine Articles affirming the Trinity and the divinity of Jesus
were to be permitted to practise their ministry; and although this measure
was not strictly enforced, and a growing number of, for instance, Unitarian
ministers functioned undisturbed, it remained an irritant. The universities

of Oxford and Cambridge had their religious tests too, at a time when some very young 'men' indeed, students perhaps not much more than 12 or 13, were required to make a solemn attestation that they assented to the Thirty-Nine Articles of Anglican belief. It was this aspect of affairs, with its attendant anomalies and invitations to hypocrisy, on which Fox on two occasions chose to speak. The nation's undergraduate youth, he protested, were being

> trained solemnly to attest and subscribe to the truth of a string of propositions, all of which they are as entirely ignorant of as they are of the face of the country said to be in the moon. I was exceedingly young, Sir [he said], when I went to the university; not however so young that the matter of subscription struck me. At the age of twelve, youths when matriculated are required to subscribe '*Articuli fidei dumtaxat*'; but at sixteen they are to subscribe the oaths of allegiance and supremacy. Now, Sir, whether it be supposed that their political creed is of more importance than their religious one, I will not take upon me to determine, but it should seem that the institution supposes them not capable of understanding the sublime mysteries of politics until sixteen, though at twelve ... they can both understand, relish, and swallow down the sublimer mysteries of religion ...[25]

'A minister who would subscribe the articles' in extreme youth 'and afterwards preach against them' would surely be ill entitled to make an impression on his congregation.[26]

It was his earliest encounter with this perennial issue of the place of dissent, whether Protestant or Catholic, in a polity still essentially and emphatically Anglican. His tone was light, as was to be expected of a man still thought of as 'the young cub' at Westminster; and he certainly owed little intellectual allegiance to many of the 'string of propositions' of which formal acceptance was still requisite for the ministry or for university studies. But Fox the freethinker was without hostility towards Christian dogma. He believed in the necessity for an established church, at least to the extent of taking for granted its integral role in society and the state. But he also believed in religious toleration and in freedom of thought, and he would always have a powerful dislike of hypocrisy. It was indeed because the obligatory subscription to the Thirty-Nine Articles forced men into hypocrisy and casual mendacity that he objected to it. In his speech on the most important of the debates on it at this time he appears not to have distinguished himself. Fox, reported Walpole, 'did not shine ..., nor could it be wonder'd at':

> He had sat up [this was a little before the crash] playing hazard at Almack's,

from Tuesday evening 4th, till five in the afternoon of Wednesday 5th. An hour before, he had recovered £12,000 that he had lost, and by dinner, which was five o'clock, he had ended by losing £11,000. On the Thursday he spoke in this debate; went to dinner at past eleven at night; from thence to White's, where he drank till seven next morning; thence to Almack's, where he won £6,000; and between three and four in the afternoon he set out for Newmarket.[27]

Fox's dismissal from his junior lordship came as a consequence of his very cavalier treatment of his own prime minister, it being generally regarded as no part of a junior minister's duty to go out of his way to embarrass his chief, even in the course of defending the sacred cause of parliamentary rights and privileges. The Commons over these years had become highly sensitive to what it saw as attacks upon its powers and dignities, whether these came from the electors of Middlesex ('the people'), the popular press, the Crown, or the mayor and corporation of the City of London. Then in February 1774 the *Public Advertiser* printed an article by John Horne (the radical parson more usually known by the name he adopted later, Horne Tooke), libelling the speaker of the House of Commons. To Fox, himself no beginner in the arts of impudence, this was an impudence not to be tolerated. When the printer of the *Public Advertiser*, William Woodfall, a respected and experienced reporter, was brought before the bar of the House, his demeanour was apologetic, which afforded one reason why most members inclined away from imposing too harsh a penalty upon him. A second reason, perhaps, was the fear that unwisely severe punishment might well provoke yet another conflict between the Commons and the authorities of the City of London. Fox, however, was adamant that Woodfall should be made an example of, and sentenced to Newgate jail. He had obtained a promise from North that he would vote for his (Fox's) amendment insisting on imprisonment in Newgate, and when North eventually came to see that wisdom lay in leniency (which would mean merely handing Woodfall over to the custody of the Serjeant-at-Arms) Fox declined to release him from this undertaking. North, as a man of honour, was thus morally obliged to go into the division lobby, for which Fox was one of the tellers, *against* his own better judgement. As it proved Fox and the hard-liners lost the vote; but although North's humiliation was hardly more than trifling, he had every reason to conclude that Fox's motive had been to score points off him, and that the services of a junior colleague given to such behaviour might well be dispensed with at an early suitable opportunity.

Fox's ministerial unseemliness, indeed arrogance, had not gone unnoticed at Court, and confirmed the King in his low opinion of this self-assertive young man. He had disliked the father. The son was proving more than merely dislikeable; the word now was 'odious' – a favourite epithet with George. The fact that Fox was a 'professed gamester' was bad enough: ministers of the Crown ought not to be. Now, and worse, his behaviour towards North had been blatantly disloyal; and George always rated loyalty very high among the political virtues. Commiserating with North on the predicament Fox had placed him in, he wrote,

> I am greatly incensed at the presumption of Charles Fox in obliging you to vote with him last night, but approve much of your making your friends vote in the majority. Indeed that young man has so thoroughly cast off every principle of common honour and honesty that he must become as contemptible as he is odious; and I hope you will let him know you are not insensible of his conduct towards you.[28]

Fox persisted with his war against what he saw as excessive press freedom, and against Woodfall in particular. A few days after the debate in which he had obliged North to vote in the 'wrong' lobby, he moved that an anonymous letter printed by Woodfall in both the *Public Advertiser* and the *Morning Chronicle* should be declared a 'false, scandalous, and traitorous libel upon the constitution of this country', tending to 'alienate the affections of his Majesty's subjects from his Majesty'. This being agreed by the House, Fox went on to move that 'the authors, printers and publishers' of the letter should be prosecuted. They were – Messrs William and H. S. Woodfall were each fined 200 marks (about £133) and given three months in jail.[29]

There was a further show of independence a few days later, when North and Fox went into opposite lobbies in a vote on a Dissenters' petition. Fox would have 'acted more becomingly', the King now wrote to North, 'towards you and himself if he had absented himself from the House, for his conduct cannot be attributed to conscience, but to aversion to all restraints'. North hardly needed the King's prompting to show Fox that he was indeed 'not insensible' to his recent behaviour. No minister was ever more laconically or stylishly dismissed: 'His Majesty', wrote North, 'has thought proper to order a new commission of the treasury to be made out, in which I do not see your name'.

Loss of office meant loss of £1,600 a year. Under the terms of his father's will, Fox would inherit substantial assets, including the Kingsgate estate, but these needed to be realized to settle debts. Then, when his brother died, he again inherited valuable property, this time in the shape of a clerkship of the Pells in Ireland, a sinecure of venerable antiquity then worth £1,700 per annum for a period of thirty-one years. As it turned out, this was a move showing uncanny nicety of judgement. Payment began in 1775; it came to an end one month before Fox's death, in 1806.

Such an annual income represents, for those days, a degree of modest affluence; but modesty was not yet part of Fox's lifestyle. Neither his dismissal from the administration nor the subsequent succession of deaths in the family seems to have much affected either his manner of life or his political stance. Only a little later, Walpole was reporting that he was seldom in bed before five in the morning, or out of it before two in the afternoon. Certainly the wagering and gaming continued unabated. Here are a few samples of the wagers: 'Mr Fox betts General Scott 50 guineas that Lord North is not first Lord of the Treasury a year from this date.' 'Mr Fox betts Mr Fitzpatrick 50 guineas that Lord Coleraine outlives Mr Codrington.' 'Lord Clermont has given Mr Crawford 10 guineas, upon receiving 500£ from him whenever Mr Charles Fox shall be worth 100,000£.' 'Lord Ossory betts Mr Charles Fox 100 guineas to 10 that Dr North is not Bishop of Durham this day 2 months, provided the present Bishop dies within that time.' 'Mr E. Foley betts Mr Charles Fox 50 guineas England is at war with France this day 2 years, supposing Louis the Fifteenth dead.' In the twenty years following Fox's financial crash of 1773–4, no other name in Brooks's club's records of bets appears as frequently as Mr Charles Fox's. Perhaps in such an entry as the following there is a touch of irony to go with the bravado: 'March 11, 1775. Lord Bollingbroke gives a guinea to Mr Charles Fox, and is to receive a thousand from him whenever the debt of this country amounts to 171 millions. Mr Fox is not to pay the 1000£ till he is one of his Majesty's cabinet.'

Sarah Lennox believed that by the year 1776 her nephew's finances had become 'somewhat better', because he had 'won enormously' during 1775 and managed to reduce his outstanding debt 'to about £1000 or £1200'. She had been told that he had given up gambling at the card-table (if he had, the self-denial must have been remarkably short-lived), and concentrated his gaming on horse-racing, which was 'such a passion of his … that I doubt he will never give it up … He is, indeed, the most agreeable of all creatures *sans exception*'.[30] These affectionate and optimistic comments need to be read side by side with, and sometimes corrected by, those of others not quite so unquestioningly devoted and perhaps by now more closely acquainted. In October 1775 Selwyn writes, 'Hare and Charles, I am told, have lost everything they had at Newmarket'. Selwyn had also been told that

> the night that Charles sat up at White's, which was that preceding the night of Lady Holland's death, he planned out a kind of itinerant trade, which was going from horse race to horse race, and so, by knowing the value and speed of all the horses in England, to acquire a certain fortune.[31]

Selwyn, who was Lord Carlisle's financial adviser, intimate friend, and tireless correspondent, was writing to him in this same year 1775:

> Charles receives money from More the attorney. He forestalls all he is to receive, and unless the importunity begins with you [Fox still owed Carlisle a considerable sum], mine will avail nothing. Besides, I fairly own that I cannot keep my temper ... When I spoke to him the other day about your demand, I was answered only with an elevation *de ses épaules et une grimace* ... I fairly own that I have so little patience with our friend's manner of proceeding ... that I am very much inclined to see to what lengths he will go ... Charles lost last night £800, as Brooks told me today ...[32]

The significant new name here is that of the wealthy wine merchant and gamester Brooks:

> Brooks, whose speculative skill
> Is hasty credit and a distant bill;
> Who, nursed in clubs, disdains a vulgar trade,
> Exults to trust, and blushes to be paid.

Selwyn reckoned him 'the completest composition of knave and fool that ever was, to which I may add liar'.[33] This Brooks was soon to set up his own establishment in rivalry to Almack's, as Almack's itself had earlier set up in rivalry to White's. Happily for Brooks's enterprise he had no difficulty in persuading Fox, Fitzpatrick, Hare, and their circle to enlist under his banner on the opposite side of the street (St James's) and eventually the opposite of the political divide from White's. Brooks's architect was Henry Holland, a favourite then among the cognoscenti and the man soon to be employed by the Prince of Wales at Carlton House, and again in the initial stages of the Prince's marine pavilion at Brighton. By 1778 Brooks's Club was fully launched, already highly fashionable, the scene of the wildest gambling in town, and established as the spiritual home of Fox and his set.

In one respect, the figure he presented to the world over these years differed from that of the macaroni Fox of the previous decade. Gone were

the high-fashion shoes, the *dernier cri* patterned waistcoats that he had
once driven across half of France to find, and the hair-style *à l'aile de pigeon*.
His hair now tended to the disorderly; he was beginning to adopt, as
something of a political gesture, a sober frock-coat and waistcoat of buff
and blue, the colours it was understood of the American rebels. He was
untidy; he was fat. A Grub Street poem of 1777, when Fox was 28,
portrays him, new style:

> In order due, Volpone next appear'd;
> Loose was his hair, unshaven was his beard;
> O'er his whole face was spread a yellow hue,
> Borrowed perhaps from some relenting Jew
> Not anxious to be paid. Gold he had none;
> The inverted pocket told that all was gone.
> But ere he made his claim to Hell's rewards,
> His right hand waved aloft the fatal cards.

And from a couple of years later there comes a picture of a matutinal Fox
emerging (perhaps after a night at Brooks's) to receive some visitors who
were likely to have been seeking his support on some political matter,
possibly concerning the position of Dissenters – for the visitors were
Henry Beaufoy, known to be interested in that problem, and a dissenting
minister, Dr Kippis:

> We accordingly knocked, and were told by the servant that his master was
> not up but that he would take our names to him, and in the meantime we
> were conducted to a handsome room in which was a portrait of an opera girl,
> a small table with an ordinary breakfast service for one person, a dirty sofa,
> and three or four chairs. After we had waited a few minutes, Mr Fox came
> in. His complexion was of the dirtiest colour and tinged with a yellowish
> hue; his hair was exceedingly black, uncombed, and clotted with the pomatures
> and small remnants of powder of the day before; his beard was unshaved, and
> together with his bushy eyebrows increased the natural darkness of his skin;
> his nightgown was old and dirty; the collar of his shirt was open and
> discovered a broad chest covered with hair; the knees of his breeches were
> unbuttoned; his stockings were ungartered and hung low upon his legs; his
> slippers were down at heel; his hands were dirty; his voice was hoarse like
> that of a hackney coachman who is much exposed to the night air. Yet under
> all these various disadvantages his countenance was mild and pleasing.[34]

A journalist in the *Public Advertiser* had been writing what would today
perhaps be called a 'profile' of Fox, in which his 'figure' was described as
squalid and disagreeable. 'I told him', said Selwyn, 'that if by his *figure* was
meant, as in French, his countenance, it was not a true picture'. Fox replied

that he never cared what was said of his person: 'if he was represented as ugly and was not so, those who knew him would do him justice'. For the opinion of those who did *not* know him, he cared not a jot. 'The *qu'en dira-t-on*', comments Selwyn, 'he holds very cheap'.[35]

Those who knew him certainly did do him justice. He was now a social lion. The Duke of Devonshire passed on to him the presumably gratifying story that 'twenty ladies had kept themselves disengaged in hopes of having him for a partner' at Lady Hertford's ball, which he failed to attend. At the great Whig country houses he was gradually becoming a frequent guest, both for business and pleasure; for business, since these were natural places for political consultation and conference; for pleasure, both varied and delightful: Fox's sporting interests were not limited merely to the horses (or to the ladies). His physical energies were strong, notwithstanding his bulk. Cricket and tennis were still minor passions with him, though a relationship was sometimes claimed between the size of his stomach and the frequency of his run-outs at cricket. The annual September partridge-slaughter was almost as capable of exciting his enthusiasm as the October meeting at Newmarket, or indeed the November re-opening of parliament.

At the Duke of Devonshire's Chatsworth, in particular perhaps, he created a brilliant impression. His hostess there, the Duchess, Georgiana (a queen of high fashion whose gambling follies, disastrous in the end, were to rival Fox's own) declared him nonpareil. She called him 'the Eyebrow'. His intelligence, she said, was always a jump or two ahead of the rest of the company's; he seemed to have 'the particular talent of knowing more about what he is saying and with less pains than anyone else'; and his conversation was 'like a brilliant player of billiards – the strokes follow one another, piff paff'.[36]

4

AMERICA,
FRANCE AND
IRELAND

1773–1779

By January 1774 news had arrived in London of the Boston Tea Party. The angry resentment which had followed George Grenville's first attempt, eight years before, to impose a revenue tax on the American colonies had somewhat cooled after its prompt withdrawal; but then had come the attempt by Chatham's minister, Charles Townshend, to gain Grenville's end by different means. Duties had been imposed on certain specified goods and articles – lead, paper, glass, painters' colours, tea. Resistance no less bitter greeted this move, and the British government again bowed to pressure, removing all but one of the taxes; that upon tea was retained. In May 1773 North's ministry next proceeded to put through parliament an ingenious Tea Act, designed to assist the troubled finances of the East India Company by allowing it to export its tea directly to America free of the British one shilling per pound duty (though not of the Townshend threepenny tax); and thus to undercut in the American market the tea being smuggled in from foreign, especially Dutch West Indian, sources. The 'tea party' – the tipping of unwanted East Indian tea cargoes into Boston harbour by radical extremists in fancy dress – was seen in Britain as at once a disreputable stunt and a dangerous gesture of rebellion. It was not only George III and his ministers who considered it so; British public opinion was nearly unanimous. Even those politicians who would come later to condone, or at least understandingly to explain, American actions – Chatham for instance, or Rockingham, or most notably Burke – stressed the need for the colonies to acknowledge their subordination to 'the mother country'. This parental approach and *maternalist* vocabulary knew no party differences. Rockingham, a principal leader of the opposition, wrote that he 'would always consider that his country, as a parent, ought to be tender and just, and that the colonies, as children, ought to be dutiful' – perhaps his last adjective was not his happiest. 'When [the Americans] are quiet and have respect for their mother country', said North, 'the mother country will be good-natured to them'. And Burke, who was by this time the London agent and correspondent of the New York General Assembly, told them that 'all true friends of the colonies' – and none surely were truer than Burke – 'have laid down and will lay down the proper subordination of America as a fundamental, incontrovertible maxim in the government of this Empire'. Fox, who would within less than a year be found alongside Burke in arguing against the policies of the parent towards the fractious children, would not at this stage have disagreed. The Boston Tea Party represented an act of childish rebelliousness, deserving punishment.

When therefore North introduced his first important punitive measure, to close the port of Boston, Fox, although he voted with the minority on one clause of the bill, sided with the majority on the main issue. This was in March 1774, and he still counted, in general and however shakily, as a government supporter. By September, however, the Treasury Secretary, forecasting his lists of *pros* and *antis* in the next session's divisions, for the first time classed Fox among those members considered to be in 'declared opposition'[1] – where indeed, with only two brief interludes in government totalling together about one year, he was to remain for the next thirty-two years, until a few months before his death. On this, Fox's close friend from early days, Lord Carlisle, who knew his Fox better than most, and whose judgement is not to be lightly dismissed, commented as follows: 'If an idle quarrel had not happened between him and Lord North, we might have seen him a supporter of the American war, a champion of the prerogatives of the Crown, and a favourite in the Closet'.[2]

That Fox was soon to become a champion of the American rebels, to the point where he welcomed their every success and lamented their setbacks, is indisputable, but the sentiments which motivated this attitude were mixed. Among them, even perhaps dominant among them at first, was the feeling that the Americans were fellow-rebels against Lord North. And indeed, for the next eight years or so, the American situation provided Fox with an ideal stick with which to beat North's back; if he gradually developed an honest enthusiasm for the rebels' cause, never the least of its virtues was that it offered by far the best tool available to him for prising North and his colleagues out of office. Unfortunately for him, the King stubbornly refused to *allow* them to be prised out. Fox's anti-ministerial activity and vituperative rhetoric were to continue tirelessly, but for a long time fruitlessly. From 1774, there was no doubting that he was 'in declared opposition', yet he kept himself unattached to the principal Whig opposition groups, if often in consultation with them. He remained the opportunist freelance, a law unto himself.

Fox had opposed the government on two key measures: the first, when he supported a motion (which was lost, 49 to 182) proposing the removal of the tea tax as an overture towards moderate opinion in America and a gesture of reconciliation; the second, when he spoke against a government bill to deprive Massachusetts of its charter and to 'vest the nomination of counsellors, judges, and magistrates of all kinds' in the Crown or the governor as the Crown's representative. On the tea tax, he held that it was imposed neither for commercial regulation nor even for revenue, but rather to assert a right. If this was persisted in, it would force open rebellion. On the second reading of the Massachusetts bill, he first allowed himself some filial fun at the expense of his father's one-time ally and later enemy, Rigby:

> Sir, I am glad to hear from [Mr Rigby, who had just sat down] that now is not the time to tax America; that the only time for doing that is when all these disturbances are quelled and the people are returned to their duty; so, I find, that taxes are to be the reward of obedience ...

On the substantive issue, while maintaining that Britain was in the wrong to tax Americans, Fox argued, they too were in the wrong to contest the ultimate authority of the British sovereign parliament. By the time the bill had reached its third reading, however, he had fallen into line with the position adopted by Burke and the Rockingham Whigs, that merit and prudence demanded the laying aside of the undoubted legislative *right* in favour of the overriding *advantage* of regaining the allegiance and affection of the Americans. Fox said:

> I take this to be the question, whether America is to be governed by force, or management? I never could conceive that the Americans ought to be taxed without their consent ... The only method by which the Americans will ever think they are attached to this country will be by our laying aside the right of taxing. I consider this bill as a bill of pains and penalties ...[3]

Fox did not yet count himself fully one of the Rockingham group of Whigs, but he was beginning to drift towards them. Edmund Burke, their chief publicist and intellectual, he now began to see much of, even if the association was not quite as exclusive or intimate as Sarah Lennox was suggesting – that Charles had 'left off all his fine acquaintances ... and lived quite with Mr Burke, etc., etc ...' From his side, Burke was discovering in Fox not only 'one of the pleasantest men in the world', but also – one of those casually extreme pronouncements in which Burke's private letters abound – 'the greatest genius that perhaps this country has ever produced. If he is not extraordinary', he went on, 'I assure you the British dominions cannot furnish anything beyond him'.[4]

To a degree the relationship was of master and pupil; Burke was by twenty years the older man. He was the author of *The Sublime and the Beautiful* and *Thoughts on the Present Discontents*; he was a powerful critic of alleged 'prerogative' and corruption; in parliament he was a leading spokesman for those Whigs who acknowledged the Marquis of Rockingham as their leader, and an orator of polished excellence. It could therefore be supposed that even as self-assertive a young man as Fox would dilute his naturally abundant self-confidence with a touch of deference. It would be some years yet before he would rank unambiguously as a Rockinghamite; and although Burke was anxious to recruit him, even as late as October 1777 he was advising Fox not to rush into a decision. Fifteen months later again, Fox was writing to explain to Rockingham how he differed with him over policies to be pursued by the opposition, and how it was impossible for 'anybody who is not *one of you* to enter into your ideas'. 'Do not be in haste', Burke wrote, 'Lay your foundations deep in public opinion.' Fox ought to realize that, for all his 'parts', he was hardly 'the man formed for acquiring real interior favour in this court or in any. I therefore wish you a firm ground in the country; and I do not know so sound a bottom to build on as our party ... I love that party very well, and am clear that you are better able to serve [it] than any man I know'.[5]

Overtures like this left him as yet unconvinced and undecided. He respected Burke and found that his views, especially on America, came close to his own. But Fox could not share Burke's enthusiasm for the notion of *party*. There were indeed parties in existence, groupings of members, allegiances, contingents, 'connexions', *factions* perhaps in the King's language. There were the 'Rockinghams', the 'Grenvilles', the 'Bedfords', the 'Chathamites'. Perhaps the synonym for 'party' used as commonly as any was, simply, 'friends': the friends of Lord Gower, the friends of the Duke of Bedford, the friends of the Marquis of Rockingham –

and, by those who disapproved of his having any in this special sense of the word, 'the King's friends'. Many Commons members, however, regarded themselves as being the 'friend' of no particular party chief. Such independents, country gentlemen mostly, would tend to vote usually, and loyally, with the administration, which was, after all, the *King's* administration. Their vote was freely given, but it might also be freely enlisted. Hence the pulling power of a good speech; a powerfully argued case could sway votes to a degree unthinkable in a modern party-regimented House. It seems likely that Fox, not unaware of his own intellectual and debating powers, was at this time contemplating an attempt to build his own group of parliamentary friends. *'I certainly am ambitious by nature'*, he readily confessed to Fitzpatrick. 'Great reputation I think I may acquire and keep.' (But he added, a little obscurely but with high-minded pessimism: 'Great situation, I *never* can acquire, nor, if acquired, *keep without making sacrifices that I will never make'*.)[6] Or again, might he find his way back to office by being once more admitted to the company of Lord North's friends? – for although he greatly enjoyed castigating, ridiculing, and even vilifying North and North's policies,* surprisingly little ill-will resulted. Once (in 1777), after he had delivered a blistering denunciation of North's Secretary of State Lord George Germain, and then afterwards happened to be passing the Treasury front bench, the ever-amiable North greeted him with 'Charles, I am glad you did not fall on me today, for you was in full feather.'

It was the large measure of agreement on the American issue between Fox and Burke – and Burke's party colleagues – which gradually eased Fox's progress towards fully acknowledged membership of the Rockingham group. The transition was not complete until 1780, although as early as 1777 he was closeted with leading supporters of Rockingham, meeting for consultation at the Marquis's great Yorkshire mansion of Wentworth Woodhouse and at his London house in Grosvenor Square.

When North early in 1775 attempted conciliation with the Americans, proposing to forgo British taxation of the colonies (excepting duties necessary for trade regulation), provided that the Americans themselves came forward with 'the means of contributing their share to the general

---

* During a debate in January 1775 Fox charged North with 'the most unexampled treachery and falsehood'. At this 'Mr Fox was called to order, and the House grew clamorous. He sat down twice or thrice, and on rising each time, repeated the same words; but at length, assuring the House he would abstain from every thing personal, he was permitted to proceed. He then repeated his former charges of negligence, incapacity, and inconsistency' (*Speeches of ... Fox*, i. 33).

defence', Fox's speech on the proposition seemed to be wholly welcoming: 'The noble lord who has hitherto been all violence and war, is now treading back his steps to peace'. However, Fox continued, the fact that North was now beginning to listen to 'reason', was not to be counted to *his* credit but to the credit of the opposition, which had brought him back thus far from his policy of 'violence'. Not altogether convincingly, Fox concluded that 'no one in this country who is sincerely for peace will trust the speciousness' of his latest proposals; and as for the Americans, they would 'reject them with disdain'. At least this last was right; and when, shortly following, North introduced a bill to restrict the commerce of the New England colonies and deny them the fishing off Newfoundland, Fox was able to clarify his position. The bill would 'give an opportunity for drawing the sword and throwing away the scabbard'. Until then, the American disorders had produced disobedience and confusion; now they were to be forced into overt rebellion – for what was the government offering them? 'Starvation or rebellion.' The question was, whether a people was 'to submit to slavery, or to aim at freedom by a spirited resistance'.[8]

Just how far his sentiments had carried him towards whole-hearted sympathy for the American rebels is seen better from his private letters than from his public speeches. In November 1775 he was writing to Lord Ossory, Fitzpatrick's brother, who was a kinsman-by-marriage now, through the second Lady Holland, and was of the Gower-Bedford connexion, once anathema to the Foxes. Ossory was, clearly, ripe for persuasion, and indeed *was* soon persuaded. Fox wrote:

> I am glad to inform you that, on Friday next, Burke will move to bring in a bill to secure the colonies against parliamentary taxation, and to repeal the obnoxious laws ... it will be the fairest test in the world to try who is really for war and who for peace. It is conceived in the most moderate terms imaginable ... I am sure, my dear Ossory, if you do think seriously enough of this matter to let your opinion regulate your conduct, it is impossible but you must consider this as the true opportunity of declaring yourself ... It does not need surely the tenth part of your good sense to see how cruel and intolerable a thing it is to sacrifice thousands of lives almost without prospect of advantage.[9]

And when the Americans, after their military successes in 1775 at Crown Point and Ticonderoga, had pushed on into Canada but were then driven back by British forces, Fox's words to Ossory show how decisively he had now taken sides:

> [The British victories] will give the fools and Tories here such spirits as to

make them insufferable. As to myself, you know little matters do not oppress me much. I am still convinced the Americans will finally succeed ... and if they do not, I am sure ... that it will check all future enterprise to such a degree as to give the completest triumph to Toryism that it ever had ... Whatever happens, let us all resolve to stick by them as handsomely (or more so) in their adversity as we have done in their glory.[10]

He was worried, he added, lest others should be *too* worried by the news: 'I see such strange dispositions in others to despond on every trifling disadvantage'.

It was important, he knew, not to greet rebel successes, when they came, with too public an enthusiasm: it could only make him unpopular. But his American sympathies were sufficiently strong and his expression of them too emphatic to be disregarded. He spoke in parliament for a minority which was regularly and heavily defeated, and was by this time severely dispirited. In the nation at large, among those whom Burke despairingly called 'the poor, giddy, thoughtless people of our country', such views as Fox held were inevitably seen as unpatriotic. For the King, too, Fox the 'odious and contemptible' gamester, the repeatedly unreliable minister, was now become the professed friend of rebels and his country's enemies. When, in 1777, the matter arose in the Commons of meeting the accumulated debts of the King (*personally* the most unextravagant of monarchs), which had by this time reached £618,000. Fox did not fail to dig still deeper the chasm of hostility between himself and the King. The motion to make good the royal arrears was passed without a division, but when a second resolution was moved, to fix the civil list at an improved annual £100,000 Fox was one of the tellers for the 'No' lobby, having spoken first in praise of the glories of George II's reign and contrasted them with 'the corruption and patronage' which had 'overspread the land' during the reign of his successor. A 'shameless prodigality' had prevailed in the disposition of the revenues of the civil list. Fox did not of course perpetrate the unthinkable, by pointing the finger at the sovereign personally. George III was 'too good a man and too great a king' to have sanctioned such corruption and extravagance. These phrases of routine obeisance were obligatory, and Fox's main fire was necessarily concentrated on George's prime minister North, whom he unamiably ranked as the equal of that 'father of corruption' Sir Robert Walpole. But he did not fail to cast blame on 'the influence of the Crown', with its 'power over the treasury'. The Commons were now being required to confirm past 'rapine and plunder'. There was sufficient irony in all this for it not to be taken

too seriously, coming as it did from a member sitting for a venal borough*
with, even in theory, an electorate of just 13: a man moreover of notoriously wild manner of life whose wanton extravagance had bid fair to ruin
himself and his family, and whose own money had derived from a fortune
made, to say the least, with dubious propriety by his father at the Pay
Office.

This debate on the civil list, however, had started Fox upon a theme
which Burke had already elaborated in his *Thoughts on the Present Discontents*, and which was to be endlessly repeated and developed in the decades
to come. It was indeed to be eventually a key element in the 'Whig
interpretation' which dominated nineteenth and early twentieth century
history books: essentially that under George III the nation's government
was rotten with the corruption which emanated from the undue and
growing influence of the Crown.

Towards the end of 1776 Fox and Fitzpatrick paid another of their visits
to Paris – 'two regular bad hats', commented Mme du Deffand; 'they have
gambled much here, especially Fitzpatrick; he has lost a lot.' On 4 July
1776 had come the American Declaration of Independence; and back at
Westminster, in the debate on the King's speech at the re-opening of
parliament, Fox for the first time in public was able to make his position
on this issue of independence unambiguously clear: 'The noble Lord [North]
said that we were in the dilemma of conquering or abandoning America;
if we are reduced to this, I am for abandoning America'. For, he continued,

> What have been the advantages of America to this kingdom? Extent of trade,
> increase of commercial advantages, and a numerous people growing up in
> the same ideas and sentiments as ourselves. Now, Sir, would those advantages
> accrue to us if America was conquered? Not one of them. Such a possession
> of America must be secured by a standing army; and that, let me observe,
> must be a very considerable army.... cut off from the intercourse of social
> liberty here, and accustomed in every instance to bow down and break the
> spirits of men, to trample on the rights and to live on the spoils cruelly
> wrung from the sweat and labour of their fellow subjects ...[11]

His contacts with leaders of the Whig opposition continued, and he
argued strongly against the tactics advocated by some of the Rockinghamites, perpetually outnumbered and outvoted as they were, that they
should mark their protest against the government's American policy by

---

*Midhurst had proved beyond his pocket at the general election of 1774 – the Fox family's
disastrous year – but he had contrived to be accepted instead at Malmesbury, which he represented
until 1780.

non-attendance at Westminster, seceding from Lords and Commons alike. When during the summer of 1777 Fox was at Chatsworth as the guest of the Duke of Devonshire, in a letter to Burke he commented on those Whig leaders whose *company* he was just then much enjoying, but whose political defeatism he deplored. 'I have been living here some time, with very pleasant and very amiable people; but altogether as unfit to storm a citadel as they would be proper for the defence of it'. This was the letter which elicited from Burke the long tutor-to-student, almost father-to-son reply[12] in which he sought to persuade Fox (but only after sober thought and in his own time) to build his political future 'upon the bottom of our [Rockingham] party'.

Fox's hostess at Chatsworth, the charming and vivacious Georgiana Duchess of Devonshire, just 20, was primarily at this time interested in Charles Fox the man, the conversational charmer and intellectual phenomenon, though Fox the politician would before long be engaging her excited enthusiasm also. 'What makes him more entertaining', she told her mother, 'is his being here with Mr [John] Townsend and the D. of Devonshire, for their being so much together in town makes them show off one another. Their chief topic is politicks and Shakspeare. As for the latter, they all three have the most astonishing memorys for it.'[13] After Chatsworth, with John Townshend now as his companion (the previously inseparable Fitzpatrick was bound for America with the Guards), Fox spent some time during September in Ireland, where he enjoyed much dining out; met Henry Grattan, then still a young barrister, beginning a friendship of some future importance; visited Lake Killarney; and bathed in the famously chill waters of the Devil's Punch Bowl.

He celebrated the reconvening of the Westminster parliament with a salvo of assaults, both on Lord North, and on the minister in charge of the conduct of the war, Lord George Germain. On 2 December came one of his fiercest maulings of Germain, 'that inauspicious and ill-omened character':

For the two years that a certain noble lord [George Germain] has presided over American affairs, the most violent, scalping, tomahawk measures have been pursued:* bleeding has been his only prescription. If a people deprived

---

* There had been angry controversy over the military use of 'Indians' against the rebels. There were indeed atrocities – 'scalpings' – perpetrated by the 'Indians'. No war, however, and especially no civil war, ever lacks conflicting stories of wickedness and evil; and there were also atrocities committed by Americans on 'loyalists'. In England, Germain would have liked to burn Boston and Philadelphia as a 'punishment'. Across the Atlantic, Silas Deane and Benjamin Franklin relished the prospect of the French burning Liverpool and Glasgow in reprisal for what the British had done in America.

of their ancient rights are grown tumultuous – bleed them! If they are
attacked with a spirit of insurrection – bleed them! If their fever should rise
into rebellion – bleed them! Cries this state physician. More blood! More
blood! Still more blood! When Dr Sangrado had persevered in a similar
practice of bleeding his patients – killing by the very means which he adopted
as a cure – his man took the liberty to remonstrate upon the necessity of
relaxing in a practice to which thousands of their patients had fallen sacrifices,
and which was beginning to bring their names into disrepute. The Doctor
answered, 'I believe we have, indeed, carried the matter a little too far, but
you must know I have written a book upon the efficacy of this practice;
therefore, though every patient we have should die by it, we must continue
the bleeding for the benefit of my book'.[14]

Germain's master plan to put an end to the American rebellion had
already encountered disaster six weeks before the onslaught upon him by
Fox. General Burgoyne had been compelled to capitulate at Saratoga
Springs on 17 October, though the news did not reach North and the
King until the very day early in December when Fox was speaking. In
retrospect, this surrender at Saratoga can be seen as a decisive moment,
perhaps *the* decisive moment of the war. Even at the time, news of it came
as a dark omen in Britain, not least because of its likely effect in France.
At the new year, 1778, Horace Walpole (keeping his friend Horace Mann,
in Italy, up-to-date with the talk of the town) was repeating something
stronger and more alarming than mere rumour – that France had 'signed
a treaty with the provincials, and the stocks look pale upon it'. But all
these rumours, he went on,

> only fill up the chinks of time, and will be forgotten when great events
> happen. By *great events* I mean foreign war and domestic calamity. We are
> on the high road to both. The present moment is only like the half-hour at
> the theatre before the play begins; the galleries are riotous, pelt the candle
> snuffers, or bawl for the overture; when the curtain is drawn up, nobody
> thinks but of the tragedy.

A month later, with a Committee of the whole House sitting 'to consider
the state of the nation', Fox, by now *de facto* leader of the Commons
opposition, moved 'That no more of the Old Corps [the regular army] be
sent out of the kingdom'. In the Lords his uncle the Duke of Richmond
moved an identically worded resolution. France was clearly sniffing at the
potential feast being promised by the British military involvement in
America. Less than twenty years earlier, in the triumphant days of the
elder Pitt, France had suffered a series of crushing defeats worldwide –
notably in Canada, in the West Indies, in India, and at sea. The time and

situation seemed ripe for her to exact some revenge. Indeed, before long the danger of a French invasion of Britain would become acute and imminent.

Fox's motion of 2 February had been well publicized in advance and, in the words of the *London Chronicle*, 'a vast multitude assembled in the lobby and environs of the House of Commons', among whom were 'the Duchess of Devonshire, Lady Norton [the Speaker's wife], and nearly sixty other ladies'. It was perhaps the first manifestation of Fox's political following among the ladies. The *London Chronicle* continues:

> Not being able to gain admission either by intreaty or interest, they forced their way into the gallery in spite of the door-keepers. The House considered the intrusion in a heinous light, and a motion was directly made for clearing the gallery. A partial clearing only took place; the gentleman were obliged to withdraw; the ladies ... were suffered to remain; but Governor Johnston observing that if the motive for clearing the House was ... to keep the state of the nation concealed from our enemies, he saw no reason to indulge the ladies ... as he did not think them more capable of keeping secrets than the men; upon which they were likewise ordered to leave the House.

Fox's reaction to these preliminaries was, in his introductory remarks, to note ironically his own 'personal good fortune in having his audience reduced'. The speech itself marks easily the greatest success so far in his Commons career. He had now tumbled Chatham from his oratorical throne, declared Walpole; 'and if he has not all the dazzling lustre, has much more of the solid materials'.[15] In an unusually full house, even the vote which followed the speech was significant. Coming after a long succession of miserably poor opposition votes, it showed 165 members now supporting Fox's motion (including several Tories, among them Gibbon), against 259. He had spoken for over two and a half hours, and in a tone of more sober moderation than had so far been usual with him. When he sat down, no one from the Treasury bench rose to make his motion the subject of debate – which caused a disappointed George III to observe to North, 'I trust that when next the Committee on the State of the Nation is resumed, gentlemen will be more ready to speak'.[16]

Four days after this motion had been defeated, Benjamin Franklin in Paris signed the 'treaty of amity and commerce' with France, which promised an alliance between France and America in the event of a future Franco-British war. For a few more days, only rumours of the signing reached the London public. Horace Walpole, however, had received intelligence more factual, and confirmed the rumour's truth privately to Fox, and it seems *only* to Fox. When therefore on 17 February North rose in the Commons to announce a new set of conciliatory propositions aimed at securing an end to hostilities in America, Fox enjoyed a tactical advantage in being able to ask an unhappy North whether it was not a fact that his administration was 'beaten by ten days', the Franco-American alliance being an accomplished fact. In any case, Fox claimed, the new conciliatory proposals – in fact, a big governmental retreat – were little different from Burke's proposals of three years before and in any case too late by this time to expect assent.

A by-product of this latest unsuccessful attempt by North at American conciliation was the dispatch of a commission to the colonies to 'treat, consult, and agree upon' the means of quieting the disorders. Appointed to head this body was that close friend of Fox's earlier days, companion grand-tourer, and financial benefactor, Lord Carlisle. Fox had been casual and remiss in failing to repay him the considerable amount of money which he morally, if not legally, still owed; and politically also the two men had drifted apart. (In 1780, the King and North appointed Lord Carlisle to be Lord Lieutenant of Ireland; in 1782, when the Whigs of Fox's party came briefly to power under Rockingham, Carlisle was to be dismissed.)

North's situation as First Lord of the Treasury, between hearing the news of Saratoga and the eventual fall of his twelve-year-long ministry in 1782, is unique in the history of the British premiership. Nowhere else is there to be discovered a prime minister over so long a period – fully four years – begging and pleading to be released from his responsibilities. On literally dozens of occasions he wrote to the King explaining the defects in his character, the weakness of his nerve, his inability to concentrate; claiming that his 'spirits, strength, memory, judgement, and abilities' were 'sensibly and considerably impair'd', and that he foresaw these failings getting worse the longer he kept at the helm. There were times when he insisted that he merited 'an immediate dismission'. His ministry could not last. It could not last the week. It could not last the next *twenty-four hours*.[17] The King must seek to build some 'broader-bottomed' administration, with someone at its head to replace his incompetent self: Lord Chatham perhaps (until his death soon removed him from consideration), Lord Suffolk, Lord Gower, Lord Weymouth, Lord Thurlow – *Lord Anybody*, Thurlow himself growled, or alternatively 'the first hackney coachman in the street'.

North's was a protracted and at times humiliating martyrdom, plumbing perhaps its most painful depths when once, coming to the Commons immediately after the death of his 2-year-old son, he broke down in tears in mid-speech. (Members volunteered in sympathy to 'put the question' there and then, but he declined the offer, recovered control, and continued speaking). The chains which held him fast were chains of honour, binding him the more strongly because it was the King personally who relieved him of the embarrassment of his private debts. North, on being appointed as George's 'principal confidential minister' in 1770, had promised him that he would not *desert*. (George was constantly reminding him that his predecessor the Duke of Grafton *had* deserted.) The tactics which the King adopted towards an often demoralized North varied from friendly encouragement with promise of full support, through gently critical remonstrance, to outright condemnation of North's inefficiency, his failure to answer letters or properly to prepare for cabinet meetings, his fits of indolence, even his vanity: '... Lord North if he will take a decided part is sure of my support ... but I fear his irresolution is only to be equalled by a certain vanity of wanting to ape the prime minister without any of the requisite qualities ...'[18]

George sternly refused to release his stricken minister from his strict obligation of honour; and the royal dependence on a largely paralysed and helpless Lord North became even greater as a number of politicians began to face the unpleasant possibility – necessity, even – of ceding American independence. 'Before I will even hear of any man's readiness to come into office', declared the King, 'I will expect to see it signed under his hand that he is resolved to keep the Empire entire.'

The King's response to the immediate crisis of April 1778, with North looking round for men of substance to reinforce his team, was once again a demand for loyalty. He would rather lose his crown, he said, than bear the ignominy of possessing it under the 'shackles' of the opposition leaders. However, although he would not 'go towards them', if they *came to him* he would accept them: 'You have now full powers to act, but I do not expect Lord Chatham and his crew will come to your assistance'.

When William Eden, the future Lord Auckland, was commissioned to sound out the probables and possibles for coming to North's rescue in a new broad-bottomed administration, one of those whom he met confidentially was Fox, who declared himself 'unconnected and at liberty'. He was not a Rockinghamite yet, and was ready to join a reconstructed North ministry provided only that Germain was excluded. He hoped also that a new government might find places for his friends the Fitzpatrick brothers,

Richard and John (Lord Ossory). In later soundings-out among the opposition groups themselves in 1779, he would add to the names of the men
whose dismissal was to be a necessary precondition for his joining a new
administration the names of the First Lord of the Admiralty, Sandwich,
and the prime minister North himself.

During the 1778 *pourparlers*, among those consulted was another key
man among the opposition parties, Lord Shelburne. He was widely
regarded as Lord Chatham's spokesman – the great man himself, ageing
and shaky, stayed aloof and virtually unapproachable, encamped on his
private Kentish Olympus. In any case, said the King, if Chatham should
ask to see him, he would refuse him audience. However, Shelburne told
Eden that *without* Chatham no new administration would work. Moreover,
any new ministry would be inadequate 'which did not comprehend and
annihilate every party in the kingdom' – in other words, an all-party and
therefore no-party government with Chatham himself in the position of
what Shelburne called 'dictator'.[19]

By 11 May Chatham was dead. The previous month, a sick man
struggling to the House of Lords to contest what he regarded as the
defeatist arguments of Fox's uncle Richmond, protesting that *any* state
was 'better than despair – if we fall, let us fall like men', he collapsed. In
Burke's unforgiving phrase, he had spat his last venom. One at least of
the options for making a new ministry to pursue the American war died
with him. Hostilities with France, however, in the maritime aspects anyway,
were dangerously alive, and promised very soon to develop into a war
also against the other Bourbon power, Spain. The French war in particular
was one for whose prosecution Fox was positively enthusiastic.

> He declared in the Commons, 'You have two wars before you, of which you
> must choose one, for both you cannot support. The war of the Americans is
> a war of passion ... supported ... by those passions of the human heart,
> which give courage, strength, and perseverance to man. The war of France
> is of another sort ... Turn your face at once against her, attack her commerce
> wherever you can, make her feel heavy and immediate distress ... She will
> find the having entered into this business a bad bargain.[20]

The Commons, he argued (unsuccessfully) ought not to be prorogued, but
should continue sitting throughout the summer to vote supplies. And why,
he demanded, was the government's policy so defensive? The navy should
seize the initiative:

> We cannot .. number ships with France and Spain. The superiority is multiplied
> by our acquiescence.... Instead of defending, let us attack. One great stroke

of policy must now be attempted, as one great, sudden, unexpected stroke can alone, in our present situation, save us ... Need I say that the capture of the Spanish flotilla would be an issue to the conflict ...

Calls for aggressive action such as this – which at least did much to remove from Fox the stigma of anti-patriotism which his American views had earned him – were doubtless much easier to make than were hard decisions at the Board of Admiralty, where Lord Sandwich, vilified though he was by Fox and the opposition, had in fact for years been doing sound work. With strong and knowledgeable support from the King, he had gone some way towards restoring the navy to battle-worthy strength after the years of neglect and deterioration following the peace of 1763. Moreover, Fox's calls for some great unexpected naval 'stroke' were, understandably, not able to be fully endorsed by Admiral Keppel at Portsmouth – who as it happened was also a Rockinghamite member of parliament and a distant cousin of Fox. Keppel, commanding twenty ships of the line, in June 1778 declined to risk the imprudence of engaging thirty-two French in the Channel. Before his fleet eventually left port, with his numbers reinforced, there had been lengthy delays, loudly complained of by the opposition. The King, who was personally present and busily active at Portsmouth, assured North that everything possible *was* being done; 'It is very absurd', he commented, 'for gentlemen unaquainted with the immense detail of naval affairs to trouble the House of Commons with matters totally foreign to truth ... From the hour I arrived here, not an instant has been lost.'[21]

During the abortive action which followed in July, misunderstandings and then recriminations arose between the commanding admiral, Keppel, and his third-in-command, Vice-Admiral Palliser. A Whig newspaper in London, the *General Advertiser*, accused Palliser of failing to respond to a signal from Keppel. Palliser lodged counter-charges against Keppel and then published them in the *Morning Post*, complaining of 'mistakes and incapacity' which had allowed the French to escape. The Board of Admiralty therefore ordered that Keppel should face a court martial, and from that moment the affair became rather more a matter of national political controversy than of strictly naval discipline. Hugh Palliser was member of parliament for Scarborough and a supporter of the administration. Augustus Keppel was a grandson of Joost van Keppel, first Earl of Albemarle, and so a member of one of the grandest of the Whig families which had arrived in England at the Revolution of 1688. Thus between the two naval antagonists political lines were drawn, and behind them stood their party supporters. In the months that followed, over the winter of 1778–9, the abortive naval engagement off the Brittany coast was fought all over again, at Portsmouth where the court martial sat, in the London newspapers, in parliament, and finally in the streets, theatres, and places of entertainment of the capital. At Portsmouth, Keppel was given encouragement and support by a strong posse of the Whig nobility, and Fox was there with them. In London, the Whig ladies wore Keppel caps at the opera, and Keppel cockades became for a time as popular in the streets as Wilkes's had been earlier. Keppel, unable though he had been to bring off any great victory, was fêted as if he had won his Quiberon Bay triumph a second time. He became the hero of the hour, and a convenient focus both of long-standing government unpopularity and of new-found Whig solidarity, however short-lived.

The climax of this Keppel-Palliser *brouhaha* was reached in February, when, upon hearing the news of Keppel's acquittal, the London mobs and rowdies, ready as ever for a little riot, celebrated in traditional style. The government and the King were discomfited; and the Whigs tasted a portion of brief and unaccustomed satisfaction. Palliser for a time was obliged to go into hiding. Late in the evening of 11 February, with the crowds of London and Westminster merrily engaged in breaking the windows of those citizens failing to display illuminations, Fox and a group of his friends emerged from Brooks's and patriotically suggested to the nearest available crowd that to break Lord George Germain's windows would be a meritorious action. This accomplished, Fox's party were glad to head them towards Lord Sandwich at the Admiralty. Here enthusiasm overstepped itself, and the unfortunate First Lord was obliged to run for it, accompanied by his mistress, Miss Ray, through the Admiralty garden to the shelter of the Horse Guards. The King thought it wise to warn Lord North to take care for himself: 'if possible', he wrote, 'come down [to the Commons] whilst I am at the House, as my guard will prevent any riot'. The broken windows were not however all suffered by the same side. A week or so later Horace Walpole was reporting that while Keppel was dining in the City, the riotous mob proved its pliabiity; or perhaps it was hired by the government party. 'It was believed,' said Walpole, 'to be at the instigation of the Court, to make the Opposition sick of such rejoicings, for many of the windows of the Opposition were broken, particularly Charles Fox's.'

England in 1779, as in 1588 and 1804 and 1940, was confronted by the imminent possibility, even likelihood, of foreign invasion. Affairs at home were in disarray: the senior naval ranks were torn apart by internecine squabbling while a Franco-Spanish fleet appeared to be lording it in the English Channel; the senior ministers were, in the popular judgement discredited and the prime minister's resoluteness was under question. Additional danger was threatening from Ireland, where the Protestant ascendancy was perceiving, in the happy combination of American example and British predicament, an inviting opportunity to exact concessions both trading and political. For a time, at about midsummer 1779, it looked as if the King himself might be thinking of taking over personal direction of affairs. He did indeed, for the first time in his reign, on 21 June preside at an emergency cabinet meeting (one of only three such in the entire reign); and when at Goodwood the Duke of Richmond 'publicly and flagrantly' refused to co-operate in plans to frustrate an invasion, the King summarily dismissed him from his Lord Lieutenancy of Sussex. If, said George, other Whig Lords Lieutenant felt like resigning in protest, let them go ahead: 'the sooner that office of dignity is in more friendly hands in every county the better'.[22] It was not 'the mere rumour of the streets', declared Richmond's nephew Fox in the Commons, 'that the King was his own [prime] minister'.[23] Of course he was not; but neither would he consent to be a cipher. He never forgot, or allowed his ministers to forget, that the position of the king at the apex of the constitutional triangle of monarch, lords and commons was historically unchallengeable. Royal authority was never to be treated as something merely ornamental or vestigial. His was a stubbornness of attitude and strength of resolve that was soon to come into headlong confrontation both with Fox personally and with Fox's own controversial and combative new interpretation of the constitution.

Spain had declared war in June 1779, which caused (according to Fitzpatrick) 'a very general consternation and a most universal acknowledgement of the necessity of changing the ministry'.[24] Fox was still being talked of as a recruit, perhaps as Navy Treasurer, and with this prospect in mind and with an acknowledgement of the acute seriousness of the national situation, Fox in the Commons spoke in terms of unwontedly prudent moderation. On this occasion it was left to Shelburne (whose Whig group were the main rivals of the Rockinghamites) to deliver what Fitzpatrick reckoned 'a most furious philippic, in the coarsest terms, against the ministers, North, Sandwich, and Germaine ... Our friend Carlisle,' he continued, 'attempted the defence of the latter ... An invasion either of England or Ireland must take place, and surely it is impossible these ministers should remain'.[25]

After parliament's prorogation, Fox hurried off to stay with friends at

Saltram, near Plymouth, where he expected to be seeing soon 'more interesting sport than partridge shooting', and where furious attempts were being made to strengthen the port's defences. On 27 August he dined on board ship in Torbay with a group of naval officers which included the future Admiral Jervis; and, sending his news back to Fitzpatrick, he reflected the sailors' own mixture of excited anticipation and bemused half-knowledge of the numerical strengths of the rival fleets. Were the combined French and Spanish fleets − for they had made a junction − of forty, or of fifty, ships of the line, or perhaps more still? The entire flotilla, with its frigates, was said to be of ninety sail. 'Jarvis thinks they are gone into Quiberon Bay', Fox wrote, ... '... to bring the troops with them that they may want for attacking the Isle of Wight, Portland, or whatever may be their object ... Others think that they are cruizing off the Lizard ... I think anything likely to happen here. The fleet to-day was a most majestic sight ... *On se sent ému beaucoup.*'[26]

Fox of course considered that if only Keppel were in charge, prospects would be more hopeful. But Keppel − and he was not alone in that faction-torn Royal Navy − had declined an invitation to command. Instead, the veteran Sir Charles Hardy had, *faute de mieux*, been appointed. He had cruised to the westward off the Scillies, playing a waiting game, but with orders specially toughened at the King's request to take *every reasonable but no unreasonable* risk in bringing the enemy to action. George did not believe scare-mongering rumours that Hardy's fleet was outnumbered by an enemy with fifty ships of the line. In fact, there were sixty-six of the enemy to the British thirty-eight, so Hardy's caution was understandable. On 2 September Sandwich reminded him that the eyes of the world were on him; yet the very next day he put in to Portsmouth to take on water. Critical voices declared it to be a retreat; and the King said that he should get quickly to sea again and give the enemy 'hard blows'. Meanwhile, however, George would have no truck with all the murmuring against Hardy. 'None of the popular names [such presumably as Keppel] would have dared to take such a part; but', he very characteristically added, 'I am not surprised, for the hand of Providence seems to be taking a part in our favour'. Like Cromwell, like Nelson, George III was ever convinced that God at heart was an Englishman. Certainly, during September, Providence declared decisively for the Royal Navy − or if not Providence, at least smallpox and 'putrid fever'. These were the 'hard blows' which finally paralysed the offensive intentions of the Franco-Spanish fleet, which was obliged to put back into Brest.

During the debate on the King's speech at parliament's reopening in November, a Scottish member, William Adam, announced that he was abandoning opposition and voting instead with the government. When Fox spoke later (powerfully, for nearly two hours),[27] he covered in his attack on the government all the ground where ministers were most vulnerable: the West Indies, where the islands of Dominica, Grenada, and St Vincent had been lost to the French; Ireland, where plainly trouble was brewing with the alarming growth of the 'Volunteer' movement, (eventually 40,000 men enlisted ostensibly to repel French invasion, but also very obviously to press for concessions from Westminster); and of course America. Fox demanded:

> What stripped Ireland of her troops? Was it not the American war? What brought on the hostilities of France and put Ireland in fear of an invasion? Was it not the American war? What gave Ireland the opportunity of establishing a powerful and illegal army? Certainly the American war!

He gave ministers their by now routine drubbing, and the King, as was becoming commoner now in Fox's speeches, did not escape a hinted reminder: it should 'never be one moment out of his Majesty's recollection' that the 'present sovereign's claim to the throne ... was founded upon the delinquency of the Stuart family'. Fox also directed some minor attention towards William Adam and his voting turnabout: he made damaging play with Adam's sanguine references to the West Indies – were we better situated '*because*, having lost three of our islands, we had less territory to defend?'; and dealt sarcastically with Adam's new-found respect for ministers – 'having once thought ill of them, a line of conduct still more disgraceful, more infamous, more destructive and ruinous, had at once done away the bad impression and had determined him to support them!'

Adam, much offended, took exception less to the speech itself than to the wide publicity the newspapers gave it. Their reporting, he alleged, reflected on him *personally*, and he therefore demanded 'the only satisfaction that such an injury will admit of'. Fox refused to apologize for newspaper reports for which he was not responsible; and four days later, in Hyde Park at eight in the morning, the matter was concluded in the manner then customary among gentlemen of honour. The cousin with whom, long before, the adolescent Charles Fox had been somewhat besotted, Lady Susan O'Brien (née Strangways), received from her husband a very detailed account of the affair, including the following:

... Mr Adam sent him a challenge on Sunday about 4 o'clock, in consequence
of wch they went out Monday morning early. Adam desir'd him to fire, wch
he refused, saying 'You think yourself injured, fire'; wch he did, and wounded
Chas slightly slantwise in the right of his belly just above the waistband,
pretty well aim'd you will say. Chas then fir'd and miss'd, on wch Fitzpatrick
step'd in and ask'd Adam if he was not satisfied, who sd 'No, unless Mr Fox
wd sign the paper he had propos'd to him'. Chas said that was impossible ...
if he was not satisfied he must proceed, on wch Mr A. with the utmost care
and deliberation level'd, fired, and thank God miss'd him. Chas then firing his
pistol in the air, the affair ended. It ... ought to be consider'd as a determin'd
plan'd assasination to get rid of an adversary they can't answer ... I heard of
it by accident abt one o'clock, and ... ran away to him, and found him lying
on the couch ... He shook me very heartily by the hand and told me he was
very well ... thank heaven it was the slightest thing in the world.[28]

Fox declared that he had been in negligible danger, since Adam was using
government powder.

While the remaining alarms in southern England subsided with the retirement of the French and Spanish fleets, and the American war still lacked
decisive issue, the crisis in Ireland mounted threateningly through the
summer and autumn of 1779. As early as May, a Londonderry newspaper
had reported, 'Scarcely a town here without its quota of volunteers, men
well armed, accoutred, and equipped'. Another Irish paper wrote, 'Under
a pretence of preparing to repell an invasion of this island, all sorts of
Protestants, but Dissenters most warmly, have taken up arms'. In October,
Lord Buckinghamshire, the Lord Lieutenant, added a still more alarming
note: 'I have been assur'd', he reported, 'that in different parts of Ireland
several have taken the oaths, and that more are inclin'd to it, but also there
are some companies [of volunteers] whose principles are determinedly
republican'.[29]

   The causes of the island's inflammable temper at this time were primarily
economic: the restrictions laid upon Irish trade had produced in the
language of a contemporary Irish petition 'the stagnation of commerce
and the failure of public and private credit', all of which had been made
more acute by the effects of the American war. But economics and politics
interacted, as ever, and among the placards placed around the pedestal of
Dublin's monument to King William III at the annual ceremony in
November celebrating that monarch's birthday could be seen several
eloquent of the situation: 'Relief to Ireland'; 'Free Trade or Else'; 'The
Glorious Revolution'; and (in Latin): '[50,000 Volunteers] Prepared to Die
for their Country'.

Among the dignitaries present that day was Fox's kinsman (his mother's brother-in-law) the Duke of Leinster, at the head of 200 men of the Dublin Volunteers, clad in the blue and buff made significant by their association with the American rebels. At the opening of the Irish parliament, just before this, the same men under the same leader had lined the street and *presented arms* as the Speaker's procession passed. Leinster was far from being a violent revolutionary, but Fox, on a six-week visit to his friends and relations in 1779,[30] could not fail to sniff what was blowing in the breeze of Irish politics. Indeed he clearly relished the atmosphere of rebellion, and resolved to make all possible use of it back at Westminster. A Commons speech of his as early as July already carried more than a hint of approval for revolution in certain circumstances. He was praising and quoting from a 'weighty and able' pamphlet (*the Extent of the Power of the British Parliament . . . in Relation to Ireland*) which declared that 'if one branch of the legislature becomes subservient to another, the people are at liberty to constitute themselves a new legislature' and, further, that 'every act of power exercised by the legislature over the people of another community is an usurpation of the fourth natural right of mankind'.

Even though they clearly leant towards support for Irish legislative independence, such words seem tame enough when they are compared with those Fox used a few months later, when he menacingly reminded George III that he sat on the British throne only because of the misdeeds of the Stuarts, and he ought therefore, it was strongly implied, to look to his own. George, he said, had acceded to the throne after the glorious reign of his grandfather. 'How sadly was the scene reversed! His empire dismembered, his councils distracted, his people falling off in their affection for his person!' If some surviving member of that house of Stuart were, in that year 1779, to look at the condition of Britain, might he not say

> 'You have banished my ancestor from the throne, and barred the sceptre from all his progeny . . . and yet the ministers of the present reign are ten times more wicked and more ignorant than those were . . .' When a nation was reduced to such a state of wretchedness . . . the people would inevitably take up arms, and the first characters in the kingdom would be seen in their ranks . . .

The Irish associations had been called illegal; legal or illegal, he entirely approved of them. He approved of manly determination which in the last resort, flies to arms in order to obtain deliverance ... He dreaded the consequences ... but whatever the effects might be, he was ready to acknowledge that such a power was inherent in men ... as a defence against the possible or actual abuse of power, political treachery, and the arts and intrigues of government ...[31]

Commenting on this two days later, the pro-administration *Morning Post* commented, 'Mr Fox in his parliamentary invocation to rebellion seems to strive as hard for a halter as any gentleman ever did in his desperate circumstances'.

By the month following, Fox was actually claiming – and at least for a space it was almost true – that the various Whig groups, Fox and his friends, Rockingham, Shelburne and their respective supporters, all were now one, and it was the *Crown's growing influence* which had united them – united indeed, so Fox declared, the whole nation; there were now, he said, only two parties in the kingdom:

'his Majesty's ministers supported by the influence of the crown, against all Britain ... The first men of rank, fortune, and character in both houses ... resolved to act in concert ... The sense of danger had brought about this coalition ... It was a lamentable contest in which his Majesty was engaged ... a contest with the whole body of his subjects.

This was language of a sort not hitherto heard during the reign (except perhaps from 'Junius' on one occasion), aimed directly at the monarch in person. For a time in mid-December it ceased, when North finally granted trade concessions to the Irish, the scope and generosity of which took both the British opposition and the Irish 'patriots' by surprise. The Irish were delighted as well as surprised; and several of their leaders failed to understand why Rockingham, Shelburne, Fox, and the rest remained so glumly critical. Could it be that the English Whigs had merely been using the Irish crisis as a ploy against North and the King and the Dublin Castle gang? Burke was even moved to complain of the 'acrimony' now being directed by the Irish patriots at their friends in Westminster. Thomas Townshend wrote in similar vein to the Irish peer, Charlemont. And Fox, apparently somewhat concerned by the voices coming out of Dublin, wrote to his kinsman Leinster: 'If , after all, we are suspected of not being friendly to Ireland, it is very hard, and upon me in particular, who certainly never missed any opportunity of declaring in public as well as in private how much I wished you success in all the points you were likely to push.'[32]

The royal influence which kept North still in office* (however much against his personal wishes), and which had now become the central object of Fox's hostility, was no figment of the imagination, though the belief that it had increased greatly during the 1760s and 1770s *was*. It existed, certainly, as it had traditionally existed; and with George III it operated through the Treasury, the secret service monies, and the civil list. In what senses it was, as Fox and Burke alleged, 'corrupt' poses questions both historical and semantic. Tradition had given such influence acceptance, just as the traditional payment of a salary to the by then obsolete Clerk of the Pells, for instance, had given Fox the sinecure that he had sold back to the Treasury in return for the sizable annual pension which supported him for the rest of his life. If political corruption is interpreted at its strictest in that any political power or position purchased by money or possessions is condemned, then a very great deal of eighteenth century politics was undoubtedly corrupt – from the Treasury or the Crown buying votes to secure the election of a candidate in an 'open' borough, to the oligarch Lord Rockingham, for instance, nominating a clutch of members for the 'rotten' boroughs under his personal control. Until 1780, Fox's very presence in parliament was thanks to the corrupt electoral arrangements at Midhurst and Malmesbury, and although Burke, his ablest ally in the campaign against the allegedly corrupt royal and governmental influence, sat between 1774 and 1780 for the 'open' borough of Bristol, faced with defeat there in 1780 he was happy to find refuge in one of Rockingham's safe but incontestably 'rotten' seats in Yorkshire. As the furious Whig attack on the blackness of 'corrupt influence' gathers momentum at this time, it is not always easy to judge between the kettle and the pot.

---

*Largely at this time by the watchful and tireless efforts of North's principal assistant and the King's invaluable servant John Robinson, Secretary to the Treasury, effectively the manager of the administration's electoral business. Robinson was indispensable to the King in his efforts to sustain North and keep him up to the mark. The King to Robinson, 6 November 1778: ' ... [North] must cast off his indecision and bear up or no plan can succeed; he must be more exact in answering letters or let others do it for him ...'; and on 11 May 1779, 'Mr Robinson must today attempt his irksome part of rouzing Lord North to act as he ought'. There are many similar letters.

5

THE PEOPLE
AND THE CROWN

1780

In the debate between opposition and government, or between Whigs and the Crown, which had so far proceeded, 'the people', except during the Wilkes troubles of 1763 and 1768–9, had played no part. But during the first four months of 1780 there came stirrings of popular activity and agitation more significant and widespread than anything that had occurred during the Wilkes episodes, and they afforded Fox an unexpected opportunity. Through 'the people' he attempted to force changes which parliament of its own had been unwilling or unable to bring about: ejecting the North ministry and pruning the powers of the Crown. Wilkes was to be involved in this 1780 movement too, but, as he was a City of London dignitary by this time, he spoke his lines now only in one of the minor roles of the drama, while Fox took his chance to move centre-stage.

The Petitioning (or Association) Movement began somewhat as the agitation of 1768–9 had begun, in Middlesex. 'Middlesex' in the eighteenth century meant, largely, London and its suburbs north of the Thames, excluding the square mile of the ancient City. However, the reform petition of the Middlesex freeholders in December 1779, threateningly though some of them spoke of 'coming to the House with other instruments than parchment', soon took second place to what was happening in Yorkshire. There, the Rev. Christopher Wyvill, a substantial landowner, having previously circularized his fellow Yorkshire freeholders, called a meeting at the York Assembly Rooms for 30 December. The Middlesex grievances had been mainly electoral; those of the Yorkshiremen concerned variously the high land tax, 'distressfully' low prices for farm produce, the waste of public money in 'sinecures and unmerited pensions', and – a late addition – the 'great and unconstitutional influence of the crown' which, if not checked, 'may soon prove fatal to the liberties of this country'.

Yorkshire was Lord Rockingham's kingdom, and Wyvill had consulted and been advised by the Rockinghamite member for the county, Sir George Savile; but at the freeholders' meeting on 30 December, although Rockingham himself together with two Dukes and four Earls attended, Wyvill managed to exclude those whom he spoke of as 'the barony' from his movement. Even so, the total annual income of the men present that day, so Rockingham himself estimated, amounted to £800,000.[1] If this was 'the people of England speaking', it was certainly not the poor 'associating' against the rich.

Only four days after the adoption of the Yorkshire petition, Hampshire followed suit. Three days later again, the electors of Middlesex assembled at the Mermaid Tavern in Hackney and followed the Yorkshire example; according to their list of grievances, the county of Middlesex 'in particular was oppressed by the house tax'. The Duke of Portland, soon from the eminence of his rank to be the titular head of the Foxite Whigs, attended this meeting, which declared publicly in favour of a *nationwide* association of petitioners. Other magnates began to patronize the movement, the Duke of Richmond proclaiming in the House of Lords that he was proud to have helped promote the Sussex petition, while Earl Temple thought it proper to *apologize* for leaving the freeholders of Buckinghamshire to their own devices. The young Lord Mahon, Chatham's son-in-law, was active both in Buckinghamshire and his own county of Kent, where his young brother-in-law William Pitt was also on the committee. The Duke of Manchester supported the petitioners at Huntingdon, but Huntingdonshire was also Lord Sandwich territory, and faction-fights resulted when Sandwich brought his own supporters to the meeting.

Wyvill, mistrustful of 'parliament-men', succeeded in frustrating the attempt by the Rockingham Whigs to take his movement under their wing. In the south, Fox and his uncle Richmond had better success, despite some embarrassment they faced in espousing a cause among whose aims were the elimination of sinecures and unmerited pensions, and a reduction in expenditure of public money – in short, what was then known as 'economical' reform. Richmond, as a descendant of Charles II, was known to be the fortunate beneficiary of a particularly valuable sinecure, the profits arising from 'a penny a chaldron' on all the coal brought into London – a prescriptive right bringing him, it was thought, £16,000 a year. (The Duke of Grafton, also descended from Charles II, deemed it wise about now to apologize in the Lords for a similarly-inherited privilege.) Fox enjoyed nothing quite so time-hallowed or spectacular; but such money as he had not already gambled away came either from recent good fortune at gaming, or from a Treasury pension converted from his sinecure, or – most notoriously of all – from his father's sensational profits made as Paymaster, for which the accounts were still not closed. To his un-derstandable vexation, Fox was repeatedly being reminded that his father was 'the defaulter of unaccounted millions'; and during the budget debate in this very year 1780, Lord George Gordon, very soon to be notorious himself in a very different sort of scandal, taunted Fox upon his 'great and superior knowledge in the business of making loans', and his ability 'to borrow money on better terms than the noble Lord [North]'.[2]

A further embarrassment for Fox, as he now prepared to become 'a man for the people' and a co-petitioner with Wilkes and other such radicals, was his record as a pro-administration anti-Wilkite, forceful and extreme in his pronouncements twelve years before. During the Middlesex election controversy of that time he had emphatically laid it down that the voice of the people ought to be heard only within the Commons that represented them. It was a complete turnabout now for him to hear 'the people' speaking, and speaking loudly, 'outdoors'.

On 27 January 1780, at Devizes, he addressed some 150 freeholders of Wiltshire, the county long associated with his family. Nothing had been done for Ireland, he reminded them, until the Irish took to looking after their own interests, so let the men of Wiltshire consider their own weight and consequence. He knew that some of them were having to deny themselves 'even the decent conveniences of life ... In God's name was the King to be the only person who was to feel nothing from the distresses of the kingdom?'[3]

This marked a quite new experience for Fox. It was the first public meeting at which he had ever spoken and – in his own angled comment – the first *uncorrupt* assembly he had ever addressed. It exhilarated him. But it was nothing to what was coming a few days later. At a big meeting in historic Westminster Hall, very heavily attended (his supporters claimed by three or four thousand) he scored a genuine triumph. Flanked by John Wilkes, John Jebb, and other radicals, he launched into the sort of speech which he perhaps of all the orators of that era was best at – spontaneous, trenchant, fiery, demagogical. It captivated his excited audience. If, he said, the House of Commons failed in its duty (which was to grant the demands of the petition) — from that moment

> they ceased to be representatives of the people; and it was legal, constitutional, and necessary for the people to assume that trust which their delegates had thrown off ... The people must be the ministers of their own deliverance and the road to it was open ... Their brethren in America and their brethren in Ireland had taught them how to act ... Were they not born from the same originals? Shall the heart of the empire be tame and lifeless while the limbs are in activity and motion?

Fox was, there and then, nominated and instructed to deliver the Westminster petition to parliament, and invited with acclamation to become Whig candidate at Westminster, the country's most 'open' borough, in the forthcoming general election.

Further, as chairman of the Westminster committee, Fox became not only a link between the Westminster petitioners and the Westminster parliament, but also the liaison between Westminster and the petitioning counties around the country — there were soon seventeen of them — as well as various petitioning cities. However, not every county proved entirely happy with the direction the movement seemed to be taking, or with the growing dominance of the three closely co-ordinated metropolitan committees of Westminster, London, and Middlesex. Wyvill particularly (who, after all, had originated the movement), and others of a like mind, not only mistrusted Fox personally, but basically suspected all 'parliament-men'. Never fully formulated, but persisting in the mind of Wyvill and his friends was the dream of what might be called an anti-parliament, an 'association' alternative to and corrective of the House of Commons. John Jebb considered that when the association of the counties was fully organized, it would be 'constitutional to declare the House of Commons dissolved', and then that the decisions of the county associations when ratified by the Lords and approved by the King would have the force of law.[4] Many differences began to arise both over the content of the reform programme to be presented and the tactics with which to pursue it. Some of the Yorkshire committee, for instance, argued for tests to be imposed on candidates proposing themselves for parliamentary election, an idea which scandalized Lord Rockingham. He himself, and most, though not all of his leading colleagues, had as their priority 'economical' reform, which meant cutting away the administrative dead wood, removing sinecures and other fossilized and expensive relics, and thereby incidentally reducing the monarch's ability to buy favours. These men — notably Rockingham, Burke, and the Cavendishes – rejected more fundamental parliamentary reform, but the Westminster and Middlesex reformers into whose company Fox had now become drawn were pushing for a variety of innovations. Two in particular they wanted: repeal of the Septennial Act with, in its place, a general election every year or every third year; and an increase in the county representation (perhaps a hundred new members) to correct the influence of the 'corrupt' boroughs. Whereas some of the petitioners went much further, a few even advocating universal male suffrage, the indifference of many of them to economical reform disappointed the Rockingham Whigs.

A speaker at a meeting in February at London's Guildhall was surely not far wrong when he argued that Mr Fox, acting now as 'head of opposition' and declaring petitions to be the voice of the people, had 'changed his opinions and his conduct as much as any man living'.[5] And Horace Walpole found himself reflecting how 'curious' it was to find Charles Fox, of late so unpopular, suddenly transformed into the people's idol, despite the fact that his family still owed the public accounts £200,000.

In the Westminster committee, Fox sided on the whole with the conservatives against the radicals, of whom perhaps the most important, as well as the most attractive, was the gentle extremist John Jebb, the man who first proposed Fox as Westminster's future parliamentary candidate. It eventually proved easier for Fox to become the idol of the people than to concert policies with even his one local committee, at Westminster, let alone those of seventeen different and differing counties, plus a number of petitioning cities. Particularly Fox was at odds with Wyvill, who persisted in standing, as he put it, with 'the independent gentlemen of Yorkshire', and wished to have as little as possible to do with not only Fox personally, but 'all great partisans and parliamentary leaders of either house'.[6] And for his part Fox could never be persuaded to lend serious support, whatever his flights of rhetoric declared, to any such anti-parliamentary campaign. Flourishing the banner of the Petitioning (or 'Association') movement for his own purposes allowed him to indulge a delightful new experience – popularity. He could exercise his new-found talent for public display and flirt enjoyably with demagoguery, but he would never agree that the decisive victory (which meant essentially the ousting of North and curbing of the King's influence) should be won anywhere but in the House of Commons.

In at least two respects, however, Fox's spell in the limelight as 'man of the people' (more realistically, perhaps, 'man of the substantial county freeholders') had lasting effects. It introduced him to the constituency of Westminster, which he was to represent for the next quarter of a century, until his death; and it converted him, however warily and with whatever provisos, to the cause of parliamentary reform beyond the merely 'economical' reform within which Burke and the more conservative Rockingham Whigs limited their endeavours.

As the petitions continued to roll towards parliament through February and March 1780, the chief business in the Commons concerned Burke's Establishment Bill and two subsidiary Whig measures of economical reform. In all this Burke excelled himslf, and during his bill's laborious progress made one of the most celebrated and brilliant of all his many great speeches; but the going was hard and exhausting. Not only Burke himself, but his supporters Fox and the Shelburnite Whig Barré, according to the *Morning Chronicle*, 'were yesterday so hoarse and so ill, in consequence of their hard parliamentary duty for these ten days that they could hardly make themselves heard'. Crucial clauses in Burke's bill concerned economies to be made in the royal household, and abolition of the office of Third Secretary of State, currently held by Fox's *bête noire*, Lord George Germain. Both these moves naturally commanded Fox's vehement support, since both, he claimed, would not only save public money but lessen 'the monstrous influence of the Crown'. When, however, these and other key clauses were defeated (less probably through 'corrupt influence' than by the votes of *uninfluenced* members), an exhausted and depressed Burke temporarily gave up the struggle. Economical reform had to wait another two years.

When the Commons reassembled after Easter on 6 April 1780, it was for the express purpose of 'taking the petitions into consideration'. Since trouble 'outdoors' was expected, a Guards regiment was held ready, 'each man provided with ten rounds of ball' – ominously, perhaps, it was the same regiment that had been involved in the so-called 'massacre of St George's Fields' in the disturbances of twelve years before. On 6 April Fox and others of his committee

> met at the King's Arms, Palace Yard, and about one o'clock went in procession
> ... preceded by ... a person bearing a blue flag, with the following words
> in large white letters: *Annual Parliaments and Equal Representation* ... Upwards
> of three thousand people ... received the Committee with three cheers.[7]

Fox then addressed the crowd for three-quarters of an hour, a sub-committee of himself, Fitzpatrick, and Sheridan having previously drawn up a 'Plan of Association' which included demands for 'shorter' parliaments and a hundred more of the 'purer' county seats. Inside the House, where the petitions were to be considered, it was to be one of the Commons' great, sensational days. It had fallen to the Shelburnite Whig, Dunning, to propose a set of resolutions, and the first of these asked members to declare 'that the influence of the Crown has increased, is increasing, and ought to be diminished'. This was *passed* by 233 votes to 215.

The very success of this famous motion poses a paradox. If House of Commons voting was as corrupt as the Whigs alleged, with so many members in the pay of the Court, how came it about that they had thus bitten the hand that fed them? Did the success of the motion invalidate what it asserted? Fox, like Burke, was always liable to explain what was to them the exasperating *wrong-headedness* of Commons votes by attributing it exaggeratedly to administrative and (especially in Fox's case) royal turpitude. In fact, both of them, and indeed the Whigs in general, appear at this time constantly to have overestimated the part played by corrupt influence, and particularly the extent to which it had recently increased. They consistently undervalued the capacity of independent members – perhaps a third of the total – to judge and vote as they thought proper.

Lord North, allegedly the very instrument of royal control, had been chronically nervous of the reliability of the votes of the country gentlemen, as indeed he had every right to be, for was it not they who at long last would topple him? It was these independents who had tipped the scales against Burke's economical reform bill, and again it was the independents – many of them substantial county freeholders themselves, sharing in most of Wyvill's Yorkshire grumbles – who helped to carry, by that still narrow margin, Dunning's celebrated first resolution. What seems to emerge from these puzzling currents and counter-currents of evidence is that, whereas there was considerable feeling that Crown influence *had* increased – which caused some concern – the political majority disapproved of assaults upon the King's dignity and had no wish to see him subjected to domination by the Whigs.[8]

To Horace Walpole, and many more, the 'blow' of 6 April seemed decisive; 'to combat on the same field of battle after being vanquished will, in my opinion, be frenzy'.[9] But the King judged otherwise; well before this, he had advised North not to lose heart because of an occasional parliamentary defeat; and now he wrote composedly to an agitated and depressed North (talking yet again of resigning) not to take the defeat 'personally' – it was all too clear against whom the vote was *'personally levelled'*. And the Commons' independent members were soon ready to show that they were far from turning Whig. By 13 April they had helped to throw out another measure of economical reform, Crewe's bill to disfranchize revenue officers. The House of Lords followed, by rejecting the Whig bill denying government contractors the right to sit in parliament – this despite an indiscreet and probably unpersuasive warning from Lord Shelburne about 'the people' in the streets 'clamorous for redress of grievances, ripe for any violence, and easy to be led to such measures as would shake the kingdom to its centre'.

Less than three weeks after the Whigs' day of triumph, with North's government apparently undismayed and certainly undislodged, Dunning tried again. (In the interim Fox had had an interview with North, trying for an 'arrangement', but without success.)[10] This time Dunning moved that the King be requested not to dissolve or prorogue parliament until 'proper measures' had been taken to correct the abuses complained of in the petitions. In the debate that followed, there were references, from both sides, to the year 1641; and Fox declared that what they were discussing was 'whether Englishmen were again to fight for their liberties, were again ready to take the field in opposition to arbitrary power';[11] if Charles I had only listened to 'the just grievances of people', there would have been no civil war. But the Whigs' temporary allies among the non-party members now deserted them; the government came home with the comfortable majority of 51.

Fox's frustration erupted in fury – and it was fury directed less against king or ministers than against those very county members whose numbers, as he had so recently declared, deserved to be increased by the addition of a hundred seats, since these were the men who represented the purer, more virtuous, aspects of the constitution. He was 'at a loss for words', he protested – but not for long:

> ... It was shameful, it was base, it was unmanly, it was treacherous ... The defection which he had alluded to originated chiefly among the county members, many of them of great weight and respect; but however high they might stand in the estimation of their friends in their counties ... he should ever judge of men by their conduct ...

He would make 'one more trial', he said, in a speech of bitter desperation,

> one effort more, in expectation that those who had deserted their principles would endeavour to retrieve their public character. If that last effort should

miscarry, he should then know what to do ... He would quit the House ...
The people had resources still left ...[12]

The Petitioning Movement did not immediately collapse, but it had passed the peak of its challenge to government and Commons. Fox of course did not 'quit the House'. Events moreover started to move somewhat the ministry's way, so that, after all, it began to look as though Lord North might be going to enjoy a political Indian summer. Germain's stubborn confidence – and the King's too – that in the end the American rebellion would be defeated gained some credibility when the British campaign in the South achieved significant successes, and captured Charleston. And then, after London's terrifying week of riots in June 1780, it suddenly appeared no longer prudent, even among the radicals and rhetoricians, to talk of 'the people outdoors' *knowing what to do* if parliamentary pressures failed.

The Gordon Riots were themselves a by-product of the Petitioning Movement. A Rockinghamite measure of Catholic relief (Savile's Act) had passed through parliament in 1778, repealing the very harsh penal act of 1699; and when analogous steps had been proposed the following year for Scotland, there was anti-Catholic rioting in Glasgow and Edinburgh which led to the measures being halted. Scottish Catholics, very reasonably frightened, themselves supported postponement. Fox, on the other hand, had taken the view that it ill became the honour and dignity of parliament to be thus deterred by 'little insurrections' in a 'small corner of the empire'.[13] It was the Scotsmen who first formed a Protestant Association to oppose further liberalization of the old anti-Catholic laws. Then in November 1779 a Commons member, Lord George Gordon, accepted the presidency of a parallel London-based association, which quickly attracted a big following, especially among some of the more ignorant and impressionable of London's poor, easily roused by the old cry of 'No Popery'. A petition was planned, which Gordon announced he would personally present in the House of Commons, but only when it had 20,000 signatures. For his part, 'he would run all hazards with the people'. Gordon's mental stability was in doubt, and his language was fanatical and sanguinary. Rumours and counter-rumours multiplied. Issues and grievances other than religious accrued. The outcome was the worst week of violence in London's peacetime history: arson, riot, and pillage, with drunken mobs at large; Catholic chapels and the houses of Catholics fired; liquor looted and distilleries raided; Newgate prisoners set free, hundreds (perhaps as many as 450) dead.

Magistrates, City authorities, and the government having lost control, it was left to the King to issue to the troops the orders which restored, though of course bloodily, peace to the London streets. The horrors of that week proved more than enough to cool petitioning ardour. More, the Gordon riots had demonstrated the potential fragility of the social fabric, and remained in the collective memory long enough to provide at least one reason – one, no doubt, of many – why, ten or twenty years later, there would be no *British* French Revolution. The majority opinion among 'the people' would approve the repressive measures which Pitt's government took against the Tom Paine radicals and revolutionary sympathizers of the 1790s.

When in the summer of 1780 the King and his advisers yet again reviewed chances of strengthening the administration, Fox's was one of the names considered. The King's objection was qualified. If he was to be admitted, he must understand that his support must be steady, and let him be offered, not a 'ministerial' post (one, that is, concerned with issues of policy) but a 'lucrative' one. Not unnaturally the King thought that Fox would be glad of the money: 'he never having had any principle can certainly act as his interest may guide him'.[14] However, after British victories in Carolina and the shock of the June riots the government's prospects had revived, and since their electoral managers were on the whole optimistic after totting up the *pros* and *hopefuls* against the *doubtfuls* and *cons*, thoughts of reshaping North's ten-year-old ministry were abandoned and, instead, a general election was called for the autumn, one year ahead of the obligatory date.

Fox was taken by surprise, as most were. He was on his way to Bath for medical attention when the election was announced. First therefore insuring his chances of getting himself nominated for what he judged a safe seat, Bridgwater,* he returned with minimum delay to Westminster, which was far from being a safe Whig seat. He faced two ministerial opponents. One, Admiral Rodney, was currently on active service off the West Indies, but his popularity almost certainly guaranteed that he would head the poll. The other, Lord Lincoln, son of the Duke of Newcastle, would be the man to beat for the second Westminster seat. North knew that a tough fight lay ahead, and wrote to his Treasury Secretary, Robinson: 'If Mr Fox stands we shall have much trouble and more expense'. (In the event they were to spend £8,000 on this Westminster contest.)[15]

---

* Neglecting to canvass there, however, he came fourth.

The electioneering proved arduous, and Fox entered with gusto into what, in this exceptionally democratic constituency, was for him a novel experience, having to earn votes from the hustings. The religious riots of three months earlier being still a vivid memory, and his supporters being nervous that Catholicism would prove a subject where his views might be judged too tolerant, they pressed him to be more outspokenly anti-papist than he found easy. 'A voter asked me publicly today', he wrote to Burke, 'whether I would do my endeavours for the repeal of the popish bill [Catholic Relief Act] declaring that his vote should be guided by my answer. I told him I would not, upon which he went away and would not vote at all.' Fox's supporters eventually persuaded him to agree to a form of words in a declaration which he published, satisfying as far as was possible both principle and prudence: 'I never have supported nor ever will support any measure prejudicial to the Protestant religion, or tending to *establish* popery in this kingdom'.

By 9 October Lord Lincoln was ready to acknowledge defeat; Fox polled 3,805, Lincoln 3,070, with Rodney comfortably ahead of them both. 'Charles is pretty knocked up', Fitzpatrick wrote to his brother Ossory. 'He was yesterday carried triumphantly through the whole town.' It was a notable victory which he had scored but, in general, Whig inroads into the ministerial majority were inadequate to threaten it yet. The glorious 6 April, six months back – Dunning's day – was dead and buried, and for Fox nearly eighteen more months of frustrated opposition lay ahead.

6

BROOKS'S

After the Prince of Wales reached the age of 18 in 1780 and was given his own establishment, his conduct began, as Walpole put it, 'to make the greatest noise'. At the Queen's weekly receptions known as 'Drawing-rooms', he talked 'irreligiously and indecently in the openest manner ... He passed the nights in the lowest debaucheries, at the same time bragging of intrigues with women of quality, whom he named publicly'. Walpole was told by George III's brother, the Duke of Gloucester, that after learning details of one particular drunken debauch of his son's at Lord Chesterfield's, the King had been so distressed that he had not slept for ten nights. And unhappily the current mentor of the young Prince in his life of dissipation was the King's other brother, that experienced roué the Duke of Cumberland. As yet, the name of Charles Fox does not much appear in company with the Prince's, though soon it will; and when someone asked the King why he did not come down harder upon his reprobate son and heir, he gave as his reason that he was afraid of *driving him into the arms of the opposition.*[1] In view of the history of the political affiliations of previous Hanoverian Princes of Wales, that was a most understandable fear. And a friend writing to Lord Carlisle after attending Court on New Year's Day in 1781 had not failed to notice which way the wind was blowing: 'The Prince of Wales was there with his new establishment, which they say he is not much pleased with. Charles Fox was there too, and the court that I take it he meant to pay seemed to be very well received'.

George Selwyn was in his sixties now, and rather out of sympathy with Fox and his hard-living, high-gambling young bloods at Brooks's. Selwyn found White's, on the opposite side of St James's Street, more to his elderly liking. White's, he told Lord Carlisle, had 300 members, with little gambling beyond the 'occasional *trente-quarante** for a few guineas'. Moreover it was very 'tolerating and agreeable', and allowed as members Scotchmen, papists, and just one Jew. Although even White's, so he avowed, afforded him 'but very little amusement', still he felt both happier and safer there than over the road at Brooks's, which he considered 'a precipice of perdition',[2] into whose abyss he had narrowly escaped falling. Brooks's prince of perdition, dangerous as Mephistopheles and as fascinating (it was 'impossible not to love him') was of course Charles Fox. It was not that he neglected his Commons duties – routine harassment of the ministry and some strongly personal attacks on Germain and Sandwich continued much as before, and Walpole reckoned Fox currently 'the first figure in parliament' – but Fox's notion of a satisfactory twenty-four hours apparently embraced a race-meeting at Newmarket, with an evening speech in the Commons to follow, and finally a nocturnal session at Brooks's with a thousand guineas or two won or lost at quinze or faro.† There was circulating a not wholly unbelievable story that he had 'levanted every soul at Newmarket' – absconded, that is, without paying his losses. Meanwhile, at Brooks's, he and Fitzpatrick, with Brooks himself as financial backer, had begun making good what they had lost by setting up as bankers themselves at the faro table.

Although Selwyn claimed that he had 'relinquished *nasty Brooks's*', he could never deny himself the pleasure of keeping one eye on its intriguing nastiness, and in his many letters to Lord Carlisle (at the time Lord Lieutenant in Dublin) we get a lively succession of White's-eye views of the *Brooksiana* of 1781. Thus:[3]

> *24 March* The play at Brooks's is exorbitant ... Charles looks wretchedly [was this perhaps from 'his old complaint in the bowels'?] ... but I have scarce seen him.

> (*27 March, Anthony Storer to Carlisle*) Lord Cholmondeley holds a (I do not know how to spell) Pharaoh bank; Charles and Richard, and I suppose Brookes and Co., have their share in another.

> *4 May Selwyn to Carlisle* Charles and [Fitzpatrick's] bank is *florissante; elle baisse*

---

* Also known as '*rouge et noir*', where 30 or 40 are respectively winning and losing numbers.
† Faro, Pharo, Pharaoh: a card game in which the players gamble on the order in which certain cards will appear when taken singly from the top of the pack. 'Pharaoh' was the King of Hearts. Quinze: a game depending on chance in which the winner is that player who obtains 15 points or comes nearest to that number without exceeding it.

et se lève, mais elle ne laisse pas d'être une ressource immense. I see old debtors
in Charles's parlour as I go by; upon the strength of it I shall desire Clegg to
move for a clearing, while there is still a shilling left. (Fox, after more than
7 years, still owed money to Carlisle).

7 May His bank thrives prodigiously, and, what is more, he has punted with
the same success that he has held the bank. He is now in prodigious affluence.
He bought last week Truth, a racehorse, for the Lord knows what ... He
comes up tomorrow for the business in the House of Commons.

16 May I saw Charles today in a new hat, frock, waistcoat, shirt, and stockings;
he was as clean and smug as a gentleman, and upon perceiving my surprise,
he told me that it was from the Pharo Bank. He then told of the thousands
it had lost, which I told him only proved its substance, and the advantages of
trade. He smiled, and seemed perfectly satisfied with that which he had taken
up; he was in such a sort of humour that I should have liked to have dined
with him. His old clothes, I suppose, have been burned ...

21 May Yesterday about the middle of the day, passing by Brooks's, I saw a
Hackney coach, which announced a late sitting. I had the curiosity to enquire
how things were, and found Richard in his Pharo pulpit, where he had been,
alternately with Charles, since the night before, and dealing to Adm[iral]
Pigott only. I saw a card on the table – 'Received from Messieurs Fox and
Co., 1500 guineas'. The bank ceased in a few minutes after I was in the room;
it was a little after 12 at noon, and it had won 3,400 or 500 g[uineas]. Pigot,
I believe, was the chief loser ... Charles says he is *accablé de demandes, comme
de dettes, et avec la réputation d'avoir de l'argent, il ne sait où donner de la tête* ...
son charactère, son génie, et sa conduite sont également extraordinaires et ...
incompréhensibles.

(21 May, same day, Storer to Carlisle) The Pharaoh bankers are in excessive
great fashion ... Charles Fox's bank thrives because he has a great deal of
money, and yet has lost a great [deal] too at all other sorts of gaming. He
lost eighteen hundred the other night at quinze. Richard and he deal by turns,
so that there is never any cessation of the bank ... The vestal fire is perpetually
kept up ... Selwyn holds a minor bank at White's, but that is ... of so little
importance that it is hardly worth mentioning.

Fox having stood as security for an annuity of Fitzpatrick's, and Fitzpatrick having failed to meet his obligations under it, the property of both
of them began now to be under siege from the bailiffs. 'Fitzpatrick's horses
were the other day taken from his coach', Lady Ossory told Selwyn, and
there had been two 'executions' in Fox's house,[4] Fox protesting for
unexplained reasons that he was not prepared to use the faro bank's profits
to pay what was owing. Then, towards the end of May, the public in

St James's Street were privileged to be spectators of an entertaining pantomime:

> While Charles, Richard, and Hare [James Hare, co-opted as banker] are holding the Pharaoh bank night and day, the bailiffs are ransacking Charles' house. I went into the house when it was pulling to pieces, in order to enquire into the fate of the books, and I learnt that they were going too to the Jews. While Charles was poor he had a comfortable house, now he is rich he is turned out of doors.[5]

This was Storer's account. Selwyn's ran similarly:

> For these two days past, all passengers in St James's Street have been amused with seeing two carts at Charles's door filling by the Jews, with his goods, clothes, books, and pictures. He was waked by [his servant] yesterday, and Hare afterwards by his *valet de chambre*, they being told at the same time that the execution was begun, and the carts were drawn up against the door. Such furniture I never saw ... Charles, with all Brooks's on his behalf, is in the highest spirits. And while this execution is going on in one part of the street, Charles, Richard, and Hare are alternately holding a bank of £3000 ostensible, and by which they must have got among them near £2000. Lord Robert [Spencer] since his bankruptcy, and in consideration of his party principles, is admitted, I am told, to some small share in this. What public business is going on I know not, for all the discourse at which I am present turns upon this bank. Offly [Lord Offaly, one of Fox's Fitzgerald cousins] sat up last night till four, and I believe has lost a good part of his last legacy. Lord Spencer did not sit up, but was there punting at four. Now the windows are open at break of day ...
>
> ... This Pharo Bank is held in a manner which, being so exposed to public view, bids defiance to all decency and police. The whole town as it passes views the dealer and the punters, by means of the candles, and the windows being levelled with the ground. The Opposition, who have Charles for their ablest advocate, is quite ashamed of the proceeding, and hates to hear it mentioned.[6]

The bank was reputed by early June to hold a balance of £30,000, and Fox asked Selwyn 'to send Gregg to him' – Gregg acting for Lord Carlisle – so that he could at last discharge his debt and 'pay off the arrears at the same time'. Fox himself told Selwyn that *at one time* his own share of the faro profits, plus his winnings at punting and quinze, amounted *itself* to £30,000 in all. However, as Selwyn and indeed everybody knew, 'Charles's property is of a very fluctuating kind', and the latest item of news was that he had just lost £5,000 to General Smith at picquet, and 'was then playing with him at £100 a game'.[7] When Selwyn dunned Fox once more on 22 June for Carlisle's money, he found the bank's tide at low ebb, and Fox put him off with saying that he *had* paid £600, and would pay 'the other six when things are mended'. *'Cela n'est pas mal'*, Selwyn added; 'I appeared satisfied, and said that Gregg and I were much pleased with his disposition to do what he could'. The misfortune was that Charles had 'not much vanity about paying what he owes'; appeals to his self-respect cut little ice; and if he was criticized to his face, he would always be disarming by refusing to take anything ill.[8] He was certainly 'in high feather, and spirits, and cash; and pays, and loses, and wins, and insures, and performs all kinds of feats ...' On 30 June, Selwyn renewed his gossip bulletin to Carlisle:

> The bank won last night considerably; the General again the loser. The small fry around the table put me in mind of all the little porpoises which you see leaping into the great one's mouth in the *Ombres Chinoises*. Charles was at the Quinze table, and seemed to be winning. I never see him but with heaps of gold before him. His house ... where he is to go soon is the sprucest to look at from the street I ever saw. I never knew such a transition from distress to opulency, or from dirt to cleanliness.
>
> There was a very warm altercation in the H[ouse] yesterday between him and [Henry Dundas, the Lord Advocate]. He then went and dined at Vauxhall. If he is at last a field preacher, I shall not be surprised.
>
> In fact ... *nothing* which can happen to him will surprise me; he seems a kind of meteor, *fait pour passer bien vite.*[9]

October meant the Newmarket autumn races. According to Hare, his fellow at the faro bank, Fox had a poor meeting financially, losing about £10,000, the greatest part of it on races, and the rest to General Smith at picquet'.[10] Next month, it was time for the new season to begin, both for Brooks's bank and the House of Commons. Members of parliament were anxiously waiting news from Cornwallis's crucial campaign in America. The Brooks's bankers meanwhile were in some disarray. James Hare reported at length to Carlisle in Dublin, with various addenda medical and sexual, such as the latest gossip concerning Mrs Benwell, the mistress Fitzpatrick was currently sharing with the Prince of Wales, and the pursuit of the comedy actress Miss Farren by the Earl of Derby,* a Brooks's 'regular' (he was soon to make her his Countess), and an assortment of news about Charles Fox. Though happily 'free from that dreadful disorder

---

* After whom the famous horse race is named.

in his bowels', he was apparently afflicted now by a different complaint, which was

> that he cannot be as foolish as he was formerly about women, and that though he takes great pains to fall in love, he cannot bring it about ... Whenever he has a fancy for any woman it makes him so unhappy and so ridiculous that I most sincerely hope his complaint may continue.[11]

As to the bankers' disarray:

> Most of the joint annuitants agreed to a proposal made to them by Richard and Charles, viz., to receive £6000 immediately, and the remainder in instalments in three years. One of them refused to accept this proposal, and seized soon after the proposal four of Charles's horses, which were of trifling value, and therefore bought in again at a small expense by Derby, in whose name they now stand ... Thus, you see, the Bankers did not meet at the beginning of the winter in the same opulent circumstances as they had parted in at the end of the last campaign ... The club at Brooks's is very ill attended, and Brookes enraged to the last degree that gentlemen should presume to think of anything but making his fortune. He complained to Charles that there was £17,000 owing to the house, which is a most important lie ... He has £15,000 belonging to the proprietors of the Bank in his hands, for which he pays no interest, though he receives at least 5 per cent, for all money owing to him.[12]

However, the news from Brooks's was not wholly bad. The 'infinitely agreeable' Fox was soon able to show Selwyn 'two of Brooks's cards; on one he was Dr. £4000, on another Cr. £11,000'. Faro and quinze fevers moreover were sweeping the fashionable quarters of the town. Reports were constantly coming in of another gaming house opening, the Duke of Cumberland's, for instance (much frequented, unfortunately, by the Prince of Wales), and one started by an army surgeon, Burlton (in which the Duchess of R___d was rumoured, scandalously enough, to have a share). And there were new clubs starting up too, such as Weltje's, also in St James's Street, for young supporters of the government, and Kenny's – and more significantly, Goostrees, 'for young men of the opposition, very nice in their admissions, discouraging gaming as far as possible'. The Goostrees atmosphere was as cool as Brooks's was fevered. Its leading spirit was William Pitt, now 22, some ten years younger than Fox. About him, Selwyn as usual was shrewd:

> Young Pitt will not be subordinate; he is not so in his own society. He is at the head of a dozen young people, and it is a corps separate from that of Charles's; so there is another premier at the starting post ... He seems to hold prudence in much higher estimation than Charles does, and in this respect

has an advantage over him; in all others is nearer in equality with him than anyone I ever saw.[13]

Pitt was just making his debut in parliament. Lord North, from the other side of the House, but unpartisan and always appreciative of quality, reckoned it the best maiden speech he had ever heard.

Fox, said Walpole, was the 'first man' among the opposition; and Selwyn said he could be the first man in the *kingdom* if it were not for certain important defects in his character. But if he was virtually leader of the opposition, he was not strictly so. The two main claimants to that position were both peers: Rockingham, who had already been prime minister once, and Shelburne, Lord Chatham's political heir. It seems, rather strangely, that Fox at this time (1781–2) did not even sit on the opposition front bench in the Commons, but usually in the third row back.[14] He was not even a fully acknowledged member of the Rockingham party, though his association with them was close. Yet in one sense he himself was head of a party, and the party headquarters was Brooks's Club. The Fox connexion – 'Mr Fox's friends' – was unique in being based (his two brothers-in-law apart) not on family relationship or territorial interest, but entirely on its leader's personal attractiveness. Selwyn, who knew well the pull of that attraction, knew also how to stand apart from it, and we can almost see his lip curling as he notes distastefully the aroma of 'incense' permeating the subscription room at Brooks's.[15] The Fox connexion numbered few more than a dozen of his mainly wealthy fashionable friends – though the wealth of one of his most interesting recruits, the playwright and theatre manager Sheridan, was seen to come and go quite as casually and spectacularly as Fox's own. The political group held together by Fox's personal magnetism included, besides Sheridan, his fellow playwright General Burgoyne, an opposition martyr second only to Keppel, after his severe usage by the King following his failure to return to America to resume campaigning; Lord Robert Spencer, the Duke of Marlborough's brother; James Maitland, the future Earl of Lauderdale; Admiral Hugh Pigot, between whom and the First Lord, Sandwich, there was strong mutual contempt; Pigot's nephew Monckton, who together with Sheridan represented Stafford; John Crewe,* who had previously paid large sums (according to Walpole, £12,000 a year)[16] to help Fox stay financially afloat;

---

* One of the 'economical' reformers. He had married the beautiful Frances Greville, Burke's 'incomparable Mrs Crewe'. Both Fox and Sheridan wrote amatory verses in her honour. Earlier, Lady Holland had seen in her a possible match for her son Stephen.

Thomas Coke, 'Coke of Norfolk', the famous agrarian innovator, and his brother Edward Coke; and young Thomas Grenville, a son of George Grenville, of Stamp Act fame.[17]

Before parliament was prorogued in the summer, Fox returned to an old family grievance, Hardwicke's Act of 1753, passed to prevent runaway or clandestine marriages, a measure which his father had so energetically and indignantly, and of course unsuccessfully, opposed: an 'absurd and improvident act', as Fox now proclaimed it, 'a disgrace to the country and to the statute-book', erecting 'an arbitrary authority in the parent and the guardian over the child and the ward'. People, he knew, would object thus,

> What! would you permit a boy of fourteen, and a girl of twelve years of age to judge for themselves? Would you suffer them to yield to the hasty emotions of desire, and marry without the consent of their parents? In all this stile and train of reasoning, there was the most palpable deception. People argued on this ground, as if there was no interval or intermediate space between the age of fourteen and that of twenty-one.

He proceeded to depict two scenarios, rather like Hamlet accosting his mother with the contrast between her two husbands: 'Look here upon this picture, and on this' ('Hyperion to a satyr'). Fox presented, first, an idyllic picture of young love, followed by early marriage, with 'connubial industry and felicity' to follow:

> A young man, a farmer, or an artisan, becomes enamoured of a female, possessing like himself all the honest and warm affections of the heart. They have youth, they have virtue, they have tenderness, they have love – but they have not fortune. Prudence ... points out a variety of obstacles to their union, but passion surmounts them all, and the couple are wedded. Their love is a sweetener of domestic life. Their prospect of a rising family becomes an incentive to industry ... The husband ... is roused into activity by the most endearing of all human motives. The wife ...makes his house comfortable, and his hours of repose happy ... Thus, while they secure to themselves the most sober and tranquil felicity, they become by their marriage amiable, active, and virtuous members of society.

So much for Hyperion: now the satyr, ugly indeed:

> View the same couple in another light. Bound together in the heart by the most ardent desires, and incited by their passion to marry without having any great prospect before them, their parents intervene; they are not arrived at the age of twenty-one; under the authority of the marriage act, their parents prevent their marriage ... but they have it not in their power to prevent their intercourse ... What are the consequences? Enjoyment satiates the man, and

ruins the woman; she becomes pregnant; he, prosecuted by the parish for the maintenance of the child, is initiated in a course of unsettled pursuits and of licentious gratifications ... He either flies the place of his residence, or he remains the corrupter and disgrace of his neighbourhood ... The unhappy female ... is turned out of doors ... comes to London, and ... is forced, much oftener by necessity than inclination ... to seek a precarious subsistence in the gratification of loose desire. Good God! what are the miseries she is not to undergo! what are the evils that do not result to society!

His bill sailed through its second reading; passed its third (tellers, Mr Fox and General Burgoyne) by 75 votes to 43; but on 12 July was thrown out by the House of Lords. Fox of course had chosen not to admit those advantages which Hardwicke's act *had* secured, by its outlawing of 'Fleet marriages' and their associated scandals, but the case he had made, however over-simplified or sentimentalized, did not altogether lack substance. Nor was this the end of the war waged by the Fox family against the 1753 Marriage Act – a war of course lacking any final Foxite victory.[18]

7

SHELBURNE, FOX, AND LORD NORTH

1782–1783

Cornwallis's capitulation at Yorktown, Virginia, which marked the beginning of the end of the American war, came three months later, in October 1781. It struck Lord North 'like a ball in the breast'; 'Oh God', he cried, 'it is all over'. He had never been more than reluctantly in favour of the war – a good deal less so than Germain or Sandwich – and he now set about the difficult and thankless task of persuading the King that its continued prosecution had become 'ruinous and impracticable'.[1] In a speech at parliament's reopening, Fox showed clearly enough that he understood North's predicament. If members were asked, he said, to lay their hands on their hearts and declare that they truly believed that Britain could ever conquer America, North and he would be found voting together, since he 'believed in his soul that the [prime] minister himself would vote against ... this accursed and abominable war'. But this did not prevent him from castigating yet once more the 'savage obstinacy' of the ministers, or from targeting once again his central object of fire:

> Though he had not enumerated our domestic grievances ... There was one grand domestic evil, from which all our other evils, foreign and domestic, had sprung. The influence of the crown. To the influence of the crown we must attribute the loss of the army in Virginia; to the influence of the crown we must attribute the loss of the thirteen provinces of America; for it was the influence of the crown in the two houses of parliament that enabled his Majesty's ministers to persevere against the voice of reason, the voice of truth, the voice of the people.

The removal of Germain from the struggling ministry, at the end of

January 1782, came less from the ceaseless attacks upon him by opposition speakers – Fox especially – than from inter-ministerial differences (Dundas did much to manoeuvre him out) and from the King's readiness to see him go – which was surprising on the face of it, since Germain on America had always been *plus royaliste que le roi*. But it was in order to obtain General Carleton as successor to General Clinton in the New York command that George sanctioned his American Secretary's departure. Germain had refused even to *write* to Carleton.[2] This left Sandwich (in direction of the naval war, now suffering new setbacks) to face a furious bombardment and the severest battering when Fox proposed a motion of censure on him on 20 February. On this occasion the opposition's forces had been co-ordinated and marshalled with unusual efficiency: 'I hear', wrote Selwyn to Carlisle, 'that all the different parties in opposition are determined to draw together on this question, how much soever they may differ afterwards'.[3] However, the total of votes which Fox and his allies managed to muster (217 to the ministry's 236 in an exceptionally full house) was still not sufficient to topple the administration. Last-minute attempts to rescue it, by once more trying to build a broader-bottomed coalition, broke down; and even the King, finding 'every description of men equally unwilling to stand forth', began to see that its demise was becoming inevitable. North insisted that he must at last be allowed to resign, though he was warned that, if he did, he would for ever forfeit the King's regard. 'Drove to the wall, hurt', his 'honour' at stake, yet 'deserted' and finding no path through his maze of difficulties, George was finally, but still resentfully, obliged to release his long-suffering prime minister. On 20 March, Lord North's government resigned.

Lord Chancellor Thurlow, employed by the King to conduct negotiations for a new administration, first made an unsuccessful approach to Gower, and then turned to Shelburne and Rockingham. Neither was *persona grata* to the King, but much the more emphatically *non grata* was Rockingham. And behind Rockingham – or perhaps, by now, one should say, at his side – stood Fox. Shelburne did not command enough parliamentary followers to give him the edge over Rockingham, whom George was thus obliged most unwillingly to accept as his new chief minister. Rockingham, moreover, came in on his own terms. These were: three measures of economical reform, including a new version of Burke's major bill defeated in the previous parliament; and *no royal veto* on American independence.

Doubtless it was apprehensiveness at the prospect of losing his sinecure 'place', with the change of ministry, which at this point gives George Selwyn's always sharp comments upon the social and political scene even more of a cutting edge. But what he has to say of his ever-admired but never quite trusted Charles, on the brink of high office at last, serves at least in some degree to give us a better picture of Fox in the round, and to qualify the adulation which was bestowed on him by some of his followers at the time and by generations of subsequent Whigs and Liberals. Certainly there is never any doubt whose side Selwyn is on in the forthcoming two-year battle of Rex *versus* Fox. Selwyn's commentary, extracted here from his letters to Carlisle (whose Dublin Lord Lieutenancy, like Selwyn's 'place', was also in jeopardy) indicates well enough the atmosphere at Court, as well as the scene at Brooks's as the old ministry fades away and the Whig aspirants hopefully try on their new ministerial clothes.

1 March 1782 At the Levee Charles presented an Address from Westminster. The King took it out of his hand without deigning to give him a look even or a word; he took it as you would take a pocket handkerchief from your *valet de chambre* ... and passed it to his Lord in Waiting ...

The truth is, I have made up my mind to whatever shall happen. I wish the King to be master ... and all whom I saw at Brooks's last night *annéantis* as politicians ... I own that to see Charles closeted every instant at Brooks's by one or the other, than he can neither punt or deal for a quarter of an hour but he is obliged to give an audience ... is to me a scene *la plus parfaitement comique que l'on puisse imaginer,* and to nobody it seems more risible than to Charles himself.

6 March: The King, I hear, is in good spirits, and went yesterday to Windsor to hunt ... But I think that if he ... heard a hundredth part of what I hear from those who are forcing themselves into his counsels, he would lose his crown, and his life too, rather than submit to it.

12 March, touching the coming disposition of 'places': These people [the Whigs], by long opposition ... are become very ravenous; and Charles ... I am persuaded, would have no consideration upon earth but for what was useful to his own ends. You have heard me say that I thought he had no malice or rancour; I think so still ... But I think that he has no feeling, neither, for any one but himself.

13 March: Charles dined yesterday, I believe, at Lord Rockingham's; I saw him about five in a great hurry of agitation ... I saw the Duke of Bedford coming out of Charles's yesterday, so there is another Duke for him to lead by the nose.

15–16 March: The bargains which are now making by venal people of both sides are innumerable ... There is to be another trial of skill [in the Commons] on Wednesday. Charles's arrogance both in the House and out of it, is insupportable. I can neither speak of him or think of him with patience ... But good God! What a government is this, if the King has not the power of choosing his own ministers!

18 March: I called in at Brooks's last night, but avoided all conversation ... Their insolence, their vanity and folly, and the satisfaction expressed in their countenance upon fancying themselves ministers ... and to drive the K[ing] from every shadow of power and dignity, is no object to me now of mirth ... The thought of a new administration is so prevalent with Charles that he would not go to Newmarket. I heard him last night tell his people that he saw no reason, when he was Minister, that he or his assistants in administration should sit upon the Treasury bench. The merry and the sad, as my Lord Clarendon says, have employment enough, while these actors are dressing themselves up for the play, and rehearsing their parts.

19 March: I saw Charles last night, and by accident was alone with him; he stretched out his hand to me with great good humour ... He spoke of all coming to a final issue now within a very short space of time. He talked of the King under the description of Satan ...

27 March: I could have seen my royal master on the scaffold with less pain than insulted as he has been today. I am going out to hear all that passed [at Court], and how he bore it. From my parlour window I saw Mr Secretary Fox step into his chariot from his office, and Lord Shelburne and Dunning from the other office ... Charles has taken a house in Pall Mall. Sheridan is his [Under] Secretary ...

28 March: I went to Brooks's last night ... The late Charles, now Mr Fox (for I think that the other name has begun to sound obsolete already even at Brooks's) was there, and as much the Minister in all his deportment, as if he had been in office 40 years. I had no conversation with him, or probably shall the rest of my life.[4]

Under the brief second premiership of Lord Rockingham, the two Secretaries of State, mutually antagonistic from the start, were Fox, Foreign Secretary, and Shelburne, in charge of domestic and colonial affairs. Fox's hatred of Shelburne, like his interest in marriage reform, arose in part from his regard for his father. In the 1760s Shelburne had been one of those rising politicians against whom the ageing and embittered Lord Holland, after early friendship, harboured a powerful grudge, which Fox inherited and maintained. This antipathy towards Shelburne, however, was by no means confined to the Fox family. Indeed his extreme general unpopularity presents one of the minor puzzles of Georgian political history.

William Petty, second Earl of Shelburne (1737–1805, later Marquis of

Lansdowne), in many respects seems to exemplify the best qualities of the Georgian aristocrat. He had wealth, private generosity, an alert and critical intelligence, an exceptional breadth of intellectual interest, a readiness to pioneer improvement and reform. Uniquely among the politicians of his day he maintained on his Bowood estate in Wiltshire his private 'think tank', which included intellectuals of the calibre of Bentham and Priestley. Why was he so very widely and heartily disliked? In part probably from his autocratic manner and lack of ease in personal intercourse. Where Fox revelled in his instant likeability, Shelburne's unapproachability was always a handicap. He had admirers and political followers, themselves sometimes men of distinction, such as Dunning and Barré and Mahon, but they were never numerous. His detractors and enemies on the other hand were legion. Burke, who was seldom at a loss for words, found himself occasionally short of them to express adequately the intensity of his detestation. And it was very generally agreed that Shelburne was devious; he was a double-dealer; he was arrogant; he was over-subtle; he was 'the Jesuit of Berkeley Square'; he was 'Malagrida'; he was at the centre of secret or sinister intrigues. The Earl of Shelburne lived and worked in a manner different indeed from that of Fox, who was all charm and ebullience, or from North (still in political business and to be reckoned with) who was, at least on the surface, all easy-going affability and disarming amiability.

North, however, for the time being was in opposition, and government forces were divided between, on the one hand, Rockingham, Fox, and their friends, and on the other Shelburne and his – and from the outset Fox was convinced that chief among Shelburne's friends was the King himself. Half the cabinet, Fox declared, Shelburne's half, was 'for the King'; the other half was 'for the people'. This was tendentious and misleading, but there was this much truth in it: George mistrusted Rockingham and hated Fox, and he could conduct business much more easily with Shelburne. His relations with Rockingham and Fox remained frigidly correct, but with them he was dealing with politicians at the heart of whose attitude was hostility to Court influence and Crown corruption. Shelburne, although he was receptive to radical ideas, had never been so transparently hostile to the King as his fellow-Secretary Fox had. Neither was he a *party* man in the sense understood and approved of by Burke and the Rockingham Whigs but detested by George III. Shelburne, like his master the Earl of Chatham, believed that governments ought to consist of unions or coalitions of groups and individuals. It is easy to sympathize with George's preference for doing business with his Home rather than his Foreign Secretary or his First Lord of the Treasury.

Ministerial wrangles surfaced almost immediately. In the eleven-man cabinet the Rockingham-Fox group numbered five, those closer to Shelburne five also. Horace Walpole's cousin Conway was eleventh man in the team (Commander in Chief) and unaligned – Shelburne commented sardonically that he was too 'innocent' to perceive that he held a casting vote. Alongside Fox and Rockingham there stood Fox's uncle Richmond, Lord John Cavendish, and Admiral Keppel. The other members of the cabinet, besides Shelburne, were Lord Chancellor Thurlow (indestructible and much trusted by the King), Lord Camden, the Duke of Grafton, and the newly ennobled Dunning, Lord Ashburton. Within a month of the new government's formation Fox was writing to Fitzpatrick (in Ireland now, Chief Secretary to Lord Lieutenant Portland):

> Shelburne shows himself more and more every day, is ridiculously jealous of my encroaching on his department, and wishes very much to encroach on mine ... He affects the [Prime] Minister more and more every day, and is, I believe, perfectly confident that the King intends to make him so. Provided we can stay in long enough to have given a good stout blow to the influence of the crown, I do not think it signifies how soon we go out after, and have him and the Chancellor to make such a government as they can ...

It seems clear from this that he was already contemplating a tactical resignation. The 'good stout blow to the influence of the crown' relates to Burke's civil establishment bill, the most important of the three measures of 'economical' reform which this short-lived Rockingham ministry achieved. It also managed to complete a successful (if, as it proved, very temporary) settlement of the Irish troubles, while final executive authority remained with the Lord Lieutenant appointed from London. These Irish reforms involved major decisions by the Westminster parliament, including acceptance of the repeal of the (Irish) Declaratory Act of 1719. Almost all of Rockingham's cabinet being peers, management of the passage of this legislation through the Commons fell to Fox, and the industry and efficiency he showed in it impressed everybody. As Burke told Portland, 'Every thing asked or even hinted at from Ireland has been yielded in the fullest measure and with the completest unanimity. Fox handled this business incomparably well.' Horace Walpole was another who emphatically approved of the new minister's performance in the Commons, praising his 'discretion' and 'address', and contrasting 'the masterly abilities of Charles Fox' with 'the intrigues of Lord Shelburne'.

The former displayed such facility in comprehending and executing all business as charmed all who approached him. No formal affectation delayed any service or screened ignorance. He seized at once the important points of every affair ... At once he gave himself up to the duties of his office. His good humour, frankness, and sincerity pleased, and yet inspired a respect which he took no other pains to attract.[5]

The dissensions between Fox and Shelburne within the cabinet arose first from their competing claims to dispense patronage, but eventually and more seriously from the complicated negotiations under way for concluding peace, both with the Americans and with France and Spain. (Preparations for a peace treaty with the third European enemy, Holland, were stalled, and had to wait two years for completion). Quite apart from trouble arising from clashes of personality, there was abundant scope for inter-ministerial conflict over disputed boundaries of departmental authority, particularly since Shelburne (Colonial as well as Home Secretary) had clear right to a say in the making of peace with the Americans – a subject, however, upon which the Foreign Secretary had very strong opinions and refused to be silenced. Fox moreover had in his own mind already ceased to regard the American provinces as any longer in a realistic sense colonies at all. In cabinet discussions he insisted that Britain must grant them independence immediately and unconditionally, while Shelburne wished to hold it as a bargaining counter, and concede it only as a constituent part of a general peace. Shelburne, moreover, proceeded to send his own representative, Richard Oswald, to negotiate in Paris, where at one stage the American commissioner Benjamin Franklin felt bold enough to hand Oswald a paper setting out ideas for the incorporation of the *Canadian provinces* in the future independent nation of America – and this without any mention of the subject to Thomas Grenville, Fox's representative in Paris. It was only by accident that Grenville came to learn of the existence of this paper; and, naturally, when he did, he wrote to inform Fox of it. Naturally also, Fox showed Grenville's letter to his cabinet allies, who registered understandable indignation and were confirmed in their conviction of the super-subtle Shelburne's duplicity. This Canada proposition was something of a red herring: it was never presented by Shelburne to the cabinet and played no part in the eventual peace settlement. But it provided one more subject of irritation; and Grenville, though confirmed in 'full powers' by Fox, continued to see Oswald in Paris pursuing parallel, but rival and uncoordinated, negotiations.

Within the cabinet a climax was reached at a meeting on 30 June, when Fox again urged that independence should be granted to the Americans straight away, *in advance of a general treaty of peace*. Later in the day Shelburne reported to the King that no final decision was taken, but both Grafton, who was at the meeting, and Walpole, whose cousin and close friend Conway was also present, declared that Fox's proposal was defeated by a single vote (according to Walpole it was Conway's). Thereupon Fox announced his intention to resign, though, he said, because of the serious illness of the prime minister he would wait a little before surrendering the seals of office.[6]

The very next day Rockingham died, and the King immediately appointed Shelburne to succeed him. Fox promoted his 'intention' of 30 June into hard fact and resigned, professedly on grounds of policy and principle, but, in the general view, much more from a rooted hatred of Shelburne. If differences of view upon policy had provided his main motive, this would have carried better conviction if all the Rockinghamite cabinet members had resigned with him. Only Cavendish did, though from the junior ministerial ranks Burke, Sheridan, and others did too. The Duke of Richmond, who thought his nephew was making a serious mistake, seemed at one point to have succeeded in persuading him to reverse his decision, provided that Cavendish were to be appointed to Shelburne's now vacated Home Secretaryship. But Cavendish refused to consider it, and on 4 July Fox attended the King to surrender the seals, stating on that occasion his opinion that Shelburne's appointment as first minister would create just the kind of mistrust among the King's servants which had already disfigured the reign. He refused the royal request that he should withdraw his resignation; and afterwards, justifying the stand he had made, he declared that it had been 'indispensably necessary that he should come forward and ring the alarm bell, and tell this country that the principle on which they had formed' the Rockingham administration 'was abandoned, and that the old system was to be revived, most probably with the old men, or indeed with any men that could be found'.[7] This, coming from one who was soon to be making tactical approaches to the chief among the 'old men', North, has an ironical touch, and in view of Shelburne's own incontestable record of hostility to North's ministry, sounds now, as it sounded to most of the Commons then, both unconvincing and perverse. That Fox himself was not altogether happy about his resignation is suggested in a letter he sent Fitzpatrick on the day he delivered up the seals: 'I wish I could see you. I shall be about all morning. I did not think it had been in the power of politics to make me so miserable as this cursed anxiety and suspense does'.[8]

Although on 4 July the King had received Fox civilly, seeking then to avoid another of the ministerial crises which had plagued his reign, he could hardly fail to conclude that there was a conspiracy among one of the main Whig parties to hound from office the man whom with undeniable constitutional propriety he had chosen as his first minister, and to force upon him their own nominee. This was to be not Fox himself (though Walpole, who also mistrusted Shelburne, still considered that Fox was 'the fittest man' to be prime minister), but the Duke of Portland, who had now become the Rockinghamites' titular chief. As Sir Gilbert Elliot said, Portland was undoubtedly 'the proper man to keep the party together'.[9]

The very name of William Cavendish-Bentinck, third Duke of Portland, proclaimed unimpeachable Whig credentials. Though of no intellectual distinction (Selwyn wrote him off as 'jolterheaded'), he was honest, conscientious, and industrious – at once, Walpole said, 'proud and bashful', with 'a thousand virtues' – and of course he was also one of the wealthiest and grandest of the 'grand Whiggery'. Two centuries ago it seemed altogether natural and proper that a party hitherto led by a great magnate like the Marquis of Rockingham should have as his successor a head – at least a nominal head – similarly acceptable to the hierarchical conventions of contemporary society. Thus the Duke of Portland now *headed* this the most important of the Whig parties, while Fox *led* it; and it was Portland who Fox claimed should have been George's choice as premier, thereby propounding, if not quite in so many words, the constitutional innovation that on the death or retirement of a prime minister the cabinet, not the monarch, has the right to nominate his successor.

It appeared that, while so briefly Foreign Secretary – and he was a very businesslike and hard-working one – Fox abjured Brooks's and gambling. But immediately on his release from office, he was back. Walpole related:

> The Prince of Wales dined with Mr Fox yesterday by previous engagement; they drank royally. Charles went thence to Brooks's, stayed till four in the morning, and it being so early, finished the evening at White's with Lord Weymouth – and the evening and the morning and the next day were the first day.

Fox's closeness to the Prince of Wales, so disturbing to the King, was now generally known and discussed. The Prince was a man of as many gifts as frailties, and there was much about him which Fox found genuinely attractive; but another motive for the ripening friendship must realistically be seen in the Prince's position as heir apparent. It was well to be on good terms with the future king, and opposition politicians had traditionally cultivated Georgian Princes of Wales. There does moreover seem to be some reason to believe that Fox thought – or at least hoped with some confidence, though why is not easy to see – that George III might not live many more years. By one account,[10] on the day upon which Fox received the seals as Secretary of State, he remarked that yes, certainly things were looking well, 'but he (meaning the King) will die soon, and that will be best of all'.

Even Fox's latest mistress Mrs Robinson, it might be said, came 'by arrangement with' the Prince of Wales. Mary Robinson, the celebrated Perdita in Garrick's production of *The Winter's Tale*, had been mistress to the then extremely young Prince, whose devotion to her had been expressed not only in the flesh, but in expansive princely prose and in one very rash undertaking. He had promised her the sum of £20,000 when he should receive his full establishment on reaching the age of 21. As for the letters, when (after the Prince's amours had led him variously elsewhere) Mrs Robinson threatened to publish them unless bought off with £5,000, the King had to ask North's government for the money. His notion of a monarchy of dignity, above public or private scandal, forbade the publish-and-be-damned response adopted at a later time in a similar predicament by the Duke of Wellington, so the public purse paid up. By 1782 – the Prince was by then 20 – Mrs Robinson, long since Perdita and now the Prince's discard, was available to star in a new role as Charles Fox's latest lady. (This tendency towards open-hearted liberality, not to say bilateral free trade, had been apparent for some time between the Prince of Wales's circle and that of Fox and Fitzpatrick. Selwyn for instance noted that another charmer, Mrs Benwell, was at about this time Fitzpatrick's *maîtresse en titre*, but that he shared her with the Prince – and others.)[11] So for much of the year 1782 Fox divided his time between St James's Street (Brooks's Club) and Berkeley Square (Mrs Robinson's). As for the former, says the plainly disapproving Walpole:

> The Prince of Wales had of late thrown himself into the arms of Charles Fox,
> and this in the most undisguised manner. Fox lodged in St James's Street,
> and as soon as he rose, which was very late, had a levee of his followers, and
> of the members of the gaming club at Brooks's – all his disciples. His bristly,
> black person and shagged breast, quite open and rarely purified by any
> ablutions, was wrapped in a foul night-gown, and his bushy hair dishevelled.

In these Cynic weeds and with Epicurean good humour did he dictate his politics, and in this school did the heir to the throne attend his lessons and imbibe them.

As for Mrs Robinson, Fox's aunt Sarah reported to his cousin and old flame Susan O'Brien:

> Charles is mad, and ruining himself I fear ... My brother [Richmond] has *talked*, and been *patient*, and tried all sorts of persuasions ... but poor dear Charles is so surrounded with flatterers that tempt him to think *he alone* can overset the whole fabric, that it's vain to talk ...
> ... I hear Charles saunters about the streets, and brags that he has not taken a pen in hand since he was out of place. *Pour se désennuyer* he *lives* with Mrs Robinson, goes to Sadler's Wells with her, and is all day figuring away with her. I long to tell him he does it to show that he is superior to Alcibiades, for his courtezan forsook him when he was unfortunate, and Mrs Robinson takes *him* up.[12]

And Mrs Robinson's house in Berkeley Square, as it happened, had upper windows which commanded a view of Lord Shelburne's town residence. Thus Fox would be admirably placed, as he observed, to combine business with pleasure by enjoying Mrs Robinson's delightful company* while keeping an eye from time to time on the prime minister. It was not Mrs Robinson, however, but another of the town's fashionable courtesans, Mrs Armistead who, more importantly, began now to attract Fox's amorous eye – and was, it turned out in the end, largely to transform his life.

Elizabeth Armistead was at this time 31. Her name, with its variety of spellings (Fox himself sometimes wrote Armitstead) was probably a professional invention to accord with the conventions of the times – as it were a *nom de guerre*. No mention or record of a Mr Armistead has ever been found (though a negative is hard to prove), and perhaps, as has been wittily suggested, he was merely 'a figure of speech'.[13] Fox's 'dearest Liz' had been another of the young Prince of Wales's favoured beauties. He is reported as 'with her at the masquerade at the Pantheon' in January 1781, and again as 'calling on her every morning' when the Court was at Windsor in August 1782.[14] She had originally been associated with what is described

---

* The story of Mary Robinson's life (1758–1800) produces some surprises: Shakespearian actress; fashionable beauty, painted by Romney, Reynolds, Gainsborough, and others; mistress successively to the Prince of Wales and Charles Fox; subsequently playwright and 'gothick' novelist; author of *Poems* (1791); admiring the young Coleridge and herself admired by him – 'she overloads every thing', he wrote, 'but I never knew a human Being with so full a mind ... a woman of undoubted Genius'.

as 'a certain notorious establishment' in Marlborough Street (in some ways her origins parallel Lady Hamilton's), and for three years in her early twenties had been the Duke of Dorset's acknowledged mistress. After the Duke ran off with the Countess of Derby, Mrs Armistead was 'taken over' by Fox's friend the Earl of Derby. Then for a time before coming to Fox she was briefly the mistress of Lord Cholmondeley. We are told that 'she lived in splendour, kept two sets of horses for her carriages, a proportionable establishment of servants; her table was the constant resort of all the young men of fashion in the kingdom'.[15]

Mrs Armistead was elegant and beautiful, as Reynolds' portraiture witnesses. (She sat for him four times during her twenties and early thirties.) She was conventionally Christian, as Fox was conventionally non-Christian; but with her background and social assumptions she saw no cause to press him to matrimony – though from early in their relationship he would habitually refer to her as his wife. Eventually, nearly twelve years away, it was he who persuaded *her* to the altar, and even then did not make the marriage publicly known until seven years later still. Above all, Mrs Armistead was kind, understanding, and loyal. Characters do not change overnight, but Charles Fox as the companion and lover of his 'dearest, dearest Liz' soon began, as they say, to settle down. And he was never in any doubt what he owed to her. After they had been together only a year or so – it was just after the Westminster election of 1784 – he was writing to her in much the same language he would be using many times over in the coming twenty-two years:

> Adieu, my dearest Liz. It may sound ridiculous, but it is true that I feel every day how much more I love you than I know. You are *all* to me. You can always make me happy in circumstances apparently unpleasant and miserable [and] in the most prosperous. Indeed, my dearest Angel, the whole happiness of my life depends on you ... And three years later: 'I never can be happy, now I have known you, but with you ... I never did know nor ever shall man or woman who deserves to be loved like Liz ...'[16]

When Fox moved over from the government benches to those of the opposition in July 1782, William Pitt, now 23, ten years younger than Fox, crossed in the contrary direction – an exchange of situations which may be seen as prophetic, since those were the relative positions (with only one brief exception) which they were to occupy for the rest of their lives. Precocious sons of fathers who were bitter rivals, they had long been foreseen as potential rivals themselves. But Pitt's earliest years in parliament were spent on the same side of the House as Fox. He opposed North; like

Fox he favoured parliamentary reform; he too opposed the American war, though his views on America were closer to those of his father than to Fox's. Again like Fox, his first contributions to Commons debates had been outstanding. He had been talked of, and approached, for a place in one or two of the governments projected but aborted to succeed or coalesce with North, but had always held out for high terms. As Selwyn noted, young Pitt, a chip off the old block, would never consent to be 'subordinate'. Shelburne, however, was one who had come to political maturity under the shadow of the old block himself, and Pitt had no difficulty in accepting office under him – *cabinet* office too, the Chancellorship of the Exchequer.

Shelburne was the new prime minister, but with only about 140 solid supporters in the lower House whereas half as many again were declared followers of North or Fox, coalition was in the air from the beginning. Shelburne himself, and then Dundas on his behalf, made flattering advances to North who, without rancour though he was, could not be expected easily to dismiss from his memory the fact that, not long before, Shelburne had been among those suggesting, if perhaps not actually demanding, his impeachment.[17] North was simultaneously being wooed by Fox, another who had not spared words in attacks on him over many years, and these approaches were at first rejected by North out of hand. Recovered from being for so long bruised and battered as George's 'confidential minister', he seemed to be enjoying life again. Gibbon, seeing him in his family territory down in Kent, reported that he was looking 'not so fat and more cheerful than ever'.[18]

Apart from North's, the only other party to which Shelburne might look for assistance was Fox's but, while Fox's detestation of Shelburne forbade thought of serving with him again, Shelburne (until he became desperate) set his face no less determinedly against having further truck with Fox – whose talents during the winter of 1782–3 were necessarily confined to guerrilla tactics against the ministry, particularly over the question of the continuing and complicated peace negotiations. These were five-sided; the British, French, Spanish, Dutch, and Americans were all involved. Perhaps artillery bombardment rather than guerrilla war better suggests Fox's part in these parliamentary hostilities, for he was back doing what he was supremely good at, directing sustained and destructive fire at an enemy in difficulties.

Shelburne was indeed in difficulties, even within his own cabinet, members of whom felt themselves bypassed or ignored. As William Grenville commented sarcastically to his brother, 'You will certainly think the mode of keeping a cabinet unanimous by never meeting them at all an excellent one'.[19] When however they did meet, dissension prevailed. In the protracted peace negotiations, for instance, the proposed surrender of Gibraltar, which had triumphantly withstood a very long Spanish siege, was greeted with dismay by the cabinet's two surviving Rockinghamites, Keppel and Richmond, and they received some support from Camden, Conway, and Grafton. Earl Temple threatened resignation, disliking being treated as a cipher; Keppel resigned; and Richmond, always a law unto himself, while not giving up his post, withdrew his presence from the cabinet.*

The prospects of Shelburne's ministry receded by the week, as 1782 gave way to 1783. Its continuing existence depended almost entirely on North, who was still being courted both by the ministry and the Foxites. So long as North held aloof from him, Fox's own position looked to be hopeless – all the more so because the King, hardened he said by his recent 3 months' experience of him as a minister, had finally determined never to employ him again,[20] and because Shelburne's premiership seemed to promise its own natural successor in Pitt. Pitt at this time, beginner though he was, seems to have been influential and uncompromising enough to veto North's inclusion in a prospective new coalition; North himself withdrew from talks with Shelburne's spokesman, Dundas; whereupon Shelburne, now almost *in extremis*, authorized Pitt to sound out Fox; and by 10 February William Grenville was writing to his brother Earl Temple:

> Pitt told me today that it being thought necessary to make a junction with Fox, he had seen him today, when he asked one question, whether there were any terms on which he could come in. The answer was, None while Lord Shelburne remained; and so it ended.[21]

The following day Fox got in touch again with North, and after several further meetings, with concessions made by both men, a mutually acceptable arrangement was reached. In the next important Commons debate on the preliminary peace agreement (which had just survived a perilously close vote in the Lords), Fox made the blandest of apologies for this famously 'infamous' coalition with the old enemy:

> If men of honour can meet on points of general national concern, I see no

---

* Another who resigned his office was Fox's sometime friend and benefactor Lord Carlisle. On being removed from the Lord Lieutenancy of Ireland to make room for the Duke of Portland, he had been made Lord High Steward, partly perhaps because Fox, knowing what he had (quite literally) owed him, spoke up for him.

reason for calling such a meeting an unnatural junction. It is neither wise nor noble to keep up animosities for ever. It is not my nature to bear malice or live in ill will. My friendships are perpetual, my enmities are not so ... When I was the friend of the noble lord I found him open and sincere; when the enemy, honourable and manly. I never had reason to say ... that he practised any of those little subterfuges, tricks and strategems, which I found in others [such presumably as Shelburne], any of those behindhand and paltry manoeuvres which destroy confidence ...

This debate also provided the celebrated occasion when Pitt, the severe and lofty – but in this case the incautiously supercilious – more than met his match in the quick-thinking repartee of Sheridan. Protesting first in terms of the deepest shock against the apostasy of Fox and North, Pitt, still the political stripling, turned aside to dispose of Sheridan, the mere playwright who should have stayed where he belonged, in the theatre. Sheridan's smart rejoinder was that if he should 'ever take up his pen again he would be tempted to improve on' one of Ben Jonson's characters – the Angry Boy in *The Alchemist.*

After his government was twice narrowly defeated in the Commons in February, Shelburne resigned – to the disgust of the King, who considered that he should have put up a tougher fight. And certainly George had no intention of inviting Fox and North, with their now combined cohorts, to succeed him. What followed therefore, over the next six weeks, was a desperate rearguard action as George sought to find, one after another, a leading politician – somebody, anybody – who would rescue him from thraldom to North and Fox; from Fox especially, the man who politically and personally stood for everything he detested, and who as he well knew detested *him.* Certainly he resented also the line North had taken, and spoke bitterly of him; yet North he *was* prepared to see first minister again, if only he could be detached from Fox; and indeed he attempted, of course without success, to enlist him. He also turned to Pitt who, after serious deliberation and consultation, concluded that a Commons majority for him was not in sight. He tried Temple; he tried Weymouth; he tried that veteran among almost-prime-ministers Gower, who now stood at the head of the old Bedford connexion and once again failed to muster sufficient backing. It was Gower who suggested to the King the name of another man worth trying, a cousin of Pitt, Thomas Pitt, later Lord Camelford; and we are told that the reply came 'Yes, Mr Thomas Pitt or Mr Thomas *Anybody'.* (Thomas Pitt's long letter, explaining why he too was obliged to decline, helpfully volunteered that perhaps the King's best policy was to give in to the Portland-Fox-North arrangement and allow them enough rope to hang themselves.)

George did not absolutely refuse to countenance Fox as minister. In fact, as early as 3 March he had resigned himself to accepting him, and by 12 March even to agreeing also to Fox's demand for Portland to head the administration. What he would not accept was the claim made by Portland – which in reality meant made by Fox – to nominate a complete set of seven principal ministers, *all* from the Fox-North 'faction'. No eighteenth century ministry could hope to last long which did not enjoy at least *some* measure of the monarch's confidence, and the ministry which Fox (through Portland) was now proposing – in fact, demanding – would necessarily have but shaky prospects. Perhaps it was Fox's hatred of the King and his gambler's temperament which persuaded him to overplay his hand and go for a grand slam when better judgement would have been content with game.[23]

The King was not just exasperated, he was very near the end of his tether, and again contemplated abdicating in favour of his son and returning to Hanover. He even drafted, but never dispatched, three messages of some dignity, one in the form of a letter to his son, one to the House of Commons, and one to the two Houses of Parliament jointly, explaining his decision to quit, and defending his conduct over the twenty-three years of his reign. At Brooks's, said Walpole, the members were laying wagers on the duration of the reign – which had in fact thirty-seven more years to go.

A second refusal from Pitt convinced George at last that the game was up, and on 1 April he bowed to the inevitable. He had stood out, so he wrote to Lord Temple (a significant name in view of the events of eight months ahead),

> till not a single man is willing to come to my assistance and till the House of Commons has taken every step but insisting on this faction by name being appointed ministers. To end the conflict which stops every wheel of government and which would affect the public credit if it continued much longer I intend this night to acquaint that *grateful* man Ld North that the seven cabinet counsellors that the coalition had named shall kiss hands tomorrow and then form their arrangements ...[24]

It was, as we know, only *reculer pour mieux sauter* but at the time it looked like surrender – or, to Fox, victory.

The threat hanging over that victory is foreshadowed in a later passage of the King's letter to Temple. The coalition ministry, it went on, cannot be supposed to have either my favour or my confidence ... I shall most certainly refuse any honours that may be asked by them ... I trust you will be steady in your attachment to me and ready to join other honest men in watching the conduct of this unnatural combination, and I hope many months will not elapse before the Grenvilles [Temple of course was a Grenville], the Pitts and other men of ability and character will relieve me of a situation [which circumstances] have compelled me to submit to.[25]

In the short run, the Portland-Fox-North victory was very nearly complete. The King tried hard to retain Lord Thurlow as Chancellor, and when he found he could not, it was agreed that the Great Seal should for the time being be put in commission. However, the seven other main offices of state all went to Fox's men: Portland (First Lord), Fox (Secretary of State), Keppel, Cavendish; and to North's: North himself (Secretary of State), Stormont, Carlisle. And the King's suppressed emotions under the shock of this undeniable defeat are nicely illustrated in one of the best-known of the Fox/George anecdotes. It originates from Lord Townshend, who was one of those present at the ceremony of the kissing of the royal hand upon ministerial appointments. When Mr Secretary Fox presented himself to assist at this ritual, the King, said Townshend, 'turned back his ears and eyes just like the horse at Astley's* when the tailor he had determined to throw was getting on him'.[26]

His determination to grant no new peerages or promotions within the peerage was not simply a trivial exercise of royal peevishness. He was an old hand by now in the political game, and knew the strength of some of the cards he still held. If Fox should try to trump the royal ace by forcing the issue of honours (and Pitt was among those who thought that this was 'a point on which almost everything depends')[27] George was shrewd enough to calculate that such an assault upon the royal prerogative would only turn the independent country gentlemen against the ministry. As he put it, he did not 'mean to grant a single peerage or other mark of favour, and if they fly out at that, I think ... I cannot fail to meet with support'.[28] This attack on the new ministers' powers of patronage, with its consequent reduction in their ability to win over votes in both the Houses, did indeed cause the coalition some initial embarrassment; and their shortage of 'places' to distribute was compounded by the effects of Burke's Civil Establishment Act of the previous year, which had swept away, among other expendables, some of the choicest commissionerships, clerkships,

---

* Astley's were the big London horse dealers.

and comptrollerships customarily providing reward for past or bait for future support. Some indication of the value attached to these inducements appears for instance from a memorandum submitted to the cabinet on 8 July, when ministers were searching for additional support: Lord Audley wanted an earldom; Lord Clarendon 'wanted *something*'; Lord Wentworth wanted '*anything* excessively'.[29]

Well aware, of course, of the coalition's uncertain future, Fox did his best on occasions to offer an olive branch, as too did the Duke of Portland. But whereas, for instance, Portland's condolences to the King on the death of little Prince Octavius received polite recognition of the Duke's 'delicacy' and 'very feeling expressions', Fox's approaches, however obsequiously phrased in the conventional 'courtierspeak' of the day, met a blank. Knowing that George regarded him as an evil influence on the Prince of Wales, at his very first audience Fox had protested that 'he had never said a word to the Prince of Wales which he should not have been glad to have your Majesty hear'.[30] Then in April he was 'humbly imploring' the King 'to believe that both the Duke of Portland and he have nothing so much at heart as to conduct your Majesty's affairs ... in a manner that may give your Majesty the most satisfaction ... and that it will be the study of your Majesty's ministers to show how truly sensible they are of your Majesty's goodness'.[31] The King endorsed this letter with 'No answer'. And when Fox offered to give him 'verbal explanation' of the definitive treaties of peace, which were completed in April, the answer came very near to a snub: 'I do not mean to call on Mr Fox for further explanations on this subject: unnecessary discussions are not to my taste and ... I do not propose to give myself any additional trouble with regard to them'.[32] The terms of peace were seen, naturally enough, by the King as representing defeat and disgrace. Fox had been powerless to obtain any substantial improvement on the arrangements so long and painstakingly negotiated by Shelburne, and had been obliged to put his name as responsible minister to treaties essentially the same as those which as opposition leader he had previously castigated as calamitous, and against which he had moved a Commons vote of censure. The King could not perhaps be expected to enjoy further discussion of them. Still, his letter was bad-tempered, and indeed untypical of the monarch-to-secretary-of-state correspondence (and *vice versa*) during Fox's tenure of office. Most of this, in both directions, was civil, correct, and businesslike.

It was however the Duke of Portland's, not Fox's, misfortune to receive what must surely be the most plain-speaking, *furious* letter ever dispatched by British monarch to prime minister (though perhaps one or two from Queen Victoria come close to it). The occasion was the financial settlement proposed by the coalition for the Prince of Wales's establishment, now that he was 21. When the matter had first arisen in cabinet, Fox as spokesman for his friend the Prince argued for an annual £100,000 to include £12,000 from the Duchy of Cornwall revenues; and although Cavendish and North both thought this claim extravagant, the cabinet commissioned Portland to present it. The King, judging it unreasonable, suggested reconsideration, but Portland repeated his proposal. At this point (15 June) George drafted a letter* to the Prince's treasurer – he was not on speaking terms with the Prince himself – complaining of his son's conduct in general, and in particular of 'his neglect of every religious duty ... want of even common civility to the Queen and me ... and his total disobedience of every injunction I had given'. The next day, 16 June, the King received a further communication from Portland, which proved a last intolerable provocation: the princely debts standing at some £29,000 had also to be included in the settlement. At this, George exploded:

> It is impossible for me to find words expressive enough of my utter indignation and astonishment ... When the Duke of Portland came into office I had at least hoped he would have thought himself obliged to have my interest and that of the public at heart, and not have neglected both to gratify the passions of an ill-advised young man ... If the Prince of Wales's establishment falls on me, it is a weight I am unable to bear; if on the public I cannot in conscience give my acquiescence to what I deem a shameful squandering of public money.[33]

He did later apologize handsomely to Portland for the excess of this outburst. But when Portland answered him that ministers were ready to ask *parliament*, not the Civil List, to find the full sum of £100,000 a year, he still would not consent. The farthest he would now go was for £50,000 a year from his own funds and a parliamentary grant of £50,000 (it eventually became £60,000) to settle debts and permit the completion of Carlton House. As he wrote separately to both North and Stormont, he would not 'forget or forgive what has passed, and the public shall know how well founded the principles of economy are in those who have so loudly preached it up ... yet, where they think it will answer their own wicked purposes, are ready to be most barefacedly lavish'.[34]

---

*Meticulous as ever, he was not fully satisfied with his first draft, slightly recast it, and did not send it until 21 June.

Fox was not mentioned by name in any of these angry outbursts. It was Portland, North, and Stormont who caught the chilliest blasts of disapproval and outrage. But of course the King knew, as indeed everybody knew, who was the powerful minister standing at the Prince's side. It was of course Fox, chief of *'my son's ministers'* who, before the hostilities began, had assured the Prince that they would request full, generous settlement.[35] And now it fell to Fox, with some assistance from the Duchess of Devonshire and others to coax him into accepting a final accommodation – which however he protested, 'will put me in a worse situation than I am at present.'

There had been a day or two in mid-June when it appeared that the affair of the Prince's establishment might even bring about the fall of the ministry. Fox himself briefly spoke of 'going out' on the issue – or possibly, it was thought, the King would treat the quarrel as a *casus belli* and dismiss his ministers. Had he been surer of Pitt and Temple, he might well have done so, but the time was not yet ripe. On (probably) 17 June, Georgiana Devonshire wrote to her 'dr brother' the Prince of Wales:

> ... The thing therefore to be considered is whether it is not in the power of the present administration to serve you more by staying in than going out – and whether the destruction of a ministry *qui vous est devoué* is not more likely to be detrimental to your interests than trusting them to serve you in the best way they can. But Mr Fox looks upon himself bound in honour to carry it thro for you and will go out rather than give it up, unless you release him ...[36]

The next day, a letter from Fox to the Prince was begging

> leave to repeat again that I think myself bound by every principle of honour as well as gratitude to take whatever part your Royal Highness chuses to prescribe me in the business.

But then two days later,

> After a good deal of conversation last night it seemed to be the general opinion that his Majesty's ministers had no part to act in the business of your Royal Highness's establishment but to submit it entirely to the King's pleasure ... I need not say how much I have felt for the manner in which yr R.H. has been treated ... Let me conjure you, Sir, to bear it with calmness and constancy'.[37]

'I believe [the Prince] was naturally very averse to it', wrote Fox to Lord Northington, 'but Colonel Lake [his Equerry], and others whom he most trusts, persuaded him to it'. There was of course not the slightest prospect, even if his prescribed allowance had been doubled or trebled, of the spendthrift Prince attempting to live within it.

Northington was the coalition's Lord Lieutenant at Dublin Castle and, inevitably, there was Irish business for Mr Secretary Fox to attend to. Only the year before, the 'patriots' of the Protestant ascendancy had won legislative independence, a notable success for them; and their parliamentary leader, Grattan, could proudly, if misleadingly, claim that he was now able to address 'a free people'. Fox's attitude to the Irish situation which confronted him in 1783 is hardly distinguishable from that of his predecessor Shelburne: they both saw the Irish, having won their big victory, threatening dangerously to be on the move again. The Irish Volunteers, in particular, were refusing to disband, and demanding parliamentary reform. To Fox this seemed to carry the menace of a breakdown of order. Enough was enough. As he wrote to Northington (after a ten-day holiday at Newmarket, for the October meeting),

> ... With respect to the Volunteers and their delegates ... unless they dissolve in a reasonable time, government ... must be at an end ... If you show *firmness* ... I look to their dissolution as a certain and not very distant event ... Recollect that this is a crisis. If they are encouraged, Volunteers and soon possibly Volunteers without property, will be the only government in Ireland.

Grattan, said Fox, had employed the Volunteers as 'a dangerous instrument for honourable purposes', and now that those purposes were 'answered, fully answered ... is he not peculiarly bound to take care that so dangerous a weapon should no longer remain in unskilful, or perhaps wicked, hands'.

However, Fox was not in office long enough to develop an Irish policy of his own. The Volunteers menace which so alarmed him subsided; but the monstrous 'Irish problem' was hydra-headed. The settlement of 1782 upon which in 1783 Fox was taking his stand quickly proved to be no settlement. The legislative autonomy of whose achievement the leaders of the new 'Protestant nation' of Ireland were so proud, even with its attendant reforms, still left Westminster's appointees in Dublin Castle in control, with the Dublin parliament entirely lacking executive authority; it functioned virtually as an opposition. The perennial Irish evils of agrarian poverty, of religious discrimination, of nationalist radicalism (soon to be fortified by French revolutionary republicanism) were to lead to the mounting violence of the 1790s and eventually to the rebellion of 1798. It was Pitt, not Fox, who was to struggle with this Irish monster.

8

THE KING
FIGHTS BACK

1783–1784

It was not Ireland but India, presenting difficulties no less complex, that offered the coalition its chief challenge. Twenty years before, North's Regulating Act had for the first time faced the fact that the state must share responsibility for what had by that time become essentially an extensive British *empire* in India. The private profits of the nearly two-centuries-old East India Company, a monopoly under royal charter, could no longer be the sole determinant of Indian policies. During those twenty years many interlocking questions had presented themselves; among them were several which demanded a speedy answer: particularly, how much political control over the government of Company-dominated India was to be exercised from Westminster; how that control was to operate; how the British parliament was to limit, and if necessary, punish the malpractices and abuses of power by the Company's servants in India. This last was to become a matter of almost obsessive concern to Edmund Burke.

It was not only in India that the Company was powerful. The wealth which its members had brought back home had purchased important property interests, in great estates and parliamentary boroughs; and in parliamentary elections its command of patronage was second only to that of the Treasury. Within the Company itself, at each of its three main headquarters, in Madras, Calcutta, and Leadenhall Street, London, there had been much internal turmoil and faction-fighting for decades past. Then too there was glaring contrast between the conspicuous wealth of the Company's servants and the chronically beleaguered situation of the Company's own finances.

Above all, a clash of financial interest, and an ambiguity of legal jurisdiction and military responsibility between parliament and government on one side and a monopolistic chartered company on the other, demanded urgent statutory attention. During the two years preceding the coalition, two separate and in a sense rival parliamentary committees, one under Dundas and one under Burke, had been collecting a wealth of evidence to provide foundation for reform. Burke's committee in particular had put prodigies of energy into its Indian investigations and published its findings in voluminous detail. Indeed it had been reckoned that Burke, a junior minister now in the Fox–North coalition, by this time knew more about India than any other man *who had never been there*. For the past five years he had become passionately involved in the politics of the East India Company, both those of the Madras Presidency in the south and of Bengal to the north, where he had already alleged villainies against the man who was destined to become his 'captain general of iniquity', Warren Hastings. And he had launched, a couple of years previously, the first of his virulent assaults upon the extortions practised in India by the banker and moneylender (and English borough-proprietor) Paul Benfield, whose 'coming into many parts of India', Burke had alleged, was likely to 'fill the inhabitants with horror as much as an irruption of Mahratta horse'.

Fox valued Burke's knowledge and judgement of Indian affairs. He was content to treat him as his Indian expert, and indeed 'Fox's India Bill' of 1783, though Fox introduced it in a masterly two-and-a-quarter-hour speech, and worked hard on it both before and during its passage through the Commons, may with justice be regarded as at least equally Burke's. 'Burke is to draw out on paper some sort of plan', Sir Gilbert Elliot reported in August, 'which Fox is to consider as soon as possible.' In Burke's hand, moreover, there is an endorsement to a letter 'from Mr Pigot' referring to Pigot 'finishing the bill from my drafts';[1] and the most closely reasoned and powerfully argued of all the many speeches on the bill came, at the committee stage in the Commons, in a big three-hour oration from Burke. In more ways than one this speech was outstanding and unusual, for towards its end Burke launched into a long eulogy – a 'studied panegyric', he himself called it when he published his speech two months later – of the man who had espoused so whole-heartedly the cause which for Burke had by now taken priority: righting the wrongs done by the Company's servants in India. Perhaps he would have made his panegyric in any case, but by the time in early December that he delivered it, popular clamour against the bill had become loud, and no doubt Burke thought that Fox both deserved and needed all his powerful words of praise:

> ... It will be a distinction honourable to the age, that the rescue of the greatest
> number of the human race that ever were so grievously oppressed, from the
> greatest tyranny that was ever exercised, has fallen to the lot of abilities and
> dispositions equal to the task; that it has fallen to one who has the enlargement
> to comprehend, the spirit to undertake, and the eloquence to support, so great
> a measure of hazardous benevolence. His spirit is not owing to his ignorance
> of the state of men and things; he well knows what snares are spread about
> his path, from personal animosity, from court intrigues, and possibly from
> popular delusion. But he has put to hazard his ease, his security, his interest,
> his power, even his darling popularity, for the benefit of people he has never
> seen. This is the road that all heroes have trod before him. He is traduced
> and abused for his supposed motives. He will remember that obloquy is a
> necessary ingredient in the composition of all true glory; he will remember
> that it was not only in the Roman customs, but it is in the nature and
> constitution of things, that calumny and abuse are essential parts of triumph.
> These thoughts will support a mind, which only exists for honour, under the
> burthen of temporary reproach. He is doing indeed a great good; such as
> rarely falls to the lot, and almost as rarely coincides with the desires, of any
> man. Let him use his time. Let him give the whole length of the reins to his
> benevolence. He is now on a great eminence, where the eyes of mankind are
> turned to him. He may live long, he may do much. But here is the summit.
> He can never exceed what he does this day.

What the Fox-Burke India bill aimed to do was to strengthen domestic
control over the East India Company without increasing the power of the
Crown — that is, of the executive arm of government under the Crown.
The proposed solution was radical, and ingeniously thought out. For a
term of years the Company was to be obliged to surrender its top-level
executive authority, not to the government, but to a body of seven
commissioners named in the bill, who would function not in India but in
London, and who, unsurprisingly, *were all supporters of the Fox-North
coalition.* They were to hold office for no fewer than three or more than
five years, after which their successors *would* be governmentally appointed.
The other Indian parliamentary committee, under Dundas, had proposed
a quite different remedy for Company misdeeds, largely by reinforcing
the power of the Governor-General in India; but this was exactly what
Fox and Burke wished most to avoid. When Fox replied to opposition
criticism — fair criticism — which had alleged that his bill was likely
to hamper 'strong' government in India by giving superior power to
commissioners thousands of miles and some six months away, he was
quite explicit. Every line of his bill, he answered, 'presumes the possibility

of bad administration, for every word breathes suspicion. The bill supposes that men are but men; it confides in no integrity, it trusts no character; it inculcates the wisdom of a jealousy of power.'[2] Such sentiments surely argue the extent to which his Indian thinking had been influenced by Burke's.

For Burke himself, the measure was intended to be India's Magna Carta – 'the great Magna Charta of Indostan'; and success with it, for the very existence of the coalition, was all-important. It was submitted in routine manner to the King, who raised no objections to it – a fact of some importance in the light of what was to happen later. 'The die is cast', wrote Fitzpatrick to his brother in mid-November, 'administration is to stand or fall upon the issue.' Fox told Northington, 'Our India business, upon which all depends, comes on Tuesday, and on that day se'nnight or thereabouts, the great contest about it upon the second reading will in my opinion be the most important question to us that is ever likely to come on'. In fact this contest ended quite triumphantly for Fox: the voting was 229 to 120. Pitt's charge that the bill combined 'absolute despotism' with 'gross corruption', and was 'one of the boldest and most alarming attempts at the exercise of tyranny that ever disgraced the annals of this or any other country' failed to persuade the majority of country gentlemen and non-party members.[3]

However, such inflated rhetoric as this of Pitt's was only matching the temper of the reception which the bill was getting 'outdoors'. The hubbub raised against it was directed partly against its violation of chartered privilege and rights of property (though the Company was to be left with its profits untouched), but chiefly against its effect of transferring patronage of great political value from the Company to the seven commissioners, all of the Fox party. It was seen as a contrivance for ensuring the coalition's continuance in office. It would substitute for the legitimate influence of the Crown the illegitimate influence of faction supported by theft.

One of the proposed Commission of Seven, Sir Gilbert Elliot (as Lord Minto a future Governor-General in India), while admitting the element of party manoeuvre in the measure (and also for himself financial reward) also recognized its honest reforming intentions. He set the balance very fairly: 'There never was a measure taken so beneficial to so many millions of unhappy people as this one. This is one good reason for my liking a part in it. There are many lesser ones, amongst which a great deal of patronage and probably a handsome salary are two'.[4]

The views of the opposition press were less even-handed. From the

Whitehall Evening Post: the bill 'left indeed the Crown where it was, but placed the Sceptre in another hand'. From the *Morning Herald*: if the bill went through, Fox would become 'the most dangerous subject in Europe'. The caricaturist James Sayers ran a series of very telling anti-Fox cartoons, the first of them showing him making off with India House on his shoulders and a list of its Directors under his feet, and the most celebrated and influential of them picturing him with that most cartoonable visage of his, as 'Carlo Khan, the Great Potentate of Leadenhall Street' making his triumphal entry into the East India Company headquarters astride an elephant bearing the face of Lord North, and preceded by Burke as herald, with banner and trumpet. Fox wrote to Elizabeth Armistead.

> They are endeavouring to make a great cry against us, and will I am afraid succeed in making us very unpopular in the city. However, I know I am right and must bear the consequences, though I dislike unpopularity as much as any man ... I know I never did act more upon principle than at this moment, when they are abusing me so. If I had considered nothing but keeping my power, it was the safest way to leave things as they are, or to propose some trifling alteration, and I am not at all ignorant of the political danger which I run by this bold measure; but whether I succeed or no, I shall always be glad that I attempted, because I know that I have done no more than I was bound to do, in risking my power and that of my friends when the happiness of so many millions is at stake. I write very gravely ... but ... do not fancy from all this that I am out of spirits, or even that I am much alarmed for the success of our scheme. On the contrary, I am very sanguine ...[5]

Events were soon to extinguish this optimism. Perhaps, when the coalition was being put together back in the spring, Fox should not have been so unconciliatory in his refusal to allow Thurlow to continue as Lord Chancellor. Thurlow was emphatically someone whom it was wise to have on your side. As an enemy harbouring a grudge he was dangerous. He stood, moreover, closer to the King personally than any of the coalition ministers or any ex-minister. In the spring Fox feared that Thurlow as Lord Chancellor would have become the King's spokesman within the cabinet, but an alternative possibility is that he might have become the coalition's spokesman in the Closet, perhaps even have helped the King at least to *tolerate* Fox. George III, after all, who had once damned the elder Pitt as 'the blackest of hearts', greeted him five years later (however temporarily) as 'my friend'. Shelburne, whom in 1778 he disliked, so he said, 'as much as Alderman Wilkes', proved four years later to be perfectly acceptable to him as prime minister. George was obstinate, but not always consistent in his likes and dislikes. If Fox had been prepared to have

Thurlow as Chancellor, and if then he had shown more quickly and decisively that he really was the King's, and not the Heir Apparent's, first minister (in particular over the question of the Prince's establishment), George's determination at the first opportunity to be rid of Fox and the coalition might conceivably have weakened. History however is not about 'might-haves'. In the spring the King had been forced into a corner, in fact into a submission. He was now shown a way to regain the initiative and perhaps reverse fortunes.

At the beginning of December, just before the bill was ready to be sent from the Commons to the Lords, Thurlow suggested to the King, in a memorandum prepared by him in collaboration with Pitt's cousin Earl Temple, that the Upper House should be 'informed of his feelings' about the India Bill 'in a manner which would make it impossible to pretend a doubt of it'. George, however, was too experienced and skilful a politician to try contriving a House of Lords defeat for the coalition (to be followed of course by dismissal) without first ensuring that he had a replacement prime minister ready and waiting. Previously, in the spring, he had made approaches to Pitt, who had then proved disappointingly cautious and irresolute. Now he tried again, but in the secrecy which both men knew was essential. Not only must he be sure of Pitt; Pitt must also be sure of him. Both knew that their movements were under constant watch. An intermediary therefore – indeed, as it turned out, two intermediaries – must be found, of adequate obscurity and discretion, to transmit the preparatory messages and mutual undertakings. This delicate negotiation was conducted through the intervening staging-posts provided by Lord Clarendon, an experienced ex-minister who was *persona grata* with the King, and Count Alvensleben, who was Hanoverian Minister in London and whose personal access to the King would be unlikely to arouse suspicion. Meanwhile a detailed survey was prepared by John Robinson, who had been North's Treasury Secretary and was immensely knowledgeable in matters parliamentary, to persuade Pitt, who would take no chances, that in the event of a change of ministry he would eventually be able to command majorities in both Houses. Robinson, Thurlow, Dundas, Atkinson (an India House director), and even Fox's own uncle, the Duke of Richmond* were all privy to the incubation of this plot, and Pitt finally was given confidence enough to agree to its hatching.

---

* The Duke's sister, Fox's aunt Sarah, was both saddened and indignant about this family rift: 'Oh! how I grieve that my dear brother was among them! It quite breaks my heart! What a head! To

On 11 December, therefore, Temple had an audience with the King, and was presented with a written statement, as follows: 'His majesty allowed Earl Temple to say that whoever voted for the India Bill was not only not his friend, but would be considered by him as an enemy; and if these words were not strong enough, Earl Temple might use whatever words he might deem stronger and more to the purpose'.[6] Such action, taken moreover in a manner at once so precise and so threatening, was certainly by nineteenth and twentieth century standards unconstitutional. Even for the eighteenth century it was unprecedented. It is true that none of the first three Georges had troubled overmuch about letting his feelings about proposed legislation remain unexpressed. George II for instance is reported by Horace Walpole as 'talking openly at his levee' against a parliamentary bill of 1759 concerning Habeas Corpus, and 'it was understood to be offensive to him to vote for the extension of it'. But he had never ventured to the extreme that his grandson was now going to, or acted so publicly. And even George III had once given it as his opinion that it would be 'unconstitutional' for the Crown to interfere in bills which had already reached parliament. Yet this India bill had not merely reached parliament; it had completed its Commons stages with large majorities. Further, where George and his predecessor had sometimes spoken openly *in favour* of ministerial measures, this time uniquely the King was intervening *against* his ministers.

It is to be accepted that a country like Britain, whose fundamental legal texts are enshrined in no one sacred document, makes up its constitution as it goes along. It certainly did, and to some extent must still do so. In December 1783 George III was attempting to give that pliable entity the British constitution a nudge towards the reassertion, even the reinforcement, of Crown prerogative. A few months earlier, Fox had essayed a considerable push in the opposite direction, by trying to deny the monarch any say in the choice of his ministers. If Fox's attempt to dictate to the King, even if 'unconstitutional' in 1783, can claim a posthumous legitimation in the slow unfolding of nineteenth century history, George III could argue, as indeed he did, that the Crown, along with the Lords and the Commons, was one of the triple pillars of the national polity; that royal prerogative had always existed and still existed; and that within the prerogative lay the power to appoint and dismiss ministers.

Unconstitutional or not, George's action was carefully prepared and

be misled by boys, flatterers, and knaves! A head capable of every good ...' (Lady Sarah Napier to Lady Susan O'Brien, 22 December 1783).

shrewdly executed. Temple passed on the royal message, with its unmis-takably minatory tone, to such of the lay peers and bishops with whom he could manage to get in touch, with the result that the Lords' first division on the bill in the early hours of 16 December resulted in a defeat for the coalition by 69 votes to 57. The Prince of Wales, probably at that time imperfectly acquainted with the form of words used by his father to Temple, was among those voting at this stage in support of his friend Fox. When however he discovered that his recorded vote put him among the King's 'enemies', he was prudent enough hastily to apologize to his father, from whom he received back a friendly acknowledgement. By the time that the very explicit nature of the royal message had been fully digested by the entire Lords' voting strength, the majority against the bill on its decisive second reading was increased to 19. Charles Fox, reported Thomas Orde, a Shelburnite member,

> was behind the throne during the whole time of the business yesterday, and seemed to be in great agitation at every turn ... I am told that his countenance, gesture, and expressions on the event were in the highest degree ludicrous from the extremity of distortion and rage, going off with an exclamation of despair, lugging George North along with him and calling out for Sheridan ... I understand that some of the bishops seemed to feel very awkward, and that those who still voted with administration cast a sad look of contrition towards those who might 'tell tales of them to high-judging Jove'.[7]

The following evening, at forty-three minutes to ten o'clock (his letters were habitually timed with this precision), the King sat down to write to North, *not* to Fox: 'Lord North is by this required to send me the seals of his department, and to acquaint Mr Fox to send those of the foreign department. [The under-secretaries] will be the proper channel of delivering them to me this night. I choose this method as audiences on such occasions must be unpleasant'.[8]

He wasted no time. The next day the not quite 25-year-old Pitt kissed hands as First Lord of the Treasury and Chancellor of the Exchequer, while Temple became Secretary of State. Fox was not to be a minister again until a few months before his death.

No presentiment of these future years in the wilderness clouded his mood after his defeat. He was angry and resentful, but also defiantly cheerful. 'We are beat in the Lords', he wrote to his mistress, 'by such treachery on the part of the King, and such measures on the part of his *friends* in the House of Lords, as one could not expect either from him or them ... However we are so strong that nobody can undertake without madness; and if they do, we shall destroy them almost as soon as they are formed.' It would be a mince-pie ministry, as the felicitous Mrs Crewe put it – all over by Christmas or soon after. When the Commons met on 19 December, the expelled coalitionists felt sufficiently confident to indulge themselves in some initial banter and sarcasm aimed at the new ministers, Fox beginning the proceedings by shepherding Dundas across the House to the ministerial front bench – he had by force of habit sat down on the opposition side.

The first question to be faced was whether there should or should not be a dissolution, with a general election to follow. Fox argued against it, and this has frequently been charged against him by historians* as an important item in the rather large catalogue of his political misjudgements, since a general election (so these writers considered, rightly or wrongly) would have been likely to result in a coalition majority. In any case Fox after his dismissal was in no position to *demand* a dissolution, but he himself was plainly somewhat unsure whether or not he had been arguing correctly on this issue. Only three days after his 19 December speech he was writing, 'I own that I am one of those who rather am sorry that the thing was not brought to a decision by a dissolution'.[9]

For some weeks yet, the Fox–North camp appear to have remained in good fettle. 'It is supposed the old ministry *must* be reinstated', Fitzpatrick told his current mistress; and optimism such as this was reinforced by an early misfortune which overtook the fledgling Pitt ministry ... 'I ... dispatch a servant to you', Fox wrote to Northington (still in Dublin awaiting his successor), 'to let you know that Lord Temple has this day resigned. What will follow is not yet known, but I think there can be very little doubt but our administration will again be established.'[10] Temple's resignation – bringing Pitt a sleepless night, and causing the King once again to feel himself 'on the edge of a precipice' – did not arise, as often used to be thought, from pique at not being offered a dukedom, but rather from fear of being impeached. His nerve had been shaken by the still only half-formed cabinet's decision *not* to dissolve parliament. Temple seems to have all along assumed that there would have to be an immediate dissolution, then a prompt election to produce a majority for the new administration, and consequently a situation in which the outraged Fox–North

---

* Among others, by Lecky, G.M. Trevelyan, and Richard Pares. John Cannon, in *The Fox–North Coalition* (pp. 146–7) puts the contrary view, on the ground that eighteenth century administrations always won elections, as Fox well knew, by virtue of their command of patronage.

battalions thirsting for his blood would be left in an ineffectual minority. Now that his openly vengeful enemies appeared likely to dominate Commons votes, he seems to have been genuinely alarmed, even afraid that his life might be in danger.[11] He was a 'damned dolter-headed coward', his understandably annoyed recent colleague Dundas reported, 'full of rashness, obstinacy and timidity by fits'.

Mrs Crewe's mince pies were to last a remarkably long time – more than three months, from 19 December 1783 to 25 March 1784. Yet on the face of it, the new administration looked neither strong nor impressive, apart from Pitt himself, who was as it were *born* impressive, and by this time had added to his inborn gifts and natural shrewdness a cool self-assurance, driving ambition, and a remarkable capacity for political calculation. With the exception of Thurlow, who was Lord Chancellor once again and was, in his own fashion, impressive too, the new cabinet contained no heavyweights. All but Pitt were peers – the Duke of Rutland, the Duke of Richmond, and Lords Sydney, Carmarthen, Gower, and Howe. The only remarkable thing about the cabinet, declared Nathaniel Wraxall, was its collective capacity for drink. Pitt's lieutenants of significance in the Commons were two only, the as yet junior ministers Henry Dundas, whose special fields were Scotland and India, and Pitt's cousin (Temple's brother) William Wyndham Grenville, a future prime minister.

Even before Christmas there were moves from several quarters for a regrouping of parties, but Fox showed no interest in them, and Pitt still refused to have any truck with Lord North. In view of forthcoming Commons divisions, and in some uncertain future a dissolution and election, both sides were soon busy offering rewards and inducements to potential supporters, whether independents, waverers, or patrons of boroughs. Here, eventually, the side with royal backing held a very substantial advantage; and, as the unfailingly picturesque Walpole had it, they were soon 'crying peerages about the streets in barrows'. Ex-Treasury Secretary Robinson, the best-informed patronage expert and opinion-watcher in the country, though still confident that Pitt would eventually win, reckoned at first that he would not be really safe until at least forty Commons votes were turned round. Before parliament reassembled on 12 January his estimates were looking better; the latest researches among the uncommitted revealed sixty-one 'hopefuls' and only forty-five 'doubtfuls.'

In the early debates of 1784, Fox hammered away at the 'secret influence' which during the previous month had been improperly and *uncon-stitutionally* exerted. There had been *intrigue* against the House of

Commons. He returned to it repeatedly: he was fighting for the *rights of the House of Commons*. Admittedly the Crown had rights too, and prerogatives; but to appoint ministers in opposition to a majority of the House of Commons was indefensible. It was 'unsafe, unwarranted, and unjustifiable'.[12] His attitude also to the dangerous prospect of a swift dissolution of parliament – uncertain and ambivalent in December – was now clarified and emphatically stated. Any dissolution of a parliament before the end of its statutory term would, he asserted, be 'unconstitutional'. Thus a further detail was supplied to the revised, if historically less than authorized, Fox version of the British constitution.

Replying in particular to the accusation of secret influence, Pitt was all blandness and unctuous virtue – mendacity too, perhaps:

> He knew of no secret influence, and his own integrity would be his guardian against that danger ... 'Little did I think to be ever charged in this House with being the tool and abetter of secret influence ... This is the only answer I shall ever deign to make on the subject, and I wish the House to ... judge of my future conduct by my present declaration: the integrity of my own heart, and the probity of my public, as well as my private, principles shall always be my sources of action ...'[13]

The first important Commons vote of 1784 gave the dismissed coalition a majority of 39, which however serious for the government at first glance, marked a significant drop from the three-figure majorities the coalition's India Bill had been enjoying before Christmas and, as Lord Palmerston noted in his diary, 'shewed on the one hand how diligent the ministry had been, in the interval of parliament, in getting over proselytes, or in the fashionable phrase, *Rats*'. On the other hand, it 'presented such an unpromising prospect as was sufficient to have made prudent men despair of their undertaking'.[14] At least the new parliamentary session afforded Fox one immediate satisfaction: an India Bill introduced by Pitt could be defeated as comfortably in the Commons as his own had been in the Lords.

The King now favoured an immediate dissolution. 'We must be men', he argued, 'and if we mean to save the country we must cut these threads that cannot be unravelled. Half-measures are ever puerile.'[15] Among the cabinet, Gower, Carmarthen, and Sydney thought similarly. Pitt however was for sitting tight, and a narrow cabinet majority sided with him. Not fully satisfied of his ministers' stomach for the fight, the King summoned them to attend him, whereupon, in the words of Secretary of State Carmarthen,

> His Majesty in a well-conceived speech of some length, and in different parts of which he appeared much agitated, expressed his wish upon all occasions

to observe the true principles of the constitution as the sole rule of his conduct ... and declared a fixed and unalterable resolution on no account to be put bound hand and foot into the hands of Mr Fox; that rather than submit to that he would quit the kingdom for ever ...[16]

Some independents continued to press for a union of parties, which realistically could only mean a Fox–Pitt coalition. There was nothing intrinsically improbable in this idea. Both men from the opposition benches had attacked North's ministry, and in particular its American policy. Both had spoken in favour of parliamentary reform. But the insuperable obstacle to such a union was the pride and ambition of both. Neither would seriously consider serving under, or even on equal terms with, the other. They were 'two young men [as Charles Jenkinson, the future prime minister Lord Liverpool, noted at the time], both of great parts and great ambition, and from their different tempers and characters, I am afraid, irreconcilable' – altogether too irreconcilable, in fact to be attracted by a suggestion of Lord Nugent's, that they should each be invited to his house, where they could get 'gloriously drunk' and settle their differences. Nevertheless, pressures behind the scenes continued through February, and the King, 'though reluctantly', went so far as 'to authorize a message to be carried in my name to the Duke of Portland expressing a desire that he and Mr Pitt may meet to confer on the means of forming an administration on a wide basis'. Even then, 'the only mode in which I could tolerate them [Portland and Fox] in my service' would be as part of some broad-bottomed ministry, and *not* as 'having the administration in their hands'.[17]

On his side, Fox was just as uncompromising: 'everybody must see', he wrote to Portland on 24 February, 'that these new suggestions lay completely open to the old objection of Pitt's being as it were an agent for the King ... You and not Pitt must be the King's agent as far as he is supposed to have one'.[18] And although of course he did not say so, Portland would also in fact be Fox's agent. Portland would provide a mask of respectability, the 'acceptable face' of Whiggism, but behind the mask, as everybody knew and the King knew best of all, lay the unmistakably individual features of Mr Fox. British public opinion never saw the political battle as being fought between Portland and George III; it was a case of Fox versus the King – a fact echoed excitedly at this time in Paris, from where Lady Clermont wrote to the Duchess of Devonshire, 'I was at Versailles last week ... They are all sure there will be a revolution, and Fox will be K'.

There were excitements too in London. That by now fervent Foxite the

Duchess of Devonshire wrote to her mother Lady Spencer:

> I was at the Opera, it was very full and I had several good political fights ...
> The Duchess of Rutland [her Duke was in Pitt's cabinet] said D— Fox, upon
> which Colonel St Leger [a friend of the Prince of Wales] with great difficulty
> spirited up Ly Maria Waldegrave [Walpole's niece] to say D— Pitt. We had
> quite an opposition supper at D'Adhémar's [the French ambassador's] ...
> There was Mr Fox, Grenville, Ld Malden, Cl St Leger, all our men in short.
> We play'd a little after supper, and I very moderately won a few guineas.[19]

Two or three weeks before these aristocratic exchanges, Pitt had received
the freedom of the City of London, and his return home became the
occasion of a minor riot. He was accompanied by his brother-in-law Mahon
and his elder brother Chatham, who many years later gave the following
account of what occurred:

> He was attended by a great concourse of people, many of the better sort, all
> the way down the Strand, as well as by a considerable mob – the populace
> insisted on taking off the horses and drawing the coach. A mob is never very
> discreet, and unfortunately they stopped outside Carlton House and began
> hissing, and it was with some difficulty we forced them to go on. As we
> proceeded up St James's Street, there was a great cry, and an attempt made to
> turn the carriage up St James's Place to Mr Fox's house (he then lived at Lord
> Northingtons's) in order to break his windows ... I have often thought this
> was a trap laid for us, for had we got up there into a cul de sac, Mr Pitt's
> situation would have been critical indeed ... The moment we got opposite
> [Brooks's], a sudden and desperate attack was made upon the carriage ... by
> a body of chairmen armed with bludgeons, broken chair-poles ... Fortunately,
> however, by the exertions of those who remained with us, and by the timely
> assistance of a body of chairmen and many gentlemen from White's who
> saw his danger, we were extricated from a most unpleasant situation ... The
> coachmen and the servants were much bruised, and the carriage nearly
> demolished ... I distinguished Mr Hare and the present Lord Crewe [Fox's
> friends] extremely active ... I never went to Brooks's any more.[20]

Naturally enough, given Fox's reputation and the involvement of some of
his closest associates, he was accused of participating in the brouhaha. This
he comprehensively denied, by offering an unanswerable alibi. He could
not possibly have played any part in the affair, having been at that hour
in bed with Mrs Armistead, who was willing to substantiate this fact on
oath.*

---

* John Ehrman, in the first volume of *The Younger Pitt* (p. 141) writes: 'The first account I have
found of this tale is in *The Olio: a Collection of Anecdotes* ... (2nd edition, 1796, p. 190). It was
therefore published, under the name of a celebrated antiquary, while Fox and Mrs Armistead were
alive'.

The confidence of the Foxites and Northites began to evaporate during February. They found no difficulty in getting comfortable majorities for a succession of critical resolutions and addresses in the Commons, and for some time Fox does not appear to have seriously considered what to do if Pitt, however frequently defeated, chose not to resign. The one, somewhat desperate, measure open to him – blocking the passage of that annual parliamentary necessity, the Mutiny Bill, essential for voting supplies – he dared not undertake, though *postponing* the voting of supplies served for a time as a compromise option. When, however, his motion for postponement came forward in mid-February, the coalition majority sank to a disappointing 12.

Worse still, public opinion began moving decisively against him. Even as early as 16 January, the corporation of the City of London, which had only recently been vigorous in asserting its own rights and privileges *against* the King's ministers, now turned smartly about, and voted congratulations to his Majesty for his 'salutary and constitutional' action in dismissing the coalition. One of Earl Fitzwilliam's electoral agents in Yorkshire reported, 'The trading part of the county are almost unanimous ... against taking from the King what they look upon to be necessary in him for the preservation of the true constitution';[21] and a trickle of loyal addresses from meetings held by town corporations and county freeholders soon grew to a flood – there were eventually more than two hundred. Moreover, when on 18 February the meeting of Cornwall's freeholders approved a form of words supporting the monarch's right to choose his own ministers, 'a pretty general murmur was heard of "Not strong enough" '.[22] In Fox's own Westminster there were 8,000 signatures for a pro-governmental address; for two addresses from Bristol, 5,000; from Glasgow, 4,000; from many smaller towns signatures by the hundred. A counter-address from Buckinghamshire, although backed by an impressive-sounding collection of Whig grandees and supported from the platform by Burke, was rejected, and the meeting 'by a great majority' voted for Pitt. Wakefield's message to Westminster travelled from Yorkshire in a coach bearing prominently a blue flag on which was 'emblazoned in letters of gold, "The King! The Constitution! The People! And Pitt for ever!" ' And an observer, quoted in the *Leicester and Nottingham Journal*, reported that when on 25 February members of the House of Commons attended the King to present an address requesting the dismissal of the Pitt ministry, they could 'with difficulty pass through the throng of delegates crowding round the throne from corporations, counties, and respectable bodies of men from all quarters, assuring their sovereign of their entire and unlimited confidence in, and highest approbation of, his newly appointed ministers'.[23]

Fox, although by 1 March his Commons motion was no longer politely requesting, but now (in whatever muted parliamentary language) demanding, the administration's dismissal, was nevertheless increasingly impotent, and sounded less than convincing when he protested that 'the people were deceived'; that they were 'causing their own ruin'; that those who 'understand the ground of the dispute' were with him. He spoke thus just after he had faced a hostile meeting in Westminster Hall and had been obliged to abandon it, adjourning to the King's Arms Tavern, from one of whose windows he harangued a crowd of his supporters. As the strongly Pittite and disapproving Charles Jenkinson informed John Robinson (whose finger was still, indeed was constantly, on the pulse of the constituencies), Fox 'was then drawn in his chariot by a low mob of about 100 to Devonshire House, but what will astonish you is that Col. Stanhope, Mr Hanger, and Mr O'Byrne were on the coach box, and that Mr George North, Mr Adam, and a third person stood as footmen behind. How disgraceful!'

The part being played behind the scenes by Robinson – helpful to the Pitt camp, deeply suspect to Fox's – produced one parliamentary exchange which nicely illustrates the Sheridan touch. It was not to be wondered at, he declared, that the coalition's majorities were decreasing 'when a member is employed to corrupt everybody in order to obtain votes'. To indignant Pittite cries of 'Name him! Name him!' the ever quickfire Sheridan replied, 'Mr Speaker, I shall not name him, but do not suppose that I abstain from any difficulty in naming him. I could do that, Sir, as soon as you could say Jack Robinson'.

The Commons' latest address, on 1 March, begging the King to bow to the will of the House – its tone, the King said, was unpleasantly 'dictatorial' – passed by 201 votes to 189. A week later there came what proved to be the decisive debate, and a general conviction that it would indeed be crucial filled the Strangers' Gallery to capacity by eleven o'clock, five hours before the proceedings were due to begin. The address which was to be debated submitted to his Majesty's wisdom, 'with all humility', that the circumstances of his ministry's appointment and continuance had 'created just suspicions in the breasts of his faithful Commons', since principles had been adopted 'unfriendly to the privileges of the House and to the freedom of our excellent constitution'[24] – which was eventually approved by a majority of just *one*. There was general agreement that this marked an end, and that soon there must be a dissolution. 'The enemy indeed seem to be on their backs', Pitt wrote to Rutland; and the King, in reply to his prime minister's routine message informing him of the voting figures, congratulated him on saving that 'most perfect of human formations', the British constitution. A one-vote victory for Fox was plainly a final defeat.[25]

Final, in that there never was any doubt that the forthcoming election was already lost. Even in January, before the movement of public opinion was fully manifest, London and provincial newspapers were predicting a majority for Pitt, and on the day of the dissolution, 25 March, the *Morning Herald* reported that Robinson was expecting a majority of 70 – rather less than he had forecast in December, but still promising wonderfully well. Of course, the election would be 'corrupt' in the sense that all eighteenth-century elections were. That is, some 'close' or 'pocket' boroughs and their patrons were available to be bought (with peerages or other honours, with *douceurs*, or simply with money), and voters in the 'open' boroughs and the counties were not always wholly resistant to corrupt persuasion, usually of a very minor, and perhaps merely alcoholic, order. But only just under £32,000 of Treasury money was spent towards winning the 1784 election, against £62,000 for instance in 1780,[26] and the outstanding feature in 1784 was that coalition candidates, Foxites and Northites alike, fared least well where genuine public opinion was best able to prevail, in the counties and the open boroughs. The most emphatic illustration of this came from Yorkshire, where Rockingham had once been supreme, and where his nephew and heir Fitzwilliam now found himself powerless to stem the tide of defeat. (One of Pitt's gains in Yorkshire was made by his friend and admirer William Wilberforce, who was to remain a member for Yorkshire for the next twenty-eight years.) Coalition candidates remained safe, of course, in most of their close boroughs, such as Burke's at Malton, but the county's freeholders and the electors of the city of York both now proceeded to vote for the King against Fox – for that was how the election was popularly seen, and even spoken of by some of the electioneering aristocracy, such for example as Lord Fauconberg, a courtier, who put it to the crowd in York's Castle Yard: was 'George the Third or Charles Fox to reign?' Or as John Carr, one of Fitzwilliam's election agents reported, people had 'no idea but that Mr Fox wants to get the better of the King and be Lord Protector'. Again, another agent reported some weeks later, 'The received notion amongst the inferiors in many parts is that Mr Fox was attempting to dethrone the King and make himself an Oliver Cromwell'. These references to Cromwell and the previous century's civil wars were in the 1780s commonly made by both contending sides of the argument. Fox and his friends liked to picture themselves as latterday Pyms and Hampdens warring against a new potential despotism, while it was all too easy for their opponents to envisage Fox as another Cromwell. Easy, and of course grossly unfair – but showing nevertheless how quickly Fox's projection of himself as 'the man of the people' had gone awry.

'Yorkshire and Middlesex', Fox once declared, 'between them make all England', and election results there always carried a special significance. In 1784 the Foxite George Byng lost Middlesex. Other results proved as depressing, and even more surprising. Sir Charles Bunbury, first husband to Fox's aunt Sarah Lennox, was returned for Suffolk at every general election for forty-seven years – except in 1784, when he stood as a Foxite. In neighbouring Norfolk the unthinkable occurred: the Foxite Thomas Coke met defeat in 1784; the only time in half a century of representing his county. The exercise of patronage and electoral management, where the sitting government always held so powerful an advantage, was likely in any case to have won the election for Pitt, but it was the weight of public opinion which turned Fox's – and of course North's – defeat into something like a rout.

9

THE
WESTMINSTER ELECTION
OF 1784

Fox's own Westminster seat always promised a close fight. It returned two members, and the 1784 contest was three-cornered. There was never any doubt that Admiral Lord Hood, a government supporter and naval hero, would top the poll; the fight would be for the second seat. Westminster was no ordinary constituency; in a variety of ways it was pre-eminent. Numerically it was the largest in the land. Uniquely it provided a vote to every 'inhabitant householder'. It housed the Court and the Palace of Westminster, which included not only the old St Stephen's parliament buildings but historic Westminster Hall. It contained the town residences of fashionable society and the political aristocracy, alongside a large middle and lower class population. Above all and more sharply than anywhere else, it brought into focus the grand political battle of the day, between Fox and North on the one side, and Pitt and the King on the other. Winning it in 1780, however narrowly, had been an important landmark in the career of Charles Fox, 'man of the people'; and in 1784, to keep it, he was prepared to fight to the point of exhaustion. And since it was prestigious Westminster, and the man to beat was Fox, winning *both* seats there became important too for the government – for Pitt personally, it was next in importance only to his own 'very near struggle' to be returned for Cambridge University.

The ministerialist whom Fox needed to beat was Sir Cecil Wray, the owner of extensive estates in Norfolk, Lincolnshire, and Yorkshire, an old political hand and a strong candidate. He had earlier for a time been a Foxite, but his hostility to North had turned him decisively against the coalition. Fox's prospects of winning were sufficiently doubtful for him to take the precaution of being nominated also for the Tain Boroughs in the far north of Scotland, which were conveniently in the pocket of a friendly Whig patron, Sir Thomas Dundas, and of course returned Fox in due course. Thus defeat at Westminster would not deprive him of a seat in the Commons, but that fact in no way lessened his anxious determination to win at Westminster.

Not only was the struggle there reckoned of particular significance, it also went on the longest – in Pitt's words, forty days of poll, forty days of riot, forty days of confusion. As Hood, veteran of some formidable naval engagements, remarked afterwards, it was 'the most arduous and unpleasant business I ever took in hand'.[1] Each side deployed its forces, oratorical, journalistic, vocal, instrumental, or muscular, with vigour and variety. Demonstrations abounded. Processions with their bands and banners paraded the streets. There were several pitched battles between rival supporters. Once, 'a gang of fellows headed by naval officers' and 'carrying his Majesty's colours' came into violent collision (in the ministerial version of events) with an opposing gang of 'Irish chairmen and pick-pockets'. In one encounter a constable was killed, a fatality alleged by each side to have been caused by the other's 'banditti of ruffians'. Bookmakers set up for business under the shadow of the hustings. Election verses and ditties, abusive jingles, cartoons and lampoons circulated by the dozen. The melody of the National Anthem, for instance, was found to adapt to some excruciating new doggerel for Foxite voices to chant:

> Time-servers, wond'ring, shall
> View us determined all,
> Spite of the Court:
> Spite of their wily tricks
> And back-stair politics,
> Fox is the man we fix
> On to support.

Or the Champion of Liberty might be hymned as follows:

> He's loyal, he's noble, he's chosen by me.
> My rights to protect and my sons to keep free.

On the other side, Fox's blue and buff coat and waistcoat, his sartorial shortcomings, and his shifts of principle might be simultaneously derided:

> One uniform suit had this whimsical fellow
> 'Twas a coat of plain blue and a waistcoat of yellow;

> For he gambled among such an infamous pack
> They left him no more than the coat on his back.
> Of principle tho' (which don't cost quite so dear)
> He had changes and suits for each day of the year.
> Thus he shifted his principles, shifted his speeches,
> But ne'er shifted his coat, nor his waistcoat and breeches.

Both sides enlisted their finest ladies for canvassing, but in this department the Fox Whigs deployed the somewhat more glamorous weaponry. For them, the Duchess of Portland, the Duchess of Devonshire, and her sister Lady Duncannon all entered the fray, while there came in for Hood and Wray the Countess of Salisbury and other fashionables. It was the celebrated Georgiana Devonshire, queen of the Foxite *beau monde*, whose participation created the most news-worthy sensation. 'She was in the most blackguard houses in Long Acre by eight o'clock this morning', declared Lord Cornwallis; and Earl Temple was of the opinion that she had 'heard more plain English of the grossest sort than ever fell to the share of any lady of her rank'.[2] Soon she came under pressure from her mother, Lady Spencer, to withdraw from disgracing herself and her family by making of her beauty and social eminence so vulgar a public display. Her mother tugged her one way, and the Duchess of Portland the other, begging her to come 'tomorrow, there are so many votes you can command and No One else'. Retiring for a while, ostensibly to be with her mother who was 'unwell', she was soon back canvassing in style and with the *éclat* to be expected from so prominent a leader of fashion – clad in her Foxite blue and buff and sporting her fox fur or tippet. She was alleged to have *shaken hands* with a cobbler – worse, kissed a butcher, which last she denied with some indignation. Her sister and one other lady were indeed kissed, she protested to her mother; so it was 'very hard that I who was not shd have the reputation of it'.[3]

It does not appear that the most devotedly and intimately Foxite of all the Foxite ladies, Mrs Armistead, took any part in these notorious activities. She stayed at her country house at St Anne's Hill, near Chertsey in Surrey, which from this time was becoming more and more to be regarded by Fox as his own true and much loved home. To his dearest Liz from the noisy confusion of Westminster, daily or every few days, he dispatched little notes telling of his latest fortunes in the polling – bad news mostly during the early weeks:

3 April plenty of bad news from all quarters ...
5 April The thing is far from being over, and I still have hopes, but their

beating me two days following looks ugly; bad news from other places...
6 April Our sanguine friends still hope, not I ...
7 April Worse and worse ... there is very little chance indeed.
8 April I must not give it up, though I wish it ...
20 April I have gained thirty-two to-day, so that we are all in spirits again.
27 April I gained forty-eight upon them today, and am now, as you see, twenty ahead ...

During the last three weeks of the poll, his score steadily improved, as his bulletin for his mistress indicates: 'I gained thirty-two to-day ... I gained forty-eight upon them to-day ... I have gained twenty to-day ... They only polled eleven to-day (4 May), and I thirty-three ... (7 May) 'we polled only nine to eight to-day, so I think it must be soon over'.[4]

Ten days later, at last it was. Hood had polled 6,694, Fox 6,234, Wray 5,998; but the high bailiff refused to declare Fox and Hood elected, as Wray had demanded a scrutiny. Undeterred by this trifle, Fox's supporters, with their hero chaired aloft, set off on their well-prepared processional march of triumph through the constituency, arriving finally at Devonshire House, whither the Prince of Wales had galloped back from Ascot that morning to share in the salutations. He had found time, before climbing to join the duchesses on their vantage point of welcome, to don the Fox insignia which were that day of all days *de rigueur* – the wreath of laurel and the fox's brush.

No detail had been neglected or expense spared in the preparations for the grand march of celebration, an impressive combination of Foxolatry and populist razmataz:

Heralds on Horseback
Twenty-four Marrow-bones and Cleavers
The Arms of Westminster
Thirty Freemen of Westminster
Martial Music
Committees of the Seven Parishes with white wands, following their respective banners, and attended by numberless Gentlemen of the Several Districts
Squadron of Gentlemen on Horseback in the Blue and Buff uniform
Trumpets
Flag. The Rights of the Commons
Grand Band of Music
Flag. THE MAN OF THE PEOPLE
Marshalls on Foot
TRIUMPHAL CHAIR,
decorated with Laurels, in which was seated

The Right Hon. CHARLES JAMES FOX
Trumpets
Flag. The WHIG CAUSE
Second Squadron of Horse
Liberty Boys of Newport Market
Mr FOX'S Carriage crowned with Laurels
Banner. Sacred to Female Patriotism!
Blue Standard, inscribed,
INDEPENDENCE!
State Carriage of their Graces
The Duchesses of PORTLAND and DEVONSHIRE,
drawn by six horses, superbly caparisoned, with six running foot-men
attendant on each
Gentlemen's servants, closing the Procession, two and two,
etc. etc.

Festivities continued into the evening – speeches at Devonshire House, dinner and more speeches at Willis's Rooms – and on the next day, in the gardens of newly magnificent Carlton House, the Prince's guests breakfasted at noon in marquees 'equally expressive of the political principle and gallantry of his Highness'. Dancing followed during the afternoon; and then in the evening the Whig leaders, having first dined with the Prince, dressed in their buff and blue, proceeded to a grand ball held by Mrs Crewe, wife of the Foxite member for Cheshire and one of the age's acclaimed beauties. It was the Prince of Wales who, at the climax of the celebrations at this ball, proposed the toast, 'Here's buff and blue and Mrs Crewe!', to which Mrs Crewe happily and memorably responded, 'Here's buff and blue and all of *you*!' Parties at Carlton House followed over the next few days, at one of which the Prince, rather the worse for drink, had the misfortune to fall flat on the dance-floor in the middle of a quadrille and on being helped to his feet was, in the midst of his distinguished company, royally sick.

In the eighteenth century disputed elections, and the scrutinies arising from them, were common. Fox's earlier Westminster victory in 1780 had for instance been originally subject to one, though it was soon aborted. In 1784 Pitt, determined as he was that Fox must not be allowed to win, was already during the last few weeks of the poll, when things looked promising for the buff-and-blue, discussing with the King the expediency or otherwise of a scrutiny. He could not then decide whether to have Wray ask the high bailiff for one, or to have all three candidates provisionally returned, and then to ask the Commons to choose two of them.

'In either case', he wrote confidently to Rutland a week after the poll closed, 'I have no doubt of Fox being thrown out, [but] the choice of the alternative is delicate'.[5]

A fortnight later, the House debated a motion which if passed would effectively sanction a scrutiny, and upon which Fox (member temporarily for Tain Burghs) made one of the ablest and most carefully prepared of all his many parliamentary speeches — ransacking historical precedents, deploying a wealth of legal expertise, but above all indignantly demanding justice and freedom from ministerial persecution. Brougham, a future Lord Chancellor, rated this the finest of all Fox's speeches, and once recommended Macaulay to learn it by heart if he wished to master the art of oratory. Even for Macaulay, however, this would have taken some little time, for Fox spoke for three hours — which prompted Pitt to ask whether 'a gentleman who had the liberty of speaking three hours at a stretch on his own cause', could really be 'a persecuted man'.

The vote, taken at 4.30 a.m., resulted in a defeat for Fox, and the scrutiny proceeded — only however at such a dawdle that after 8 months a mere quarter of the votes had been examined. Moreover, among the votes now deemed invalid, there proved little to choose between those which had been given wrongly to Fox, and those wrongly to Hood or Wray; nor was the total for any of them large. It began to appear that even a complete examination, effectively disenfranchising Westminster for years, would be very unlikely to change the result of the poll originally declared. But Pitt would not give up. Unwisely, and many thought vindictively, he continued to press for Fox's exclusion. In February 1785 Fox's friends twice tried to have the scrutiny terminated, and although the decision of the Commons both times went against them, Pitt's majority within the space of twelve days was reduced from 39 to 9. Opinion, both in parliament and 'outdoors', was moving against him as emphatically as it had moved in his favour a twelvemonth before. On 3 March, he was defeated in the House by 38, and the next day Hood and Fox were at last declared elected. Tain Burghs could go back into Sir Thomas Dundas's pocket. For Fox this defeat of Pitt had been quite a triumph. He would do well to cherish it, for it would be the last major victory he would be able to enjoy for the next twenty years and more.

10

PITT AND FOX

1784–1789

Over those two decades (1784–1806), Fox and Pitt stood head and shoulders above their fellows in the House of Commons – or at least (until his retirement in 1793) above all but Burke. Not until the heyday of Disraeli and Gladstone a lifetime later would there again appear two such incontestably dominant party leaders, or two so well-matched and so strikingly contrasted. It was an opposition and confrontation of appearance, of manner, and of personality: Pitt angular and spare, holding himself stiffly upright, his face impassive, his aspect frigid; an essentially *public* persona and, as the memoirist Wraxall commented, 'without suavity or amenity'; Fox fat and Falstaffian, his coat carelessly worn and often largely unbuttoned, his hat aslant (as in the well-known Hickel portrait), his gait tending to a wobble, his seated posture lolling or with legs crossed; his face always mirroring his swift changes of mood; gregarious, accessible, warm, energetic, impulsive, genial. Whereas Fox, before taking his place on the opposition front bench, would often stop here and there for a nod of recognition or an exchange of news or views, or perhaps a joke, his great adversary's entry was altogether different. 'From the instant that Pitt entered the doorway of the House of Commons', wrote Wraxall, himself a long-serving member, 'he advanced up the floor with a quick and firm step, his head erect and thrown back, looking neither to right nor to left, nor favouring with a nod or a glance any of the individuals on either side, among whom many who possessed £5,000 a year would have been gratified even by so slight a mark of attention.' The two men were opposite also in their style of oratory and manner of delivery. Pitt, so Fox himself said, was 'never at a loss for *the* word, and I am never at a loss for *a* word'. Or as the celebrated Greek scholar Richard Porson once put it, 'Mr Pitt conceives his sentences before he utters them. Mr Fox throws himself into the middle of his, and leaves it to God Almighty to get him out again'. Both men were excellent classicists, but Pitt did not choose to match Fox's interest in contemporary writing. While lacking Fox's eclecticism and intellectual range, Pitt's mastery of financial and economic detail was much the superior.

Fox basked in the adulation which was so freely accorded him. Pitt, although in public he was imperturbably self-confident, in private made a quite different impression. He was, said Wilberforce, 'one of the shyest men I ever knew'. Fox was attractive to women; Pitt was not. Predictably his apparent lack of susceptibility to feminine charm gave rise to much comment, including suggestions that he was homosexual – which however seem to carry slender plausibility. He never married, nor did he keep mistresses. Fox, of course, until he 'came to rest on the experienced bosom of Mrs Armistead'[1] enjoyed the company of a succession of them. Strangers and political opponents never managed to pierce the Pitt façade, although among his few close friends he could be convivial, and drink himself under the table with the merriest of them. Fox needed no façade, public or private; he was always unmistakably and unambiguously himself. With few exceptions, even his political opponents allowed his charm and respected his shining abilities. Pitt himself conceded that Fox possessed 'magic'. Gibbon's testimony was almost extravagantly laudatory: nobody 'was ever more perfectly exempt from the taint of malevolence, vanity and falsehood'.

Lord Carlisle, who had known Fox continuously from boyhood, disputed the then widely held theory that ambition was his ruling passion. No, said Carlisle, it was pleasure; and pleasure is no doubt a term sufficiently broad to be accepted, broad enough to embrace equally delights intellectual and sensual. But gradually from about his mid-thirties Fox's pursuit of the pleasures seems to undergo, if not a sea-change, at least a change of emphasis and to a degree of direction too. He still gambled, but less frantically and on the whole less disastrously, though he continued from time to time to need baling out of trouble by his friends; for example, one of these living in Sackville Street was towards the end of 1784 helpful in giving him temporary asylum from pressing creditors. He was far from deserting Brooks's. It was an unusual year when he missed his September partridge shooting, and of course he was still to be found at Newmarket with fair regularity. Whether the following story refers to horse-racing or the faro table is not entirely clear, but its relevance to the essential and probably unchangeable Fox is hardly affected:

> It must have been about this time that some ladies who were calling upon Mrs Armistead were startled by the sudden appearance of Mr Fox, who danced rapidly into the room to a chant of 'Great run! Great run! Finest thing you ever saw! Pay the Jews! Pay 'em all! Great run!' and disappeared with undiminished velocity.[2]

When away from the Commons, he now spent an ever-increasing proportion of his time at St Anne's Hill – and parliament seldom sat for more than half the year. The house there, with its 30 acres of farmland, its secluded gardens, trellised verandah, and fine views over the green and wooded Surrey countryside, had nothing pretentious about it. It was a long way from the style of grandiose splendour favoured by his father at Holland House or at Kingsgate, his ambitious Kentish retreat. In Fox's letters from St Anne's Hill there begins to emanate a strong impression of middle-aged, quasi-married bliss; begins, and long continues. 'I believe that if ever there were a place that might be called the seat of true happiness', he wrote to his nephew Henry (third Lord Holland), 'St Ann's is that place'. Or again, 'Here am I, passing a most comfortable week of holidays, the weather delicious, and the place looking beautiful beyond description, and the nightingales singing, and Mrs A. happy as the day is long – all of which circumstances combine to enable me to bear public calamities with wonderful philosophy'. Still to his nephew: 'I need not tell you that Mrs A. is as happy as I am, and she says she only wants to see the young one [Henry himself] to make her completely so'. And again, 'I am perfectly happy in the country. I have quite resources enough to employ my mind; and the great resource of all, literature, I am fonder of every day; and then the Lady of the Hill is one continual source of happiness to me. I believe few men, indeed, ever were so happy in that respect as I.' And after the two of them had been together for ten years he was writing:

> Mrs A. and I had each a letter from you last week, I need not say how much pleasure your letter to her gave me. You were never more right than in what you say of my happiness derived from her, I declare I think my affection for her increases every day. She is a comfort to me in every misfortune, and makes me enjoy doubly every pleasant circumstance of life; there is to me a charm and delight in her society, which time does not in the least wear off, and for real goodness of heart if she ever had an equal, she certainly never had a superior.

If there were conjugal felicities and consolations rural and literary at St Anne's Hill, at Westminster there was to be little cheer. After the 1784 election the forces of the Foxites and Northites, even when fully combined, could never hope for anything but minor successes. The Northites had been left in as poor shape as the Foxites. North himself was a sick man (he eventually went blind also) and the loyalty of his followers was far from secure. Fox was unchallengeably leader of the opposition. At first, after the electoral disaster which had followed hard upon a politically hectic 8 months he was (as he told Portland) 'completely tired out with it, body and mind', and felt himself to be 'totally unequal' to acquit himself adequately either for the good of the party or for his own reputation. It was not 'caprice or laziness' which kept him at St Anne's Hill, he explained. 'Great injustice is done to me if I am suspected of any want of zeal for the cause, but I *know* that ... I can serve it better by lying by for a little while.'[3] His appetite for politics was soon somewhat restored, and he never ceased to be regarded as principal leader of the Commons opposition. Even so, throughout the remaining years of the decade, although he would sometimes experience bouts of optimism when his political adrenalin would surge, he would at times be weighed down in pessimism or exasperation, leaving the business of party organization and tactical decision either to the Duke of Portland or to William Adam, the Scottish Whig, lawyer, and sometime Northite – and the man with whom Fox had once fought his duel in Hyde Park.

An opposition, and above all an opposition leader, must oppose, and be seen to oppose. This doubtless encouraged Fox over the next four or five years to adopt attitudes and put forward arguments which sometimes now appear factious, unconvincing, or carping. Early in the new parliament he was placed in an awkward predicament by an initiative from Pitt. Fulfilling a promise he had given to Christopher Wyvill, and to satisfy his own convictions, Pitt (as a private member, not as prime minister) introduced a bill to reform parliament. It could not be a government measure, since the cabinet was divided on the issue, as also were the opposition Whigs. But on many earlier occasions Fox had spoken – spoken sometimes vehemently – in favour of such reform: not root-and-branch democratic reform, of which he never dreamed, but just such practicable and modest changes as Pitt was now proposing. These were to disfranchise thirty-six of the rottenest boroughs and redistribute the seats among the counties and some of the large towns still unrepresented, such as Birmingham and Manchester; to compensate the dispossessed borough-proprietors; and to give the county vote to copyholders – previously it had been freeholders only. Fox's speech on this bill[4] proclaims his embarrassment. It was strong on generalization, devoid of warm commendation, full of marginally relevant debating points to discredit the foe, critical of Pitt's proposals for compensation, but lacking any clearly suggested alternatives of Fox's own. But of course, seizing though he did on every detail of the bill in any way to be criticized, he could not possibly, with his record, vote against it. At least he did not abstain. He thus became one of the 174 members who voted in favour. 248, among them North and Burke, voted against.

Probably Pitt had no realistic expectation that his parliamentary reform bill would succeed. His other main objective during 1785 was the Irish Propositions for which he did certainly have high hopes, but it too was to come to nothing. Pitt, whose notions of political economy took much from Adam Smith's *The Wealth of Nations* (published some nine years before) and something also from Shelburne, was aiming in these ambitious Irish Propositions to kill two birds with one stone. By reciprocal reduction, and in some cases abolition, of custom duties between Britain and Ireland he sought to add to the wealth of both nations. In fact, so he told his colleague Rutland, his fiscal and commercial reforms ought to make the two countries for the most essential purposes united. At the same time, he hoped that the stimulus given to Ireland's trade and manufacture would help to remedy the current unhappy state of Anglo-Irish political relations. The granting of strictly *legislative* independence three years before – largely the work of Fox – had failed to solve Ireland's problems; but he had come to regard it as untouchably final. 'The account must be considered as having been closed', he wrote to the Lord Lieutenant in November 1783.[5]

Fox, with none of Pitt's grounding in the still novel Smithian arguments, was guided by notions of commercial policy which were strictly conventional – what came later to be called mercantilist: crudely stated, that commerce might be regarded as a non-military branch of war. Like his colleague Burke, and like the elder Pitt earlier, he never questioned the idea, despite his sympathy for the American rebels, that colonial trade should be regulated in the interest primarily of the home country. But unlike Burke, and even more emphatically unlike Pitt the younger, he was never able to recognize that the freeing of trade, or at least some freeing of trade, between Britain and quasi-colonial Ireland might benefit the prosperity of both countries.

Pitt's 1785 Irish Propositions, imaginative and forward-looking as they were, still contained an important safeguard for the British imperial treasury: any Irish surplus of revenue arising from the scheme, above an annual £656,000, was to be earmarked for 'the support of the naval force of the empire' – which, particularly as later modified to Ireland's disadvantage, was to become a major sticking-point for Dublin. But it was the opposition which Pitt's proposals aroused, not in Ireland but in Britain, which Fox was able to seize upon and exploit. There were fears among British manufacturers that Irish products would under-sell the British market, and fears too among merchants that the Irish would win from the British important advantages accruing to them from foreign and colonial trade, especially since Pitt was proposing to allow such trade to pass between the two countries without any increase of duty.

Pitt thought at first that he had met and removed these and other fears. He was rewarded too by the Dublin parliament's initial acceptance of the propositions. Soon, however, there was a loud assault upon them in Britain, though it was not Fox who began it. 'The truth is ... and you best know it', wrote William Eden to Lord Sheffield (John Holroyd, Gibbon's friend), 'that if you and I had not work'd up that Irish business, Ld North would have slept thro the session at Bushy, and Mr Fox at St Anne's Hill.' Sheffield's pamphlet 'working up the business' concentrated chiefly on the threat to the Navigation Act, that Holy Bible of the mercantile interest. His influence particularly with the West Indies lobby was powerful. Meanwhile alarm grew also among the manufacturers (Josiah Wedgwood was one of the movers here), and if Fox really had needed waking up to be shown his opportunity, as Eden suggested, he was too good a politician to fail to grasp it in time.

As protests and addresses to parliament poured in from dozens of English and Scottish towns – sixty-four of them eventually – opposition at Westminster mounted too, and Fox's own part in it contributes some ninety pages to the published version of his speeches.[6] Burke, the Irishman, saw value in Pitt's propositions. Fox would see none. As Burke himself wrote later, 'Fox declared he would fight the whole of it inch by inch', insisting on carrying to a division every resolution, every amendment;[7] and Pitt was forced to make important concessions. One of these, to placate the mercantile interest, proposed obliging the Dublin parliament to consent to any future British legislation relevant to the Navigation Act. Although it was the opposition which had squeezed such changes out of a reluctant government, the temptation to Fox to condemn this particular concession proved irresistible, since it became obvious that the spirit of it ran quite against the grant of legislative independence negotiated in 1782 by Mr Secretary Fox himself. Surely Fox was wanting to have his cake and eat it, and surely therefore his claim, a proud and celebrated one, made in the debate of 30 May, does not fully convince:

> I wish to appear what I really feel, both an English and an Irish patriot ... I considered the whole plan as a lure to divert the Irish from constitutional points by throwing the trade of England at their feet ... If this conduct, Sir, constitutes an Irish patriot, then I am one; and if to struggle to save the trade of England from annihilation gives any claim to the appellation of an English patriot, I possess that claim ... I will not barter English commerce for Irish slavery; that is not the price I would pay, nor is this the thing I would purchase.[8]

By concessions to British vested interests and by ever more elaborate safeguards extracted to ensure an adequate Irish contribution to imperial defence, the Irish Propositions became distorted enough to turn the Irish sharply away from their previous readiness for acceptance, and when in August the Dublin parliament threw them out, the streets of *both* capitals saw many bonfires and illuminations of joy.

It came as near to being an important success as Fox was to see for a long time, and he was more than pleased with the share he had had in it. Recounting a month or so later the story of his part in one episode of the agitation against the Irish reforms, he wrote to Mrs Armistead:

> Our reception at Manchester was the finest thing imaginable, and handsome in all respects. All the principal people came out to meet us, and attended us into the town with blue and buff cockades, and a procession as fine, and not unlike, that upon my chairing at Westminster. We dined with 150 people ... The concourse of people to see us was immense; and I never saw more apparent unanimity than seemed to be in our favour; and all this in the town of Manchester, which used to be reckoned the worst place for us in the whole country.[9]

Fox's antipathy to Pitt's Irish Propositions of 1785 is closely paralleled by his hostility to the Pitt-Eden trade agreement with France, of 1786–7, although the grounds of his opposition were different and in this second matter Pitt had little difficulty in brushing it aside. Over Irish trade, Fox had had the merchants and manufacturers on his side, especially the northern cotton and hardware men, but when the substance and likely effects of the Anglo-French treaty of commercial reciprocity came to be examined, it became clear that the very men who had most excitedly opposed the Anglo-Irish measures had most to gain from the Anglo-French treaty. In France the economy was in trouble, and the French were glad enough to gain what advantages they could by British concessions over their wine exports. In general, Pitt's negotiator in Paris, William Eden, was consequently able to get much the better of the bargain. He and Pitt even managed to extract better terms out of the French for the Irish linen trade. None of this impressed Fox. All his arguments on matters affecting international trade depended on a basic thesis: that France always had been, and remained, Britain's 'natural' enemy. She aimed at the hegemony of Europe – as under Louis XIV, so now under Louis XVI – and therefore at the 'destruction' of Britain. As he expressed it in the debate of 12 February 1787, 'France was the natural political enemy of Great Britain. What made her so? – not the memory of Cressy and Agincourt ... It was the overweening pride and limitless ambition of France; her inevitable and ardent desire to hold the sway of Europe.'[10] From this powerful conviction came the enthusiasm with which he had greeted war with France when she intervened as partner of the American rebels in 1778; hence also his unsuccessful attempt in 1782 as Foreign Minister to forge an alliance of northern powers against France; hence his refusal now in 1787 to accept that a purely commercial agreement with France need do nothing to strengthen France diplomatically or militarily, and thus threaten Britain.

Fear of French ambition also dominated his speeches on the Netherlands crisis which came to a head in 1787, but in this matter he was content to find himself for once following the ministerial line. A struggle for power in the United Provinces had for some years been waged between Prince William V of Orange, the Stadtholder, who was looking for support from Britain and Prussia, and an alliance of patrician merchants and 'patriot' republicans who looked towards France. Naturally enough, Britain saw once again the old alarming spectre of French influence extending northwards through the Netherlands. Threatening and actively preparing for war, Pitt nevertheless hoped to avoid it and trusted that his manifest readiness to wage it would deter the French. Prussia went one better and actually began military operations. Accordingly France took the course of prudence, and withdrew from her attempt to take over 'protection' of the Netherlands. Fox found himself in, for him, the unusual position of enthusiastically supporting the session's inaugural speech from the throne. He rose to express

> his satisfaction at the system of measures lately adopted ... and he hoped, when we should have connected ourselves with the United Provinces by a solid and substantial treaty ... the government would pursue the idea of taking the most effectual steps to preserve the balance of power ... The best

means to insure the continuance of peace was to add to our strength rather than to trust to the weakness of our oldest and most inveterate rival. Let us enlarge the number of our alliances ... improve our marine, cherish and preserve it and all that belonged to that favourite service, and we might then consider the ambition of the House of Bourbon, its imbecility, or its power, as matters of equally trifling consideration ...[11]

A few months later, it was less France than her Bourbon ally Spain whose hostility threatened; and Fox a second time was ready to give Pitt his backing. Spain had never abandoned her ancient claim, hallowed by the Church, to sovereignty over the entire western cost of the American continent. Now therefore, challenging the existence of a small settlement of hunters and fishermen, the Spaniards arrested some British ships in Nootka Sound, off Vancouver Island, and Pitt was faced with a diplomatic poser: how to protect British rights without provoking war. Spain being weakened by her reluctance to tackle the British navy on her own and by the revolutionary turmoil then beginning to incapacitate the navy of her French ally, he was eventually successful in negotiating an agreement. The British were permitted to keep trading posts on the western American seaboard, but not within ten leagues of any existing Spanish settlement.

While giving Pitt general support in this affair, Fox saw no reason to refrain from criticizing him for lack of toughness, and appears to have been much the readier of the two to risk war. He ridiculed the centuries-old 'papal line', demarcating the New World between Spain and Portugal – what he called 'this exploded claim': 'occupancy and possession should be considered as the only right to title ... We should not rest contented merely with a satisfaction for the injury, but obtain a renunciation of the claim set up with so little ground of reason'.[12]

In the protracted proceedings against Warren Hastings, at first in parliament, then in Westminster Hall for the impeachment trial (this *cause célèbre* spanned nearly a decade in all) Fox's role was always subsidiary to Burke's. It was not that he was indifferent to the affairs of India. In the India Bill debates of 1783, his mastery of the measure's provisions and of the conditions in India which had promoted them was well recognized, not least by Burke, who did the drafting. Fox moreover had been genuinely convinced of his bill's beneficent purpose, even if its ulterior motive – command of political patronage – is not to be denied. But he had none of Burke's passionate indignation at Indian wrongs and East India Company malefactions. Most of the early running in the campaign against Hastings beginning in February 1786 was made by Burke, then perhaps hardly less by Sheridan, whose virtuoso oration of February 1787 captivated and astonished the House. The sensational brilliance of this speech had the effect of creating immense popular interest and also potential for what was eventually to become prime public entertainment, as the unfortunate Hastings soon had cause to complain. When the impeachment proceedings at last, after two whole years, began in Westminster Hall, seats for what has to be called *the show*, particularly to listen to Sheridan's second marathon performance on Hastings and the Begams of Oudh, were going for anything up to £50.

Fox's main part in the preliminary parliamentary stages concerned the charge against Hastings that by attempting to fine Chait Singh, the Rajah of Benares, half a million pounds merely for *delay* in paying a due sum of £50,000, he had acted indefensibly and criminally. Burke had presented the first of the twenty-two charges (later reduced to twenty) alleging Hastings's high crimes and misdemeanours, but the Commons had rejected this. In the following month, the notable and surprising success of Fox's handling of the important Benares charge concerning Chait Singh – winning a majority of 40 – undoubtedly owed much to the skill of his presentation, which served finally to clinch in Pitt's mind the conclusion which he had been moving towards 'after long and laborious study': that Hastings had indeed acted in a manner 'disproportionate, arbitrary, tyrannical, shamefully exorbitant, repugnant to principles'.[13]

Twice, during the long summer and autumn recesses of 1786 and 1787, the House of Commons rested its case against Hastings, though by mid–1787 it had arrived at instructing Burke to inaugurate impeachment proceedings, and Hastings had first been arrested and then released on bail of £40,000 pending trial before the House of Lords. Not, however, until 1788 did the curtain rise on the high theatre of the spectacle in Westminster Hall, and by the end of the first session just *two* of the twenty accusations had been heard. The first was the Benares charge, presented again by Fox, this time with the assistance of the young Charles Grey. The second was Sheridan's repeat performance on the Begams of Oudh. By turns it astounded, delighted, curdled the blood, and reduced to tears the fashionable crowd assembled in Westminster Hall, among them the Queen and the Prince of Wales. Sheridan's was 'a display of genius', declared Gibbon.

However, after the thrills of its opening scenes, the very complicated plot of the Warren Hastings drama began to lose its grip, and the audience first yawned, and then stayed at home. Fox and his fellow managers of the prosecution persevered, and Burke would remain tireless for years to come. But even among most of the committee of managers, and notably with Sheridan, boredom with the *longueurs* of the impeachment set in early, some months even before the French revolutionary explosions in the summer of 1789 put all rival excitements in the shade, and years before Hastings was at last acquitted in 1795. Even so, as late as May 1795 Fox was still pressing the Benares charge, in a speech which lasted three hours.

Fox's position on the contentious religious issues of the 1780s was uncomplicated and liberal-minded. His own disposition was far from religious, and scriptural or theological controversies resided in territory foreign to him upon which he had no inclination to intrude. The sources, Greek and Roman, which nurtured the riches of his intellect and imagination, were necessarily more pagan than Christian, and it is doubtful if, pressed into an intellectual corner, he could have given honest and full assent to any of the current versions of the Christian creed, still less to the Thirty-Nine Articles. Belief itself occupied him little; religious speculation hardly at all. 'Poor fellow, how melancholy his case', Wilberforce once said of him, 'he has not one religious friend or one who knows anything about it'. Yet he was in no way anti-Christian, and on the whole he approved of the Church of England. It was a guarantor of the nation's moral well-being, and provided a degree of 'moral policing' for the lower classes. (The similarly unreligious Horace Walpole believed in attending church to set the servants an example.) Moreover, the Church's record since the Revolution of 1688, with its Toleration Act of 1689, and particularly since the Hanoverian Succession of 1714 had in general, he judged, been good – 'latitudinarian' and relaxed. There were some indeed, John Wesley for instance, who had reckoned it far *too* relaxed, to the point of sleepiness. But the old conventional wisdom concerning a 'torpid' Georgian Church of England is wisdom no longer, and certainly the Church commanded the devotion of many, perhaps most of the leading lay as well as clerical minds of the century – men of the intellectual calibre of Samuel Johnson, for example or Edmund Burke. Further, it had both the allegiance, if only from unquestioning habit, and the respect, however conventional and low-key, of a majority of the population. The mental character and intellectual outlook of the 'enlightened' freethinker Fox were very different from those of a Johnson or a Burke, but equally with them Fox saw the Church of England as part of the fabric of the state, and he would never scoff at it or seek to weaken its influence.

He was ready to give credit to the established Church for its rejection of persecution, but he deplored its refusal to allow its increasingly liberal spirit to be reflected in law. The Test and Corporation Acts – that old legislation enacted during the reign of Fox's great-grandfather Charles – remained on the statute book. Their original intention had been to disbar Protestant Dissenters and Roman Catholics from playing an active part in public life, but in practice these laws were largely inoperative, since year by year parliament passed indemnity acts protecting those who transgressed the law. For Fox and many others, this merely made the Test and Corporation Acts nonsensical as well as wrong-headed. Members of denominations other than Anglican should be given, not an annual *ex-gratia* dispensation, but a *right*.

Parliamentary resolutions to repeal these discriminatory acts were introduced unsuccessfully many times before at last they disappeared in 1828 (when Fox's nephew, 'the Young One', the third Lord Holland, played a part in their removal), and Fox constantly pleaded the liberal cause. Religion, he argued, was 'not a proper test for political institutions'. Men should be judged by their actions, not by their opinions. It was 'irreverent and impious' to hold that the Church of England should seek to be supported as 'an engine or ally' of the state, rather than on the evidence of its doctrines based on the scriptures and on the beneficent moral effect of its teachings. The very safety of the Church of England's position, as well as the general happiness of the people, demanded 'moderation', 'indulgence to other sects', and 'the most candid allowance for diversity of opinion'. Religious liberty was a prime prerequisite of civil and political liberty.[14]

The one major reform with which Fox was to be in the end successfully associated was the abolition within the British empire of the Atlantic trade in black slaves. In the end it was just three months before his death that he was able to say, moving an anti-slave-trade resolution in the Commons, 'If ... I had been so fortunate as to accomplish that, and that only, I should think that I had done enough, and could retire from public life with comfort and conscious satisfaction'. A few months later again, parliament finally outlawed this traffic, though the institution of slavery itself had still to wait a quarter-century before becoming illegal.

It was during the 1780s that Fox began interesting himself in the matter,

1. The young Fox, with his aunt Sarah Lennox and his cousin Susan Fox-Strangways, in the garden at Holland House in 1761. Sarah Lennox is at the window. By Joshua Reynolds

2. Holland House from the south in 1752, by John Vardy

3. Henry Fox, 1st Lord Holland, Charles James Fox's father, studio of Reynolds

4. (*below left*) Lord North, by Nathaniel Dance

5. (*below right*) George III, by Johann Zoffany

6. (*above left*) Lord Rockingham, studio of Reynolds

7. (*above right*) Lord Shelburne, after Reynolds

8. Perdita Robinson in 1781, after Romney

9. Burke and Fox, by
Thomas Hickey

10. Richard Fitzpatrick in
later life, after W. Lane

11. The Duchess of
Devonshire and her sister
Lady Bessborough, by
Thomas Rowlandson

12. A miniature of Fox in 1787, by Thomas Day

13. St Anne's Hill, near Chertsey in Surrey; Fox's rural retreat

14. Mrs Armistead, artist unknown

15. Fox the revolutionary, caricatured by James Gillray in 1797

Le Coup de Maitre. — *This Print copied from the French Original, is dedicated to the London Corresponding Society.*

16. Bust of Fox in 1791, by Joseph Nollekens

17. The Duke of Norfolk and Fox in May 1798 (see pp. 199–200), by Richard Dighton

MEMBERS of the WHIG CLUB.

CHARLY, Keep a CIVIL Tongue in your Head.

Jocky of NORFOLK be not so BOLD.

18. Fox's nephew, the 3rd Lord Holland in 1795, by F. X. Fabre

19. Mr and Mrs Fox received by Napoleon in September 1802. Lord and Lady Holland are on the extreme right. By James Gillray

cautiously at first, though he was never in doubt of the rightness and necessity of abolition. 'I am very much inclined to undertake the business', he wrote, 'but I must both read and hear more before I engage. I should very much like to put down so vile a thing, if it be possible.' Here Pitt and he were speaking with the same voice. 'The more I reflect upon it', Pitt wrote to Eden in December 1787, 'the more anxious and impatient I am that the business should be brought as speedily as possible to a point.' Pitt and Wilberforce were intimate friends – they belonged to the same club, Goostrees, and had holidayed together – and after Wilberforce's religious 'conversion' during 1784–5 he had first espoused and soon become the parliamentary leader of the slave trade abolitionists. Pitt gave him all possible encouragement and support short of introducing a government bill, for which majority backing would be unobtainable from cabinet, Commons, Lords, and King alike.

Even those who agreed that the practices publicized by Wilberforce and his associates were barbarous and shameful were divided upon the practicalities of reform. Was there to be regulation and control of the trade, or outright abolition? If abolition, how was it to be enforced? And would unilateral British action be effective without the goodwill and concurrence of other powers, France especially? Both Pitt and Fox were for full abolition. Regulation, Pitt decided, would be as difficult to supervise as abolition. Moreover, if 'the principle of humanity and justice ... is in any degree compromised, the cause is in a manner given up'.[15] Fox agreed: abolition would be more in keeping with the nation's good name and would probably be *easier* to enforce than some merely palliative measure. He professed optimism, perhaps without much justification, about the prospects of French collaboration; and in any case if foreign nations would not follow Britain's example, she had the naval strength to compel their cooperation. This was in 1788; but in the following year came the French Revolution, reaction to which coloured all politics for years to come. Abolition of the slave trade, though its advocates continued tirelessly campaigning for it, had a long time yet to wait.

11

FOX
AND THE
PRINCE OF WALES

1784–1789

The old problem of the Prince of Wales's debts surfaced again in 1784. His extravagance in the rebuilding, extending, and adorning of Carlton House had run wild. What had begun as a relatively small town house in Pall Mall for the Dowager Princess of Wales (George II's daughter-in-law Augusta) and had then taken in Bubb Dodington's house next door, was now in the process of becoming, under the direction of the connoisseur Prince and his architect Henry Holland, nothing less than a palace superb enough to satisfy demands of the 'magnificence' of his 'rank' (words never long absent from the Prince's vocabulary) and the wide-ranging eclecticism of his aesthetic inclinations. As new splendours were added by the month – and would be, for the next two or three decades – there was talk of an English Versailles. Adjoining properties were acquired and demolished; new wings and ranges of servants' quarters were added, and stables which alone were costing £31,000 a year.

Carlton House's entrance hall, leading to an octagon and double stair-case, was resplendent in Ionic columns of Siena marble; the finest craftsmen were imported from France; the rooms were embellished with Sèvres ware and Gobelins tapestries, the walls hung with a splendid display of pictures, some commissioned, more purchased by the Prince's agents abroad. Eventually it comprised the finest collection of French art ever assembled by British royalty. One agent was dispatched to the Far East to buy furniture for the 'Chinese' drawing room, for which the mercer's bill came to £6,817, and during 1783–4 it was reckoned that the Prince was spending over £1,000, on average, per month on furnishings alone. The fan-vaulted

Gothic conservatory assumed the dignity of a small cathedral. The gardens sprouted statues, a marble-floored temple, waterfalls, and an observatory.

Much of all this was accomplished very quickly, and hence his annual allowance, agreed at last in 1783 after the crisis which had come near to unseating the Fox-North coalition, was now engulfed in debts conservatively estimated by the Prince's treasurer at £147,293, with new 'torrents of expense' likely.[1] The King and Commons were thus faced with a fresh crisis, and again the King judged that he had to intervene. The Prince's conduct was 'reprehensible', he wrote to him; it was growing 'worse every year, and in a more glaring manner since his removal to Carlton House':

> If he has deranged his affairs he ought to take a manly resolution to diminish his expenses and thus establish a sinking fund to clear those debts, which would in some measure palliate with the public for an extravagance which everyone but his flatterers have universally blamed; the Prince of Wales ought to know ... that if he once loses the good opinion of this nation it is not to be regained.

But rather more than these enormous Carlton House debts was at stake. The Prince had informed his father on 24 August that in view of 'the peculiar and very embarrassed situation' of his affairs, he proposed 'putting in full practice a system of economy by immediately going abroad'. The King's lengthy reply of 27 August[2] ('the Queen is as much hurt as me') sharply forbade 'this impossible plan'. If the Prince went ahead with it, 'his character would be forever blasted in this country, and in all Europe. I therefore insist on his giving up a measure that would be a public breach with me ... and my people shall know that this shameful flight is in defiance of my express prohibition'. The King, who always kept himself well informed, knew that his son was proposing to go abroad, not to practise some improbable 'system of economy', but to live with the latest object of his devotion, which would threaten serious political trouble less easily disregarded than earlier parental condemnations.

The Prince of Wales was 22. The lady was Maria Fitzherbert, now 28, a charmingly attractive woman who had been twice widowed while still very young. She came from a well-to-do Catholic family, convent-educated in Paris, had been amply provided-for by her second husband, and returned eventually from France with the intention of settling down in Park Street, London and at Marble Hill in rural Twickenham, the house which had originally been built for George II's mistress, Henrietta Howard. She was attracted, as few failed to be, by the Prince – by his person, his personality, his liveliness, his rank – but her religious convictions forbade her to fill the role which Fox for one, and naturally many more, thought would suit her – *maîtresse en titre* to the Heir Apparent, a respectable and traditionally enviable position. If that admirable lady Mrs Armistead was content to be *his* mistress, why should not the no less admirable Mrs Fitzherbert be happy, and indeed honoured, to be the Prince's? And it was probably the knowledge that this was Fox's view which helped to incline Mrs Fitzherbert against him from the outset.

After she had persistently refused on religious grounds to become his mistress, the Prince, in a show of despairing passion, was alleged by his attendants to have stabbed himself, and certainly succeeded in covering himself with a considerable quantity of well-witnessed blood. His own version was that he had 'fallen on his sword'. Whatever the genuineness of this supposed attempt at suicide, there was no doubting the desperation of his thwarted love, acted out frenetically as it had been, not only to Mrs Fitzherbert herself, but before the perturbed gaze of his staff and his friends. He could not, would not, live without her. He had become ill, hyper-emotional, feverish, lachrymose, and to Mrs Fitzherbert repeatedly threatened to kill himself. He would sacrifice *everything* for her, the throne included. (This last was, however temporarily, quite serious.) The self-stabbing was a final half-crazed attempt to force her hand and prevent her from escaping abroad from his importunings. When his surgeon and others among his staff, together with the Duchess of Devonshire as chaperon, brought her, reluctant and protesting, to Carlton House to confirm their story of the Prince's gory plight, she still at first maintained that she could not, must not, would not marry him, but then sufficiently relented, in the face of his disturbed condition, to allow him to place a ring (helpfully provided by the Duchess) on her finger in token of future union. Back in Park Street and better able to ponder what she had been induced to concede under shock, she and the Duchess prepared a statement, penned by the Duchess, signed by them both, to the effect that 'promises obtain'd in such a manner' must be considered void. Next day, Mrs Fitzherbert fled to France. It was thither that the Prince now intended to pursue her, while still claiming to the King that his motive was merely to practise 'a system of economy'.

There were two statutes which stood in the way of his marrying a Roman Catholic. The first, the 1701 Act of Settlement was surmountable, but only at the price of his forfeiting succession to the throne. The second, the statute of 1772 (whose passage Fox had spoken strongly against, and whose enactment George III had obliged North to implement in the light of earlier impolitic royal marriages) necessitated the monarch's prior consent to any royal marriage. In this instance, of course, such consent was completely unthinkable.

The reputation of the Prince of Wales was important for Fox. After his crushing defeat of 1783–4 and the known strength of the King's resolve not to employ him again, his best hope for a ministerial future lay with the Heir Apparent. Kings did not live for ever, and George III would soon be 50 – he was eleven years older than Fox – in an age when the average expectation of life was by modern standards low. A self-interested eye to the future was bound to play a part in the close relations between the Whigs and the Prince of Wales. It might well be terminal for Fox's ambitions if the Prince's amorous obsession led him to disqualify himself from the succession. In a mood of combined pique and desperation, the Prince did more than once say that he would retire, to allow his brother Frederick (George III's next oldest and favourite son) to succeed.

Fox and he were kindred spirits to an only very limited extent. They had often enjoyed one another's company, and they both relished the fashionable sports and amusements and luxuries of the *beau monde*. They had shared a propensity to live much beyond their means and rely for rescue in the one case on parents and friends, and in the other on the public purse. They had even shared mistresses, though sequentially, not simultaneously. But intellectually and increasingly in their lifestyles they were poles apart. As Fox grew older, no longer the somewhat outrageous 'phenomenon of the age', he became steadier, soberer, one may reasonably claim wiser, while the Prince of Wales became (if that were possible) ever more unreliable, undisciplined, self-righteous, and – despite his undoubted cleverness and artistic flair – foolish.

If Fox and *gravitas* were still far from constant companions, at least one no longer heard of him the sort of story persistently being reported of the Prince of Wales, like Thomas Orde's account of his drunken helplessness and spectacular public vomit at one of the Carlton House celebrations for Fox's Westminster victory, or his demeanour at a grand ball somewhat later:

> Lo! at twelve o'clock in reeled H.R.H. as pale as ashes, with glazed eyes set in his head, and in short almost stupefied. The Duchess of Cumberland made him sit down by her, and kept him tolerably peaceable till they went down to supper, when he was most gloriously drunk and riotous indeed. He posted

himself in the doorway, flung his arm round the Duchess of Ancaster's neck and kiss'd her with a great smack, threatened to pull Lord Galloway's wig off and knock out his false teeth, till some of his companions called for his carriage.

During the year when Maria Fitzherbert was abroad, the Prince's courier was constantly posting to find her and deliver a steady torrent of letters compounded of self-justification, self-praise, amorous entreaty, and always, always promises of eternal devotion. She was his 'dearest and only belov'd Maria', his 'dearest wife'. He implored her not to marry anyone else, as her companion Lady Anne Lindsay had suggested she should. 'Until the latest moments of his existence' he was *'unalterably thine'*. The first of these verbose effusions ran to eighteen of the Prince's letter-pages, the last – after conspiratorial arrangements for her return had been all but completed – to forty-two, or nearly 7,000 words. When he was not writing them, so Mrs Armistead told Fox's nephew Holland, he

> testified the sincerity and violence of his passion and his despair by ... rolling on the floor, striking his forehead, tearing his hair, falling into hystericks, and swearing that he would abandon the country, forgo the Crown, sell his jewels and plate, and scrape together a competence to fly with the object of his affections to America.

Mrs Fitzherbert came back to London in December 1785 and just before Christmas was secretly married to the Prince by an Anglican clergyman, who was paid danger-money of £500 and promised in good time a bishopric.* The ceremony was canonically acceptable but inescapably illegal. Learning on 9 December that Mrs Fitzherbert had returned and reasonably enough suspecting the worst, Fox took fright, and immediately sent to the Prince (still some days before the wedding) a long letter of advice, warning him against 'a mock marriage, for it can be no other':

> I hope that your Royal Highness does me the justice to believe that it is with the utmost reluctance that I trouble you with my opinion ... upon a subject where it may not be agreeable to your wishes ... I was told ... there was reason to suppose that you were going to take the very desperate step (pardon the expression) of marrying [Mrs F.] at this moment. If such an idea be really in your mind, and it is not too late, for God's sake let me call your attention to some considerations ... Sir, this is not a matter to be trifled with, and your Royal Highness must excuse the freedom with which I write ... Consider the circumstances in which you stand: the King not feeling for you as a father

---

* His part in the marriage celebration made him in law a felon. He died long before the promised bishopric could stand any chance of materializing.

ought; the Duke of York professedly his favourite, and likely to be married to the King's wishes; the nation full of its old prejudices against Catholics, and justly dreading all disputes about succession. In all these circumstances your enemies might take such advantages of any doubt of this nature as I shudder to think of ... [Moreover], it will be said that a woman who has lived with you as your wife without being so is not fit to be Queen of England; and thus the very thing that is done for the sake of her reputation will be used against it ...[3]

The Prince's reply came immediately. It was intended to mislead, and it did. 'Make yourself easy, my dear friend; believe me the world will soon be convinced that there not only is not, but never was, any ground for these reports which of late have been so malevolently circulated ... I believe I shall meet you at dinner at Bushy on Tuesday ... At all times, my dear Charles, most affectionately yours, George P.'[4]

Throughout 1786 he and Mrs Fitzherbert were constantly together, and the public prints, respectable newspapers and scandal-sheets alike did not go short of transparently disguised hints that the pair were already married. Although they lived in separate houses – she in a newly rented mansion in St James's Square conveniently near to Carlton House – they appeared in public inseparably, and reports of their union, as Horace Walpole said, stretched 'from London to Rome'. Yet only a handful of people could be absolutely sure of it, and Fox, trusting to the Prince's assurance, could only cling to the belief that the rumours must be false. This however did not allow him to escape from depiction in cartoons as having connived at the marriage – Gillray for instance picturing him giving away the bride (in a French church) while Sheridan and the notorious rake Colonel Hanger prepare to serve the wedding breakfast. Pitt, like many more among leading politicians and the aristocracy, strongly suspected the dangerous truth, but was unable to confirm it. As Lord Lothian told the Duke of Rutland, 'I think it has all the appearance of being true ... Most people believe it, and I confess I am one of the number ... I am very sorry for it, for it does him infinite mischief, and particularly among the trading and lower sort of people, and if true must ruin him in every light'.

The debts meanwhile continued to soar. When Colonel Hotham, the Prince's treasurer, eventually rendered his 1787 account, they had mounted high above the 1785 reckoning, now standing at what for those days was the extremely large sum of more than a quarter of a million pounds, in fact precisely at £269,878 six shillings and seven pence and a farthing. When it was put to the Prince that his father would be more likely to come to a financial arrangement with him if he agreed to a suitable marriage (which meant to a Protestant foreign princess), he excitedly exclaimed, 'No, I will never marry . . . Frederick will marry, and the Crown will descend to his children'. Then suddenly in July 1786 he decided, by way of a dramatic public gesture, to close Carlton House, to dismiss all but five of his staff, and 'not to appear again in public' until he could do so 'with that dignity and splendour' to which his rank entitled him. Fox, although he tactfully suggested that it would be prudent to set aside £35,000 or £40,000 of any agreed annual allowance towards a fund for paying creditors by instalments, nevertheless had no hesitation in siding with the Prince against his supposedly cheeseparing father.* The proposed retirement from London (most people thought it would be to Hanover) was 'a manly and judicious step' which Fox considered would convince in his favour 'the universal opinion of all descriptions of men'. The Prince of Wales, as it happened, chose not to go to Hanover, but instead to what until the mid-century had been a fishing village but was fast becoming a fashionable resort, Brighthelmstone (as he was still spelling it), where he and his 'dearest wife' both had houses already.

By the spring of 1787 his financial situation was once more demanding the attention of the House of Commons. While Pitt tried to stonewall, a Devonshire Tory member, John Rolle (Fitzpatrick and others among Fox's friends had recently been lampooning him in their *Rolliad*), embarrassed ministers and opposition leaders alike by pressing 'the Prince's matter' in language which, however veiled, bore an unmistakable meaning. The situation of the Heir Apparent, Rolle insisted, tended 'immediately to affect our constitution, both in church and state'. For the Fox party, Sheridan then assured the House, more hopefully than truthfully, that the Prince wished 'every part of his conduct to be laid open without ambiguity or concealment'. Two days later Fox, now present himself in the House, boldly declared that the rumour of the Prince's marriage was a 'calumny destitute of all foundation . . . and propagated with the sole view of depreciating the Prince's character'. Pressed by Rolle, he went further: he had *direct authority* for what he had said.[5] The next day at Brooks's he was taken aside by a fellow-member, who must have been one of the extremely few present at the secret ceremony sixteen months before. 'I see by the

---

* The final settlement was generous. The Prince was to receive a further £10,000 a year from the King's Civil List, £161,000 towards paying off his debts, and £60,000 towards completing Carlton House.

papers, Mr Fox', he said, 'you have denied the fact of the Prince's marriage to Mrs Fitzherbert. You have been misinformed. I was present.'

In more ways than one, the fat was in the fire now. Mrs Fitzherbert was furious with Fox for, in her view, destroying her reputation, and angry too with her husband for leaving her in so ambiguous a position. On his side, Fox was annoyed and exasperated by the Prince's failure to be honest with him, which had made his own words seem rash and misinformed, and landed him in considerable trouble. The two men did not speak to one another throughout the ensuing year. Fox, moreover, could hardly intervene further in the Commons debate on 'the Prince's matter' without worsening his situation. It was to Charles Grey that the Prince first avowed the fact of his marriage, asking *him* rather than Fox to speak on his behalf. Grey refused, so it was left to Sheridan, that expert word-spinner, to make a speech which, without actually confirming or denying anything, would aim at contriving simultaneously to restore goodwill towards the Prince, flatter the good taste and restraint shown by the Commons, and apply some balm to Mrs Fitzherbert's injured feelings. As a member reported, 'Sheridan ... said today in the House her situation was truly respectable, at which every one smiled.' Fox perhaps did not smile.

During the 1788 parliamentary recess he set off on a continental holiday, touring through France, Switzerland, and Italy in the company of his 'dearest Liz' – or as a hostile writer had it, 'in the arms of faded beauty'. One of their staging posts being Lausanne, Gibbon, now resident there, seized the opportunity to arrange a meeting. As he wrote to his friend Lord Sheffield, on 24 October:

> I was informed that he was arrived at the Lyon d'or. I sent a compliment, he answered it in person; we returned together to the Inn, brought away the fair Mrs Armstead, and settled at my house for the remainder of the day. I have eat and drank and conversed and sat up all night with Fox in England; but it never can happen again, that I should enjoy him as I did that day, alone (for his fair companion was a cypher) from ten in the morning till ten at night ... Our conversation never flagged a moment ... We had little politicks, though he gave me in a few words such a character of Pitt as one great man should give of another his rival: much of books, from my own on which he flattered me very pleasantly to Homer and the Arabian Nights; much about the country, my garden which he understands far better than I do, and upon the whole I think he envys me and would do [even] were he Minister ...
> The people [here] gaze on him as a prodigy but he shews little inclination to converse with them: the wit and beauty of his companion are not sufficient to

excuse the scandalous impropriety of shewing her to all Europe ... Will Fox never learn the importance of character ...?[6]

Fox was thus far distant from Westminster when George III's health, which had been troubling him since midsummer, deteriorated drastically. In June he had merely suffered from 'abdominal spasms', but by the beginning of November his condition had grown desperate, with fever, debility, breathlessness, sleeplessness, 'a hoarseness of voice', as Fanny Burney (the Queen's Mistress of the Robes) described it, 'a volubility, and earnestness – a vehemence, rather – it startles me inexpressibly'. He found his eyes, his legs, and – spasmodically and terrifyingly – his reason deserting him. He was beset by compulsive fidgeting and began to gabble uncontrollably. Then delirium, severe mental confusion, and hallucinations followed. It was clear that the King had gone mad.* It even appeared possible that he might very soon be dead. 'As the poor King grew worse', wrote Miss Burney, 'general hope seemed universally to abate, and the Prince of Wales took the government of the house [Windsor] into his own hands. Nothing was done but by his orders' – one of which was to bring in as consultant his own physician, Dr Warren (whom the King had always much disliked). 'Warren is strongly inclined to think the disorder permanent', William Grenville told his brother; and probably, he added, the Prince would be regent with full royal powers, which meant that he would 'dismiss Pitt without hesitation'.[7]

The Prince was already in communication with Sheridan, of all the Whigs the closest to him now that Fox was abroad and in any case *persona non grata* to Mrs Fitzherbert. By contrast, Sheridan was allowed to move temporarily into Mrs Fitzherbert's house when the bailiffs evicted him from his own. It was Sheridan too who was in negotiation at this time with Lord Chancellor Thurlow, a minister on poor personal terms with Pitt and (correctly) judged to be the likeliest of the cabinet to desert him for the confidently expected new Portland-Fox Whig ministry under the aegis of the Prince Regent-to-be. The fact that obstacles and complications abounded before such a consummation could be achieved did not prevent it being widely and optimistically discussed. The *Morning Post* on 28 November even printed a list of the expected cabinet, naming among others Portland First Lord of the Treasury, Fox and Stormont Secretaries

---

* The now generally accepted diagnosis of the royal malady is porphyria, a rare hereditary disorder causing in its more virulent manifestations the variety of painful and distressing symptoms, including mental derangement, which the King experienced.

of State, Sheridan Navy Treasurer, Cavendish Chancellor of the Exchequer, and Burke Paymaster.

Among the many difficulties to be surmounted before these buds could blossom was the unfortunate fact that Portland had fallen out with the Prince over his debts; that the ambitious Charles Grey claimed very strongly that he and not Cavendish should be Chancellor of the Exchequer; that there was a bitter feud between Grey and Sheridan, and for good measure a quarrel between Grey and Fitzpatrick; that Loughborough (whom we might call the Whigs' 'shadow' Chancellor) was justifiably afraid that Thurlow was about to be lured by Sheridan into *remaining* Chancellor: in short that the postulant Whig cabinet was far indeed from being a band of brothers.* None of all this however precluded much premature celebration and jollification. The Prince himself, who had behaved tolerably well at the onset of his father's afflictions, had by now reverted to habit, and spent happy and sometimes riotous evenings, some of them at Brooks's, with his expectant Whig associates. But as one of the more thoughtful men of the party, Sir Gilbert Elliot, wrote to his wife: 'I do not much relish ... this triumphant sort of conversation, especially before the battle is won, or even fought; for I remember that just such triumphs preceded by a very few days our utter defeat four years ago'.

Sheridan was now acting as self-appointed ministry-maker-in-chief, and the messages which arrived from the King's two eldest sons and their men at Windsor gave grounds for much optimism. 'The pulse is weaker and weaker', wrote the Prince of Wales's Comptroller, 'and the doctors say it is impossible to survive long'. By the beginning of December the unfortunate and ill-used patient had been tricked into consenting that he should be brought from Windsor to Kew (for everybody's convenience but his own), and on 3 December the faithful Colonel Greville's diary was recording 'the worst day H.M. has experienced'. But at this time Pitt, who had good cause to be alarmed, had succeeded in getting Dr Anthony Addington, earlier for a time family physician of the Pitts and once a keeper of a madhouse, introduced as royal fellow-consultant; and Addington forecast an eventual recovery. This opinion was reinforced when another 'mad-specialist' was brought in, the Rev. Dr Francis Willis. (The luckless King,

---

* At about this time Grey was the lover of the Duchess of Devonshire, Sheridan of her sister Lady Duncannon – a coincidence doubtless without political relevance. But the Duchess herself was in the thick of this Whig ill-temper and disarray and her diary becomes at this point a prime historical source.

bled, blistered, cupped, and strait-jacketed, eventually underwent the attention of seven men, yet, as we know, lived.) With Addington and Willis firmly optimistic, Pitt's strategy now was to play for time, to postpone for as long as possible a decision on the necessity and nature of a regency, and to trust that the King's sanity would return.

Fox was in Bologna when news reached him of the King's grave illness. When he first was told that an express message was on its way to him, he was in dread that it was going to tell him of the death of 'the young one', his much-loved nephew Lord Holland. Relieved to learn of the falseness of this alarm, he set off for home immediately, hearing at Lyon a rumour that the King was already dead. Over poor roads in a vehicle less well-sprung than his own, the journey to Calais punished him badly. Then the rest of the hurried, arduous journey worsened his already poor physical state to such an extent that by the time he arrived in London on 24 November his appearance shocked all who saw him. Wraxall describes him as emaciated, sallow-faced, and swollen-eyed, 'while his stockings hung upon his legs', and he 'rather dragged himself along than walked'.[8] He was suffering from dysentery, and was still much too ill ten days later to attend a meeting of the Privy Council, when the rival doctors presented their differing judgements on whether the King would or would not recover.

By 10 December, though looking the ghost of his normal portly self and still very unwell, Fox felt able to take part in an important Commons debate on the King's incapacity and the regency question. This began with a predictable taking of sides parallel to the doctors' own, with Sheridan and Burke supporting the pessimistic Warren ('*Rex noster insanit*') and the ministerial speakers echoing the more cheerful prognoses of Addington and Willis. Fox then tackled the issue of the regency head on. The Prince of Wales, he insisted, all too rashly as it proved,

> had as clear, as express, a right to assume the reins of government and exercise the power of sovereignty, during the continuance of the illness and incapacity with which it had pleased God to afflict his Majesty, as in the case of his Majesty's having undergone a perfect and natural demise . . .[9]

Pitt, we are told, smiled as he listened to these uncompromising words and, slapping his thigh, vowed that he would '*unwhig* the gentleman for the rest of his life' – because Fox's claim that the Heir Apparent had absolute, inherent right to the regency seemed to deny any parliamentary role in the matter. Fox, 'man of the people' and supposed champion of parliamentary rights and privileges, had laid himself open to be pilloried as the defender of hereditary royal prerogative, the highest of high Tory principles. 'Only think of Fox's want of judgement', wrote William Grenville the following day, 'to bring himself and them into such a scrape as he has done'.[10] Without fully retracting, Fox tried to correct his tactical error, not very successfully. His line of attempted escape was sophistical: although the Prince did have the 'right' to the regency it was not his 'possession', and the 'adjudication' of his right belonged to the two houses of parliament.[11] He drew back from adopting the dangerous but logical extension of his original argument, embraced vehemently by Burke, that the Prince, possessing indeed the hereditary right, ought himself to take the initiative to exercise it. Pitt meanwhile, shrewd, consistent, and of course playing for time, took the line that the Prince's *claim* to the regency was beyond dispute, but historical precedents should be exhaustively investigated before any parliamentary decision was reached. Further, the question of 'limitations' should be considered. What powers should an incoming regent be given, and what deprived of?

The restrictions on the Regent's powers proposed by Pitt and approved by Commons vote would have placed care of the King's person not with the Prince but the Queen; would have drastically curbed the regent's power to award 'places' and pensions; and most importantly, would have denied him the right to create peers. This last made highly problematical the prospect of ensuring a Lords majority for any incoming Whig ministry and, taken together, these statutory limitations would have tied Fox's hands most uncomfortably.

The Whig opposition continued to be at sixes and sevens throughout December and January, with complicated cross-currents of mutual suspicion and mistrust. At one point Fox lost his temper with Sheridan over a difference concerning tactics, and when Fox came to apologize for his part in this tiff – 'Oh', said Sheridan, 'for all I care you can be as cross as you like'. But at least when he was writing to his 'dearest Liz' Fox could sound determinedly, even obstinately, cheerful. He wrote on 15 December,

> Though I am fatigued to death, and ought to go to bed, it being near three, I cannot let go the opportunity of Carpenter, who sets out in a few hours, to write a few lines to my Liz with more freedom than I can do by post. We shall have several hard fights in the H of Cs this week and next, in some of which I fear we shall be beat, but whether we are or not, I think it is certain that in about a fortnight we shall come in … At any rate the Prince must be Regent and of consequence the ministry must be changed. The manner in

which the Prince has behaved throughout the whole has been the most steady, the most friendly, and the handsomest that can be conceived. You know when he sets his mind to a thing he can do it well ... I am sure I cannot ... advise him to give up anything [from] the full power of a King, to which he is certainly entitled. The King himself (notwithstanding the reports you may possibly hear) is certainly worse and perfectly mad ... Adieu, my dearest Liz. It is so late that I can only write here what I dare not by post. The sooner you come the better, but ... this next fortnight will be such a scene of hurry that I should have little time to enjoy what I most value in the world, my dearest Liz's company. I take for granted you will want some money and will, if I can, send you some by next post, but I have hardly a minute to myself, either to get the money or to write, adieu my dear Liz, indeed, indeed, you are more than all the world to me.[12]

His illness – indeed, perhaps illnesses – persisted. The *Times* informed its readers that Fox was suffering not only from dysentery but also from 'an obstruction on the neck of the bladder'. Before the end of January 1789 he had removed to Bath for the 'cure'. Soon after he had gone there, unmistakable signs began to appear that the King was mending, and this at just about the time when Pitt's regency bill, with its restrictions, completed its passage through the Commons and was due to come before the House of Lords. The prospect of royal recovery soon began to look convincing enough in the eyes of Lord Chancellor Thurlow to make him decide that, after all, he would resume his position on Pitt's side of the fence – which pleased Fox, who had always mistrusted Sheridan's policy of intrigue and enticement. For Pitt, the medical news from Kew was reassuring and heartening. For Fox, away at Bath, it was too depressing to be believed, and he seems to have convinced himself that it was merely enemy propaganda, a strategem of Pitt's. In mid-February he sent letters to Portland, to the Prince, and to Fitzpatrick with the aim of stiffening Whig morale. To Portland: he had 'no belief in the K's recovery, but I dare say some of our friends are a good deal alarmed'. To Fitzpatrick:

I hope by this time all ideas of the Prince or any of us taking any measure in consequence of the good reports of the King are at an end; if they are not, pray do all you can to crush them; and if it were possible to cure that habitual spirit of despondency and fear that characterizes the Whig party, it would be a good thing, but I suppose that is impossible.[13]

To the Prince of Wales:

The report of the great amendment in the King's health will I doubt not be made use of by Mr Pitt and his friends to justify the restrictions, and consequently will be much exaggerated; but I humbly submit to your Royal

Highness that it is wisest for you to act precisely as if the King were in the same state as he was a month ago.[14]

On 20 February the King was well enough to receive a visit from Thurlow, and three days later from his two eldest sons. The letter which he was able to write to Pitt later that day, 'with infinite satisfaction', could hardly be more circumspect, or better considered, or saner. 'I chose the meeting [with his sons] should be in the Queen's apartment', he wrote, 'that all parties might have that caution which at the present hour could but be judicious.' It was not to be concealed from him that the public and private conduct of his sons, even of his favourite Frederick, had lacked judgement, and that their behaviour towards their mother had been, to say the least, insensitive. And when the royal doctors before the end of February ceased issuing bulletins; when the King was known to be conducting 'business as usual'; and when the public began preparing to celebrate a grand national thanksgiving, the royal princes had no option but to feign a full share in the general joy. However, on their proposing to be present at a concert in Windsor Castle to mark the royal recovery, they were sharply informed by the Queen that the occasion was intended only for those who had supported the King and herself through the terrible months just past. Both Portland and Fox hastened to express their anger on hearing of this rebuke from the Queen, and Fox's letter to Mrs Armistead which told her of it and appears to be wilfully blind to the reality of the new political situation, is both strange and revealing: 'As to the poor man he is mad, but the mother seems to me to go beyond the worst woman we ever read of ... Liz would not be such a mother if she had a son, and ... I do not believe except our Queen there is another in the world that would be ...'[15] Though Fox persisted in shutting his eyes to it, the reality was plain to the public or, more accurately, to that fairly small politically interested portion of it known for convenience as 'the people'. In 1783–4 Fox and his party had been defeated by the King and Pitt. Now, in 1788–9 they had been worsted again, first by Pitt in debate, then by the King's remarkably complete recovery. Moreover, their frustration had served to widen already existing cracks in the party. These had first appeared when opinions diverged over the wisdom of continuing the lingering prosecution of Warren Hastings. Then the regency fiasco exacerbated both political and personal differences. But it was the French Revolution which was to be the main agent of Whig disintegration.

12

'HOW MUCH
THE GREATEST
EVENT ..!'

1789–1793

The grand thanksgiving for the King's restoration to health and vigour was held in St Paul's Cathedral on 25 April 1789. Nine days later came the meeting at Versailles of the French estates of the realm, the States General, summoned by Louis XVI in response to the deteriorating crisis, financial and civil, then facing the nation. Six weeks later, the Third Estate (or Commons) took the Tennis Court Oath, and constituted itself the National Assembly. In Britain, meanwhile, the political tension which had persisted through the winter had slackened. It was proving a sunny summer, and by 13 July George III, by now hailed as 'the good old King', and certainly much more popular than he had been earlier in his reign, took his first dip in the sea at Weymouth, while a band of music housed in a bathing machine close by (so Miss Burney tells us) struck up 'God Save Great George our King'. On the day following, the Paris mob stormed the Bastille, slaughtered half its garrison, and joyfully decapitated its Governor – an event which, if only in its symbolic significance, may reasonably be seen as loosening the first stone in the ancient fabric of the French monarchy, which in little more than three years was to be utterly destroyed.

Fox could not foresee such an outcome, still less the Terror which was to follow it. The events of July 1789 seemed to him to be presaging a French revolution broadly on the lines of Britain's in the previous century, whereby a potential Stuart despotism had been averted, first by the resistance of parliament in the 1640s, and then again by parliamentary action – and in particular by the Whig aristocracy – in the Glorious Revolution of 1688.

Much of his own political career had been devoted to the cause of limiting the monarch's power and influence. How excellent it now seemed to him that the French should be following in the footsteps of the English Whigs. As for the fall of the Bastille, 'how much the greatest event' it was 'that has ever happened in the history of the world!' So he wrote to Fitzpatrick in a sudden access of extravagant enthusiasm – and if Fitzpatrick went to Paris, as he was proposing, he ought, said Fox, to tell the Duke of Orleans ('Philippe Egalité') and Lauzun 'that all my prepossessions against French connexions for this country will be at an end, and indeed most part of my European system of politics will be altered if this revolution has the consequence I expect'.[1] Such a friendly reaction was close to the majority view at this still very early stage of the revolution. A dissentient voice was that of Burke, to whom it did not appear that the National Assembly had 'one jot more power than the King' – and how could they exercise 'any function of decided authority' with 'a mob of their constituents ready to hang them if they should deviate into moderation?'[2] The elements which composed human society had dissolved, and 'a world of monsters' had taken its place.

The Revolutionary Society, an association in which Dissenters were well represented, and which met annually on 4 November to celebrate the Glorious Revolution of 1688, judged very differently. Their very existence would hardly be acknowledged in history books by this time if their meeting in November 1789, addressed from the pulpit of Old Jewry by Dr Richard Price, once a *protégé* of Lord Shelburne, had not provoked the angry contempt of Burke, and launched him on his passionately eloquent and wide-ranging *Reflections on the Revolution in France*. 'I have lived', Dr Price had said, 'to see the rights of man better understood than ever, and nations panting for liberty which seemed to have lost the idea of it. I have lived to see thirty millions of people ... demanding liberty with an irresistible voice, and an arbitrary monarch surrendering himself to his subjects.' The Revolution Society proceeded to adopt an address of congratulation to the French National Assembly. Fox's publicly stated views on the situation in France, threatening as it must the cohesion of his party, were by now more cautious and temperate, but some of his friends, Sheridan in particular, were running dangerously ahead of him in enthusiasm.

When Burke, with his *Reflections* only just begun, spoke on 9 February

1790 in the debate on the Army Estimates, he went out of his way to praise Fox's 'remarkable understanding', his 'natural moderation', his temper which was 'mild and placable, even to a fault', his disposition which did not have in it 'one drop of gall'. But all this was only the prelude to a fierce attack on the 'fraud and violence' of what was happening in France and on those in Britain who professed to admire 'the excesses of an irrational, unprincipled, proscribing, confiscating, plundering, ferocious, bloody, and tyrannical democracy'. Fox replied with his own mollifying, placatory eulogy of Burke, a man he said from whom he had learned more than from all the men with whom he had ever conversed. On France his words were now carefully moderate, unequivocally rejecting out-and-out democracy. He was 'equally the enemy of all absolute forms of government, whether an absolute monarchy, an absolute aristocracy, or an absolute democracy'. He claimed opposition to all extremes – and Burke, to his own Whig party members in particular, was looking more and more like an extremist. After Fox had thus done his best to damp down the flames of inter-Whig controversy, Sheridan proceeded to pour paraffin on them. Burke, he insultingly suggested, must now be regarded as 'the friend of despotism'. Replying to this more coolly than might have been expected from one of such notoriously warm temper, Burke declared – ominously for any prospect of future party unity – that Sheridan and he were now 'separated in politics', Sheridan having apparently lined up with those who held 'theories of government incompatible with the safety of the state'. Struggling to maintain a show of party unity, and reconcile his two Irishmen, Fox arranged to bring them together at Burlington House, when at first it seemed that an apology offered by Sheridan might satisfy Burke, until some reservation within it which Burke fastened upon left the antagonists still at odds.

Fox next proceeded to tackle once more the religious discrimination written into the century-old Test and Corporation Acts, whose repeal he and his friends had earlier come near to achieving in May 1789, when they had failed by only twenty votes. Even if these laws had in practice ceased seriously to oppress Dissenters, their retention on the statute book represented to Fox a national disgrace, a negation of the claim to religious freedom of which the British were properly proud. But here too the French Revolution and its ramifications were beginning to engender fears and bolster conservative caution. Some of the most vocal among the British friends of France's fast-developing revolution were Dissenters professing radical opinions wholly uncongenial to the majority of Commons members, who considered it no time to be tinkering with the country's constitution. Thus this latest resolution for repeal was emphatically rejected by 294 votes to 105. Burke was among the 294, though conceding that he had earlier been in favour of repeal. In fact, the more contentious among Dissenting controversialists had for the past five or six years been forfeiting Burke's sympathies, because of what he condemned as their 'warm, animated, and acrimonious hostility to the Church of England'. Dissenters, he said, ought to regard the established church as 'a jealous friend to be reconciled', not as 'an adversary to be conquered'. Further, a 'considerable party among them' – he meant of course Priestley, Price, and their radical friends – were 'proceeding systematically to the destruction of some essential parts of the constitution'. Once more, Fox had gone out of his way during the debate to heap compliments upon Burke, but nonetheless did not omit to award himself a measure of credit for retaining his own views on the subject in debate 'ten years longer than his right honourable friend'.

The political tension between Burke and Fox was being aggravated by Fox's obvious *ennui* and indifference in the matter of Warren Hastings's impeachment proceedings, where Burke, after four strenuous years, was untiring. But it was Burke's furious denunciation of events in France which finally destroyed the two men's political relationship and with it their personal friendship. Burke's *Reflections* was published in November 1790, became immediately a best-seller, and was considered alike by Fox and by most of his party to be the product of overheated brains – brilliant but extremist, wrong-headed, even fanatical. Inside the Whig party Burke's reputation, already heavily criticized by the time of the regency crisis, was now at its lowest. The heckling and mockery which of recent years had constantly interrupted his speeches in the Commons had come more from his own side of the House than from the government benches, and especially from the men he dismissed resentfully as Mr Fox's 'light troops', that group largely of fellow-members of Brooks's for whom their much loved Charles could do no wrong. Fox himself, whose admiration for Burke was sincerely held and several times publicly insisted on, stood apart from such behaviour, but his private verdict on the *Reflections* was hostile. He remained convinced that Burke's fears were exaggerated and that his attacks on the French revolutionaries and their British sympathizers were misguided. Although in private he was beginning to express alarm at the increasingly violent turn of events across the Channel, he still considered that the French would ultimately arrive at a constitutional monarchy not too different from the British model.

On 15 April 1791, during a debate on British policy towards Russia and Turkey, currently at war (which, however, like almost every other topic at this time inevitably included consideration of affairs across the Channel), Fox was betrayed into another outburst of enthusiasm for what was happening in France. First comparing existing conditions there with those under the old regime, and observing that even 'those who detested the principles of the revolution had reason to rejoice in its effect', he proceeded in his least restrained vein to declare that the French Revolution, 'considered altogether', was 'the most stupendous and glorious edifice of liberty which has been erected on the foundations of human integrity in any time or country'.[3] This sort of talk was beginning to alarm some of the more conservative-minded members of his party, not least its titular leader the Duke of Portland, who wondered whether Mr Fox was not going rather too far and too fast, and apparently trying to drag the main body of the Whigs along with him. Portland however was so heavily under the spell of Fox the charmer, the magician, that he still professed unwavering confidence in 'the superiority of F's talents and the rectitude of his heart and head'.[4] Not so Burke, at least so far as concerned head; but he too remained on sufficiently good personal terms with Fox for them to stroll along together to the House on the way to the next important debate (on the committee stage of the Quebec Bill) in amicable conversation. The Quebec Bill was proposing a new constitution for Canada, but this proved no bar – and, after all, Canada was peopled largely by Frenchmen – to allowing the debate to include discussion of the current turmoil in France. Consideration of the bill was then postponed for a fortnight, and fears during that interval of probable Whig dissensions were prevalent enough to prompt the Foxite *Morning Chronicle* on 4 May to hope that 'no altercation on the subject of French politics' would intrude on the Canada debate due two days later and thus weaken the 'virtuous' opposition. Fox, unwilling to waste the fortnight of delay, accepted it as a holiday and went off to Newmarket to enjoy the pleasures and excitements of the spring meeting.[5]

The famous debate of 6 May 1791[6] was to bring its own measure of excitement, even of drama, but certainly no pleasure for Fox. Burke's opening speech, substantially not on Canada but on France, successfully survived continual protests about its irrelevance, some noisy heckling, and numerous interventions on points of order. He attacked the 'spurious' and 'mischievous' rights of man 'imported from a neighbouring country', and alleged (though he thought the nation still sound at heart) the existence of dangerous plots against the British constitution.

Most of the hostile interruptions greeting him came from the Foxite squadron of 'light troops' on the benches behind him, and at one point he broke off in anger and no little contempt to quote at them Lear's cry, 'The little dogs and all, Tray, Blanche, and Sweetheart, see, they bark at me!' Fox rose to reply. Burke's speech had done him 'a direct injustice', seemed eager 'to seek a difference of opinion', anxious 'to discover a cause of dispute'. As for the rights of man, they underpinned 'every rational constitution', including the British. And once again Fox stressed his admiration for the French Revolution, 'one of the most glorious events in the history of mankind'. There was more to come, some of it, so Burke thought, hitting him below the belt – with debating points recalling out of context earlier opinions of Burke apparently inconsistent with what he was now saying.

Burke spoke again, at first (according to the *Parliamentary History*) 'in a grave and governed tone of voice', protesting against the reception which some members had given his first speech, developing some of his previous arguments, and praising monarchy as 'the basis of all good government'. Fox's speech, he complained, had

> ripped up the whole course and tenour of his private and public life, with a considerable degree of asperity ... A personal attack had been made upon him from a quarter he never could have expected, after a friendship and intimacy of more than twenty-two years ... He had met with great unfairness from the right honourable gentleman ... [who] brought down the whole strength and heavy artillery of his own judgement, eloquence, and abilities upon him to crush him ...

He reminded the House of other occasions on which he and Fox had differed with no damage to their mutual relations – the Royal Marriage Act for instance, parliamentary reform, repeal of the Test and Corporation Acts. In the matter however of the danger presented to Britain by the French Revolution ... At this point Fox leaned over towards him, and said in a lowered voice (the *Parliamentary History* says 'whispered') that there was 'no loss of friends'.

For Burke, whose politics were built on passionate conviction, this debate had been the last straw. With him, a great issue overrode any personal relationship. Upon the subject of the danger to the British constitution and to European civilization itself now arising from events in France, he was overwhelmingly convinced of the correctness of his own judgement, and in despair at the *bien pensant* gullibility of the revolution's British sympathizers. Moreover, the latest debate had come at the end of a sequence of topics on which he had felt increasingly isolated within his own party, distanced from its leading spirits, at best tolerated as a high-minded bore by some of them, at worst ridiculed and harried. His temper had always been held on a taut thread, and now it snapped. 'Yes, there *was* a loss of friends', he said; he 'knew the price of his conduct – he had done his duty at the price of his friend – their friendship was at an end.'

That Fox was surprised, vexed, shocked, indeed stunned, is clear from his reaction – an inability, surely unique for him, to command his own voice in reply. Some little time passed before he was able to compose himself and regain control. In the words again of the *Parliamentary History*:

> Mr Fox rose to reply; but his mind was so much agitated and his heart so much affected by what had fallen from Mr Burke that it was some minutes before he could proceed. Tears trickled down his cheeks, and he strove in vain to give utterance to feelings that dignified and exalted his nature. The sensibility of every member in the House appeared uncommonly excited upon this occasion.

Recovered, and launched afresh, he tried to assure Burke, despite what had passed, that *he* at least refused to consider their friendship dead. But he repeated once more how he rejoiced at the ending in France of 'a tyranny of the most horrid despotism'. In the immediate future, he said, he would keep out of Burke's way, till time and reflection had 'fitted him to think differently upon the subject'. There was of course little chance of that. Burke in fact was already busy renewing his campaign – one might well say crusade – publishing his *Letter to a Member of the National Assembly*, a defence of his conduct and opinions which left him more isolated among the Whigs than ever. Fox wrote to his nephew, 'I have not read Burke's new pamphlet ... It is in general thought to be mere madness, and especially in those parts where he is for a general war for the purpose of destroying the present government of France'.[7] Then, three months later, Burke brought out a further fighting apologia, *An Appeal of the New to the Old Whigs*, his third important publication within ten months. As well as seeking to demonstrate how the radical wing of the party had deserted time-honoured Whig principles, the *Appeal* challenged especially the most basic of democratic concepts, the claim to sovereignty 'of a majority of men, *told by the head*', and denied the right of such a mere numerical majority even to be considered 'the people'. (Fox, though deeply suspicious of democracy and on the whole hostile to it, was always proud to be hailed as 'the man of the people'.) Who were 'the people'? Burke now asked. No head-count would give for him the correct answer. Where 'great multitudes of people', he wrote, acted together in a state of civil society under the direction of 'a true, natural aristocracy' – as in Britain, but not, alas, as currently in France – such an aristocracy being 'an essential, integrant part of any large body rightly constituted', *there*, Burke said, he did recognize 'the people'. But when this natural harmony was disturbed, when 'the common sort of men' were separated from 'their natural chieftains' you were left not with 'the people', but merely with 'a disbanded race of deserters and vagabonds'.[8] Burke's *Appeal* of August 1791, where these fundamentally anti-democratic sentiments appear, had renewed the quarrel with Fox. The political and philosophical matters in hand were much too serious for him to be content to allow time's healing hand to scab the wound. Instead he raked it over, protesting anew against Fox's attack on him in the debate of 6 May.

So Burke's *Appeal* made him few new friends and mended no rifts with his old ones. Even the Duke of Portland, though he was nervous of Fox's oratorical excesses and discovered a few 'excellent and admirable' touches in Burke's latest polemic, deplored his 'calumniation' of party colleagues. *Colleagues* was in fact no longer an appropriate word. Burke saw himself as 'excommunicated'. Only a very few Whig friends such as Elliot and Windham retained connection with him, and even they were not in full agreement. As Fox's nephew Lord Holland observed sourly many years later, any of Burke's future intercourse with the Whigs was 'for the purpose of disuniting them'.[9] Burke told his son that there *were* more in the party who agreed with him, but that they 'dare not speak out for fear of hurting Fox'. Portland, though he longed to preserve party cohesion, was quite incapable of exerting decisive influence. He persisted in believing that Fox's publicly expressed enthusiasm for violent revolution would be kept within bounds; so admirable and withal so brilliantly perceptive a man was surely indulging a brief political flirtation merely. And that other principal aristocrat-chieftain among the Whigs, Rockingham's heir and Burke's patron Earl Fitzwilliam, judging the *Appeal* to have been tactless, was sure too that Fox was sound at bottom.

Fox himself, though still tending to see in the French Revolution a parallel to what he regarded as his own earlier battle against the power of the Crown in Britain, was doing his best to steer a middle course between the conservative and radical wings of his party. He chose not to be one of the company at the Crown and Anchor tavern to celebrate the second anniversary of the attack on the Bastille. He even began to admit, if only privately (to Fitzwilliam) that the 'present state' of France alarmed him very much. It was to Fitzwilliam too a little later that he confessed his *private* hesitation in the support he still felt bound to give publicly to the cause of parliamentary reform. 'I am more bound by former declarations and consistency', he wrote revealingly, 'than by any strong opinion I entertain in its favour. I am far from being sanguine that any new scheme would produce better parliaments than the present mode of election has furnished.' Perhaps Fitzwilliam's own more conservative position on this subject, he admitted, was 'upon the whole the more manly and judicious'.[10]

Internal differences were aggravated by the Whigs' conflicting reactions to some new radical bodies and publications which were beginning to appear on the scene, and especially to Tom Paine's *Rights of Man* and the growing, though still small, band of Paine's followers. Part One of the *Rights of Man*, the most powerful counterblast yet to Burke's *Reflections*, came out in March 1791 – revolutionary and republican, a landmark in the history of radical politics. Then there was the London Corresponding Society, founded by the shoemaker Thomas Hardy, a pioneer association of working-class advocates of universal suffrage. But more disturbing to the conservative Whigs was The Friends of the People, a club founded by the radical wing of their party, prominent among them Grey, Lauderdale, Sheridan, and Erskine. Grey, in particular, chose to ride immediately towards the sound of gunfire by tabling a Commons motion for parliamentary reform.

Fox, equivocal and studiously ambiguous, concealed his irritation at this last development as far as he could, but certainly he was annoyed. Neither he nor his closest associates joined The Friends of the People, and he made it known that he thought them 'injurious to us as a party'. He referred to them in April 1792, in a letter to Fitzpatrick, as contributing to 'several unpleasant things going forward', and to his nephew at this same time he confessed that 'things here are very very bad'. The *Public Advertiser* on 18 May predicted that Fox and the Whig reformers would probably soon be parting company.[11] Yet in the preceding debate on the reform of parliament, the Whigs had managed to tread warily enough through their self-sown minefield to avoid any further explosions of public dissension. Fox's own speech gave only the vaguest and least controversial support to the general principle of parliamentary reform – though its tepid tone did not deter the London Corresponding Society from distributing 500 copies of it. Fox 'saw nothing in any human institution so very sacred as not to admit of being touched or looked at'. Grey's motion 'afforded time to inquire into the facts'. 'If the people of the country really wished for a parliamentary reform, they had a right to have it'. Unexceptionable sentiments; but Fox was at pains to stand somewhat apart from Grey – 'the right honourable gentleman had in his warmth outrun himself' – and he specifically condemned Paine's *Rights of Man* as 'a libel on the constitution'.[12]

With affairs in France growing ever more violent during 1792, there was some spread of alarm in Britain at the importation of French-inspired republican ideas, and the Friends of the People could easily be perceived however mistakenly, to be at least flirting with them. After Grey's reform motion was safely out of the way (defeated, of course) Fox felt more cheerful about his party's chances of continuing cohesion; but – unknown to him at first – it was just now being threatened from a different quarter. Lord Loughborough was a prominent Whig of conservative inclination, and he was also generally known to be hungry for the Lord Chancellorship which he came so tantalisingly close to gaining when George III went mad in 1788. It was also well known that Lord Chancellor Thurlow was on very difficult terms with Prime Minister Pitt. Pitt therefore, wishing to broaden his 'bottom', made overtures to Loughborough in the spring of 1792, suggesting that opposition leaders should attend a meeting of the Privy Council to consider measures appropriate to 'present circumstances'. Pitt and some of those nearest to him, such as Dundas and Lord Auckland (William Eden), thought for some weeks during May 1792 that they stood a fair chance of hiving off the more conservative of the Whig leaders from the Friends of the People wing of the party. Everything would depend on the attitude of the man who stood by general consent at the head of the Fox party, the Duke of Portland. But Portland, all caution and propriety, would not reply finally to Pitt's offer before consulting Earl Fitzwilliam and Fox, whose advice held him back – as it would continue to do for more than two years yet.[13]

They proved to be two years of intricate party and intra-party manoeuvre. Portland was struggling to preserve as much Whig unity as was practicable and to resist as long as possible becoming fully absorbed within ministerial ranks, long determined to stay loyal to his infinitely admired and loved Fox. Pitt was quietly and obliquely, but repeatedly, offering to such conservative Whigs as seemed susceptible inducements to join a coalition or multi-party ministry which would guarantee good order and – after war began early in 1793 – patriotic solidarity. Many middle-of-the-road Whigs, such for instance as Fitzwilliam, were torn painfully between, on the one side, the attractiveness of such a prospect and, on the other, their party links with the Friends of the People Whigs such as Grey, Sheridan, and Erskine; and some of these moderates, notably Windham, got together for a short time in a semi-independent 'Third Party' of some thirty-eight members, twenty-six of them Whigs. Fox himself was willing at least to toy with the notion of joining forces with Pitt and allowing his friends to do rather more than toy, but often gave the impression that his main task was to avoid taking crucial decisions. His conviction of Pitt's deep hostility towards him, malevolence even, stood in the path of any genuine attempt at coalition. If ever he and his associates were to join Pitt's ministry, he insisted, they were 'only to go in as equals', 'on fair and even conditions to share equally with him all the power, patronage, etc'.[14] He had personally resolved never to serve *under* Pitt, although at one point there was some discussion of Pitt and himself becoming joint Secretaries of State in a rearranged government under a 'neutral' First Lord much as he and North had served under Portland in the coalition of 1783. Given Pitt's record, his ambition, his ability, and his prodigious self-confidence, there was small prospect of such an arrangement being seriously considered by him, and of course no prospect whatever of his serving *under* Fox. His tactics, increasingly successful, were to lure away by such slow stages as proved necessary all those Whigs who were alarmed by the domestic unrest stemming from French revolutionary ideas – or who, like Loughborough, were specially hungry for office. Loughborough indeed was Pitt's first important catch. He became Lord Chancellor, at last, in January 1793, just three days before war was declared on France, but for a long time he proved the only Whig to go the whole way and join forces with Pitt. His was a move which met with emphatic approval from Burke who, hardly regarding himself any longer as a Whig at all, was in despair at Portland's indecision. 'The whole edifice of ancient Europe' was being 'shaken by the earthquake', and he was passionately urging war to save European civilization, 'a general war against Jacobins and Jacobinism'.[15] By this time he was busily working to assist counter-revolution in France.

Although with Fox, as with Pitt, it was always *aut Caesar aut nihil*, each of them during the 1790s did promote measures which the other supported. There were for instance the annual occasions when Wilberforce's motion to abolish or limit the slave trade came before the Commons. Again, both men were to be found in the same division lobby during the passage of a bill relieving Catholics from some of the old restrictions judged out-of-date and unnecessary. This small step towards full Catholic Emancipation was to be legalized conditionally upon the taking of an oath of allegiance. (The Test Act itself had another thirty-seven years to run.) In the same year, 1791, common ground was found again in Fox's own bill to transfer from judges to juries the right to decide the verdict in certain cases of libel. This judge-versus-jury quarrel was an old one, and the rights of juries as representing the judgement of 'the people' had long formed part of that 'palladium of liberties' in whose creation the Whigs always claimed a lion's share. Pitt's own support for the 1791 Libel Act may well have owed something to his paternal upbringing and respect for his father, who had fought a well-remembered battle on this same issue with the man who (next perhaps to Fox's own father) had been his foremost enemy, Lord Mansfield.

Fox followed French events, as they grew in savagery during 1792, with fluctuating feelings, of pleasure and anxiety, of revulsion and relief. But he was consistently determined not to be betrayed into seeing the trees rather than the wood. For him the wood meant that essentially, despite its excesses, the revolution would prove a blessing, and that the *ancien régime*, with its 'Bourbon despotism', had been a curse which everyone should be happy to see destroyed. When the *fédérés* from Brittany and Marseille, along with Santerre's revolutionaries from the Faubourg St Antoine, stormed the Tuileries on 10 August and killed some 800 of the nobility and the King's Swiss guards, themselves losing 300–400 dead, Fox was initially shocked, but three weeks later was telling his nephew,

> I do not think nearly so ill of the business of the 10th August as I did upon first hearing it. If the King and his ministers were really determined not to act in concert with the Assembly, and still more if they secretly favoured the Invasion of the Barbarians [the Duke of Brunswick, that is, and his Prussian army now threatening Paris], it was necessary, at any rate, to begin by getting rid of them.[16]

In the same letter, however, which was written a day or two before he learned of the September massacres in Paris (with the mob at large for five days, butchering indiscriminately well over 1,000 people, some 300 of

them priests), he writes disapprovingly of the behaviour of National
Assembly members:

> When the enemy is in a manner at their doors, to be amusing themselves
> with funerals and inscriptions, and demolitions of statues, and creations of
> honorary citizens, is quite intolerable; and to talk so pompously of dying for
> liberty and their country, before one single action has been performed by
> any part of their army against the enemy, is worse than ridiculous. And yet,
> with all their faults and all their nonsense, I do interest myself for their
> success to the greatest degree. It is a great crisis for the real cause of
> liberty ...[17]

He was still judging the relationship between Louis XVI and the National
Assembly in terms closely similar to that between George III and the
House of Commons. 'From the moment of the dismission of the Jacobin
ministry', he wrote, 'I have thought that it was absolutely necessary either
that the Assembly should come round to the Feuillans,* or (which seemed
most according to our Whig ideas) that the King should be forced to have
ministers of the same complexion with the Assembly.' But even Fox, for
all his disinclination to accept that events in France were running steeply
away from British parallels, was repelled and perturbed by some of the
news from Paris. It was impossible, he wrote on 3 September 1792, 'not
to look with disgust at the bloody means which have been taken, even
supposing the end to be good, and I cannot help fearing that we are not
yet near the end of these trials and executions'.[18] As it happens, those
words were written to his nephew during the week of the September
massacres, but before he learned of them. When news of the butchery
arrived, he wrote that 'the horrors of that day and night [2–3 September]'
made them 'the most heart-breaking event that ever happened to those
who, like me, are fundamentally and unalterably attached to the true cause'.
Unalterably: the point was crucial. He had taken his stand for 'the cause',
and no news of violence or atrocity would budge him. It was only very
shortly after this that Gibbon, away in Lausanne but well briefed in the
current politics of Westminster, was giving his friend Lord Sheffield a
considered view of Fox's attitude to the French Revolution:

> The behaviour of Fox rather afflicts than surprizes me: you may remember
> what I told you last year at Lausanne when you attempted his defence, that
> his inmost soul was deeply touched with Democracy. Such wild opinions

---

* The Feulliants were a group in various ways less extreme than the Jacobins, aiming broadly to
establish constitutional monarchy.

cannot easily be reconciled with the understanding, but tis true tis pity and tis pity tis true.[19]

Back from some strenuous games of tennis which rather fatigued him (not lawn tennis of course, but the older and more complicated game of 'real' or 'court' tennis); then some 'very good sport' partridge-shooting in September; and then the Newmarket meeting, where that year he had no luck at all with his horses, Fox was soon communicating to his nephew his keen joy at hearing of the French victory over Brunswick's invading Prussian army at Valmy:

> As you wished, as you say, against the invaders, you must be almost as much (for *quite* is impossible) rejoiced at [the Prussians'] flight as I am. No! no public event, not excepting Saratoga and York Town, ever happened that gave me so much delight. I would not allow myself to believe it for some days for fear of disappointment.

In Paris politics, the Feuillant moderates were emphatically out of favour with him. Still writing wholly in the spirit of an English Whig, he condemned them for supporting King Louis when he used his vote 'and other prerogatives in opposition to the will of the Assembly and the nation'. Was he recalling King George in 1784 sustaining Pitt in office against the will of the assembled House of Commons? An English Whig, so Fox now pronounced, 'must disapprove the Feuillant party or quit his English principles'. Indeed, the behaviour of the Feuillants even 'went a great way' towards palliating the violent conduct of the Jacobins – unless it could be conclusively shown to him that the Jacobins had any hand in the September massacres. For such 'cruelty and extreme baseness' there could be 'no excuse, no palliation'.[20]

His deeply ingrained mistrust of French expansionism revives again when he reads of the conquest by Dumouriez of the Austrian Netherlands (Belgium) and the looming threat to the Dutch. The French disclaimer of aggressive intentions, 'even if sincere', was hardly to be relied on. All the same, he would think Pitt's government *mad* if they allowed this or *anything* to draw them into a war with France. But at the beginning of December a British order in council activating the militia signalled the reality of such a 'madness'. On learning of it, Fox dashed off a letter to Fitzpatrick – 'only time to write two words' – condemning this 'detestable measure ... I will not believe there will be war; if there is, I see dangers innumerable'.[21]

It was not so much foreign war as domestic insurrection which, to many, now seemed to threaten the worse evil. There were growing though exaggerated fears, among both the public and the government, of a French-inspired republican rebellion. (This was the very month, December 1792, in which Louis XVI was on trial for his life, though news of his execution did not reach London until 24 January.) As Burke was constantly insisting, the heart of the British public beat to a loyal and monarchist pulse, but it is true that there were some radically 'democratical' opinions in circulation, some of them advanced enough to alarm even Grey and his 'people's friends', and to provoke the formation of opposing Associations, loyalist and patriotic. At the Whig Club Fox denounced these last, pooh-poohed any threat of a 'British rebellion', and declared that the real danger to the country 'chiefly consisted in the growth of Tory principles' such as were being evinced in the government's 'abominable' Aliens Bill,* targeted against the importation of republicanism by French agents. The successful launch of the loyal Associations which so infuriated Fox was now moving Grey and Erskine to found yet another Association, this one for Preserving Freedom of the Press.

The order to embody the militia was widely interpreted as a precaution against civil tumult, and to Portland on 1 December Fox wrote in controlled exasperation:

> If they mention danger of *Insurrection*, or rather as they must do to legalize their proceedings, of *Rebellion*, surely the first measure all honest men ought to take is to impeach them for so wicked and detestable a falsehood. I fairly own that if they have done this I shall grow savage, and not think French *lanterne* [lamp-post, i.e. gallows] too bad for them. Surely it is impossible for such monsters, who, for the purpose of weakening or destroying the honourable connections of the Whigs, would not scruple to run the risk of a civil war! I cannot trust myself to write any more, for I confess I am too much heated.[22]

And in the House, a fortnight later, after the King's speech had referred to 'seditious practices', 'a spirit of tumult and disorder', and 'acts of riot and insurrection', Fox protested forcefully. There had been, admittedly, he said, 'some slight riots in different parts of the country, Shields, Leith, Yarmouth, Perth, Dundee'; but 'was there any gentleman in England' who honestly believed that these were attempts to overthrow the constitution, rather than complaints at low wages?

... Now this, Sir, is the crisis which I think so truly alarming. The question

---

* One of those eventually expelled under the terms of the Aliens Bill was Talleyrand.

is, whether we shall give to the king, that is, to the executive government, complete power over our thoughts, ... whether we shall maintain that in England no man is criminal but by the commission of overt acts forbidden by the law ... I know well that there are societies who have published opinions and circulated pamphlets containing doctrines tending, if you please, to subvert our establishments. I say that they have done nothing unlawful in this ... Show me the law that orders these books to be burned, and I will acknowledge the illegality of their proceedings; but if there be no such law, you violate the law in acting without authority ... You neglect in your conduct the foundation of all legitimate government, the rights of the people: and, setting up this bugbear, you spread a panic for the very purpose of sanctifying the infringement, while, again, the very infringement engenders the evil which you dread. One extreme naturally leads to another. Those who dread republicanism fly for shelter to the crown. Those who desire reform and are calumniated are driven by despair to republicanism. And this is the evil I dread![23]

Not only would he oppose the Aliens Bill, but he proposed for good measure to proclaim his convictions louder and louder, abandoning his earlier prudent equivocation. Further, he would persist in efforts to reform parliamentary representation, and make one more attempt to repeal the Test Act. He declared that Britain ought officially to recognize the French Republic. To cooperate with Austria and Prussia in an attempt to restore the French monarchy would be wrong and wicked. It was disgraceful that Britain should be 'supporting rather the cause of kings than the cause of the people'. Indeed the violence of his language directed against the European monarchs lent support to the suspicion that he was hostile to monarchy itself – which logically would have to include the British monarchy. He was never in danger of adopting so extreme a position, though in the debate of 1 February he did argue that in Britain it was 'the people' who were sovereign, and that the monarch was elective. He expanded further: 'The people are the sovereigns in all countries ... They might amend, alter, and abolish at pleasure the form of government under which they live'.[24] Strongly defending the actions of the French 'people' over the previous few months, he stopped short of excusing the execution of Louis XVI.

The voting support for him in the Commons was by this time thin, varying between something under 40 and a little over 60, while it was currently estimated that the more conservative Whigs, moving regretfully even further away from Fox, numbered over 100.[25] However, as he observed in his *Letter to the Electors of Westminster*, of January 1793, 'to vote in small minorities is a misfortune to which I have been so much accustomed that I cannot be expected to feel it very acutely.' He was still voting in company with 'a small minority' when in May he supported Grey in the Commons on another motion for parliamentary reform. This time he was even prepared to support 'universal' suffrage *in principle*, his objection to it lying only in the lack of 'any practical mode of collecting such suffrage' without the intervention of 'influence'.[26] May 1793 also marked the first occasion when he publicly sided with the Friends of the People. 'Parliamentary reform', however, continued to mean widely different things to different people. Neither the aristocratic Friends of the People nor of course Fox himself approached anywhere near the radicalism of the Westminster Association (of 1780) in Fox's own constituency, who first formulated the 'six points' which sixty years later were to become the central demands of the 'People's Charter': universal manhood suffrage, annual general elections, equal-sized constituencies, secret ballot, abolition of the property qualification, and payment for members of parliament.

By now, of the Whig leaders, Windham (with his short-lived Third Party), Fitzwilliam, and most importantly Portland, were all in varying stages of dismayed reaction against the man who was still ostensibly the Whig leader in the Commons. Burke, of course, had been lost to the party for two years already, and was now regarded by Fox and his followers as merely the creature of Pitt – and more than a little out of his mind.

With France and Britain at war from February 1793, and with hostilities going badly both for Britain and her continental allies, Fox saw no need to allow either his patriotic feelings or his dyed-in-the-wool mistrust of the power of France to deter him from voicing approval as the list of allied military failure lengthened; and he protested angrily when Prussia and Austria combined with Russia in the two later partitions of Poland, which extinguished her for over 100 years as an independent state. Together with Sheridan he attempted to intercede with the current rulers in Paris to prevent the execution of Marie Antoinette; but lack of success here, and afterwards the onset of the Jacobin reign of terror, did not inhibit him from lauding the 'liberty' which the Revolution was bringing to the French. He would never, he repeated, never be *converted* from his love of liberty. But privately, at Christmas 1793, he confessed to his nephew his predicament:

> There is such a barefaced contempt of principle and justice in every step we take, that it is quite disgusting to think that it can be endured. *France is worse* is the only answer, and perhaps that is true in fact, for the horrors grow every

day worse. The transactions at Lyons seem to surpass all their former wickedness. Do you remember Cowper? –
    'Oh for a lodge in some vast wilderness', etc.

This et cetera from *The Task* has, a few lines down, and pertinently enough:

> My soul is sick with every day's report
> Of wrong and outrage with which earth is filled

A fair example of such outrage had just been perpetrated in Scotland, where Thomas Muir and the Rev. Thomas Palmer had been given sentences respectively of fourteen and seven years transportation for the seditious 'crime' of advocating parliamentary reform. In this same long letter ('God bless you, my dear Henry') Fox continues:

> ... I do not think any of the French *soi-disant* proceedings surpass in injustice and contempt of law those in Scotland. And yet ... [they] are to be defended in Parliament ... Good God! that a man should be sent to Botany Bay for advising another to read Paine's book, or for reading the Irish address to a public meeting! for these are the charges against Muir ...*

Then, the Fox of old reasserting himself,

> If all these horrors at home and abroad can be endured with the bad success of the war, what will, or rather what will not, be the power of the crown if chance should ever make us prosperous?[27]

When in December 1793 news of the loss of Toulon by the British and counter-revolutionary forces finally brought home to public opinion that the war was going to be long and difficult, Portland, Fitzwilliam, and Thomas Grenville together informed Fox that they judged the time had come 'to take a more decided line ... in support of the administration'. Fox interpreted this message realistically, as formally declaring 'the separation, or rather the dissolution, of the Whig party'. It was to be another six or seven months before the leading Portland Whigs could bring themselves actually to accept office under Pitt, but the schism between them and the small band of Foxites was henceforth an accomplished fact.†

---

* In Edinburgh Muir had read out to a national assembly of Scottish reformers an allegedly seditious address from the revolutionary United Irishmen.

† Fox's opposition to the war and championing of radical reformers under threat from the law may have received little support in parliament, but it is interesting to find at this time a somewhat wild young undergraduate of Jesus College Cambridge, Samuel Taylor Coleridge, reporting Fox as 'quite the *political Go* at Cambridge'. Coleridge, just before fleeing the university for his brief sojourn of black farce with the Dragoons, was active with other young radical idealists in support of William Frend, who had published a pamphlet attacking both the Church of England and the war against France. The university expelled him. (R. Holmes, *Coleridge, Early Visions*, 47–9)

When they at last joined the ministry that summer, Fox wrote, 'I think they all behaved very ill to me, and for most of them, who owe much more to me than I do to them, I feel nothing but contempt' – from which he exempted only his old friend Fitzwilliam.[28] To his nephew, a little before this, he wrote rather less harshly and more resiliently:

> You will easily imagine how much I felt the separation from persons with whom I had so long been in the habit of agreeing. It seemed some way as if I had the world to begin anew, and if I could have done it with honour, what I would best have liked would have been to retire from politics altogether, but this could not be done, and therefore there remains nothing but to get together the remains of our party, and begin, like Sisyphus, to roll up the stone again, which, long before it reaches the summit, may probably roll down again.[29]

And the following month, from St Anne's Hill now:

> Politics go on, according to the Irish translation of *semper eadem*, worse and worse ... However, here am I, passing a most comfortable week of holidays, the weather delicious, and the place looking delicious beyond description, and the nightingales singing, and Mrs A. as happy as the day is long; all which circumstances enable me to bear calamities with wonderful philosophy; but yet I cannot help thinking now and then of the dreadful state of things in Europe, and the real danger which exists, in my opinion, of the total extinction of liberty ...[30]

13

FROM
SCHISM TO
SECESSION

1793–1801

Politically powerless as he was, and bitter at what he judged to be the desertion of the majority of his old party, he largely managed to escape the return of similarly hard feelings. Even Burke, from whom political bitterness was liable to flow freely, and who regarded Fox's *politics* now with passionate hostility, felt bound to admit (though, as it was said, 'with a deep sigh') that he was a man 'born to be loved'.[1] Gibbon expressed feelings not dissimilar. He was afraid, he wrote, that 'the powerful genius of Mr Fox, instead of being useful', would be 'averse to the public service'. And yet, and yet – 'Let him do what he will, I must love the dog'.[2]

There had just occurred a remarkable demonstration of this wealth of affection in the shape of a large-scale financial rescue, organized by his friends. Although he had been brought up amid great and ostentatious wealth, the middle-aged Fox was not by the standards of the Georgian aristocracy rich. Despite a reduction in the recklessness of his gambling, his carelessness with money never left him, nor could he ever quite lose old habits of easy-come, easy-go. But unlike his wealthy Whig compeers he was not a big property owner – though indeed he might have been, had he not thrown away his chance when he gambled away his inheritance (including the prospect of Kingsgate) in his profligate twenties. His aristocratic life-style was never cushioned by rents from the rolling acres attached to a Woburn or Wentworth Woodhouse or Goodwood or Chatsworth. He had, of course, his house in London – just now it was in South Street – but his 'little corner of Paradise' in Surrey, at St Anne's Hill, laid no claim to rival the country mansions of the Whig grandees.

He lived among a circle where lending and borrowing came readily; which saw no great stigma attached to running into heavy debt, and whose members had little compunction in begging a sometimes quite substantial loan. There is an air of almost casual insouciance in the sort of request that we find Fox making more than once in his early forties to a friend and admirer, the rich merchant J. B. Church. He explained first, though without elaborating, that he was 'in a very awkward situation at the moment', and proceeds: 'Two thousand guineas would extricate me in great measure, but would not supercede the necessity of my applying to some other friend for money to begin the Newmarket campaign. Four thousand would put me quite at my ease'. We may presume that Church's money was forthcoming, for two years later there follows a request for 'a further £2,500'. It is not always easy now to avoid a blink of incredulity, but such very tangible benefits of friendship within Fox's circle were, it seems, not at all unusual. Modern research has unearthed several parallel instances. 'A pattern emerges', writes Leslie Mitchell, 'of the talented and indigent being assisted by their more inarticulate, but wealthy friends'.[3]

Fox's debts, some of which he admitted were 'burthensome', had by 1793 become mountainous, and a few of his friends therefore got together to promote a fund which would be substantial enough, not only to discharge everything he owed, but to provide him also with an annuity adequate to ensure a comfortable income for the rest of his life. This, it was hoped, might come to £2,000 a year.* To William Adam, the old Northite lawyer-politician who fourteen years before had been Fox's opponent in his Hyde Park duel and was now Whig party manager, was assigned the task of organizing and soliciting subscriptions. £100 was the suggested minimum, but it is not surprising to find the impecunious Sheridan among those who could only manage to raise £25. The total amount initially aimed at was £55,000, of which £40,000 was already subscribed by June 1793. By October the full £55,000 had been either paid or promised; but then Adam found, to his annoyance, that he was expected to find a further £10,000, to ensure that the annuity was sufficient. But the Duke of Bedford together with other prestigious figures, busied

---

*Probably the best way of estimating the monetary value of this is to compare it with some average incomes of contemporaries. A farm worker might expect between £20 and £30 a year, a skilled workman perhaps £90. A man and wife with a small family and one servant could live comfortably on £200.

himself in keeping up the charitable pressure, and the full £65,000 was eventually found.[4]

On earlier occasions when Fox's friends had been discussing how they might jointly rescue his finances, one of them had put it to Fox's old friend (and one of his severest critics) George Selwyn, that perhaps to be the object of such well-meant largesse might prove an embarrassment. How would Fox take it? 'Take it?' answered Selwyn, dry and wry and shrewd as always, 'Take it? Why, quarterly to be sure.'[5] Whether quarterly or otherwise, Fox certainly had no hesitation in accepting, and with gratitude. He regarded it, he said, as recognition for his services to the party, 'the most honourable thing' that had ever happened to anybody; and he saw no reason to refrain from making a relevant political point: it bestowed on him an additional obligation, 'if any were wanting, to continue steady in the principles' which he claimed to have 'uniformly professed'.

First among those principles now was peace with France. It is not surprising therefore to find among those consulting him at this time, Talleyrand, originally in his role of unofficial or perhaps semi-official emissary of the French government, having been commissioned by them to try to keep Britain out of the European war. (Talleyrand paid two quite long visits to London, although the second of them, beginning immediately after the September Massacres, arose more from his pressing necessity to keep away from danger.) Oddly, it is through a casual remark of Talleyrand's that we get a surprise glimpse of Fox's domestic circumstances. Mrs Armistead bore him no children, yet round his dinner table in South Street, in the company of Sheridan and others, Talleyrand was astonished to see 'the first orator in Europe' conversing with his *son*, but 'only with his fingers'. This boy was deaf and dumb. The poet and man of letters Samuel Rogers, through whose *Table Talk* this anecdote surfaces, was told by Talleyrand that throughout dinner that day Fox confined his attention almost entirely to his son, talking to him in sign language while their eyes (according to Rogers) 'glistened as they looked at each other'. This boy, said to be 'the very image of his father', died at the age of 15.

Fox did have another 'son'. It was his nephew Henry, the baby orphaned in the family's time of disasters, 1773–4. Henry was now 20, recently down from Oxford; third Lord Holland, future Whig minister of the 1830s, and to him, 'Young One', Fox was effectively both parent and mentor. Indeed the many and often long letters he sent him sometimes read as much tutorially as personally, embracing classical and Italian literature and the great painters equally with family trivia or political opinions. Back in

May 1791, a week or two after his clash in the Commons with Burke, the tutorial vein in his letters is already evident:

> I am glad you have begun Herodotus ... There is a flow, and ease, and pleasantness in him that I know in no other prose writer ... If you do not like algebra, I cannot help it; the liking of such studies or not is mere matter of taste, and if one does not feel them pleasant, I know no way of being persuaded that they are so. But with respect to Demosthenes, if you go on ... I think you cannot but see in him superior force of understanding and expression to all other writers ...[6]

Later, when the young Lord Holland was on a tour of Italy, there was a constant flow and counterflow of opinion on the relative merit of this or that great writer or painter. When Fox in October 1794 (he was Coke's guest at Holkham, for the shooting) begins by acknowledging that *three* of Henry's letters await an answer, he proceeds to make amends in an outpouring not far short of 2,000 words. He discusses Correggio, Domenichino, Raphael, Rubens, Titian, Veronese, and Parmegiano; laments the current condition of English politics; argues at some length the general advantage of a system of party government; praises the virtues of his faithful Whig friends then at Holkham with him – Coke himself, Lord Derby, Lord Guilford,* and the Duke of Bedford, who had beaten him at tennis, 'though last year I gave him near fifteen'. 'What a length of a letter', he ends; 'you need not read it all at one sitting'.[7] 'To doubt about Correggio', he writes on another occasion, 'seems to me just as if a man were to doubt about Homer, or Shakespeare, or Ariosto'. And elsewhere, 'There are parts of Virgil which I think fully equal to Homer, but then he has not in any degree [Homer's] freedom of manner, which I prize so much ... Ariosto has more of it than any other poet'. Just now, he wrote in April 1795, his mind was 'full of poetry', but he was afraid Henry must have grown out of the habit of reading, since he never replied with 'a word either of Ariosto, or Dante, or Tasso, or indeed of any poet at all' – and this despite the fact that he could write 'remarkably well'. Particularly Fox praises some translations from the classics which his nephew had made earlier (though two lines in his *Medea to Jason* had 'failed very much'). A month or two later: 'I have been reading Ariosto again, and I declare I like him better than ever. If I were to know but one language besides my own, it should be Italian.'[8]

---

* George North, 3rd Earl of Guilford. The prime minister Lord North had become 2nd Earl in 1790; blind in his last years, he had died in 1792.

Fortunately, his nephew's political opinions on the whole agreed with his own, and more than once he presses him to enter politics when he returns from abroad, stressing how convinced he is that his own political line has been correct. In June 1794, from St Anne's Hill, he writes:

> In these bad times, here am I with Liz, enjoying the fine weather, the beauty and (not its least beauty) the idleness of this place, as much as if these horrors were not going on ... When one has done all one can, as I think I have, to prevent mischief, one has a right I think to forget its existence if one is happily situated, so as not to be within its reach; and indeed I could not name any time of my life when I was happier than I am now, but I do not believe I should be so, if I had acted otherwise than I have done ... I wish you were here to enjoy it with us and, faith, for myself, that is almost the only wish I have. There is your picture on the other side of the room ready to say, I *say* my Uncle, and I do assure you that Mrs A. looks at it with almost if not quite as much pleasure as I do. Addio carissimo, this is a very long letter considering the weather and the idleness it produces ...[9]

Two months later:

> Here I am perfectly happy. Idleness, fine weather, Ariosto, a little Spanish, and the constant company of a person whom I love, I think, more and more every day and every hour, make me as happy as I am capable of being, and much more so than I could hope to be if politics took a different turn. Though the death of Robespierre took place on the 28th of last month, we have yet no regular account of it here ... Whoever comes in Robespierre's place cannot be worse than he was ... I am afraid too that they are not likely to be much better ... I am sorry you have not made more progress in Italian...

What he had learned of Robespierre's reign of terror had nauseated him, as had the news earlier of Marie Antoinette's execution, which he denounced as an act 'more disgusting and detestable than any other murder recorded in history'. Yet he still considered that even the rule of Robespierre, 'or a worse if worse can be', was preferable to a Bourbon restoration. And in fact on Christmas Day 1794 he was telling his nephew, 'the general conduct of the French since Robespierre's death seems to be extremely good, and has reconciled them to me wonderfully'.[10]

His books, his mistress, and his garden amid the Surrey woodland held him increasingly. 'I have quite resources enough to employ my mind', he said; 'and the great resource of all, literature, I am fonder of every day; and then the Lady of the Hill is one continual source of happiness to me.' As companion on his visits to friends, Mrs A. had been as socially acceptable as if she had been Mrs F. – or almost everywhere so. An exception was Holkham, where Coke, though among the closest of Fox's friends, seems to have declined the company of his mistress. Generally, in all but name Mrs Armistead had been accepted as Mrs Fox for over a decade now, and their need of one another had increased rather than lessened as the years passed. What should prevent her therefore from *becoming* Mrs Fox?

There would have been nothing at all unusual in a Georgian aristocrat taking his long-established mistress to wife, with or without any attendant publicity. But Fox and his Lady of the Hill chose to be married in secret, and in a place far distant from either Westminster or their country house. She had feared that, if they were to marry, he might love her less; but no, he insisted, he would 'never, never repent of being married to her'. Besides, if he should die first, her situation as his widow would be 'less uncomfortable' than as his former mistress. He was willing to go along with her wish that the wedding should be secret, but would it much matter if the secret got out? 'Indeed after the first talk it would be pleasanter that it should be known than not', he wrote.[11] It was eventually arranged that she should spend the statutorily prescribed (though by Fox resented) period of local residence before the marriage. They chose a parish where the rector, a Rev. J. Pery, was known to Fox, and there – it was at Wyton in Huntingdonshire – on 28 September 1795, 'Charles J. Fox of the parish of Chertsey in the county of Surrey' was married – not indeed to Elizabeth Armistead, but to 'Elizabeth B. Cane of this parish'. That was the name by which, somewhat smudgily, she signed the register; but any answers to the question of her parentage and origins, or to the previous existence of any putative Mr Armistead or Armitstead or Armstead were thereby little advanced. The marriage ceremony was witnessed by one of Fox's maid-servants and Wyton's parish clerk. That there now existed an undoubtedly legitimate and unchallengeably respectable Mrs Fox did not at all inhibit her husband from still sometimes referring to her in letters as 'Mrs A.', which to the world in general and even to the 'Young One' she continued to be. It was only when they were preparing to visit France in 1802, during the mid-war interlude of peace, that Fox at last chose to let it be known that they had been married for nearly seven years.

At about the time of his uncle's marriage, the 22-year-old 'Young One' was constantly to be seen, in several of the towns of Italy and Austria, in the company of Elizabeth, the wife of Sir Godfrey Webster. Married at the age of 15 and by now detesting her much older husband, she had already pursued amours with an assortment of devoted lovers. In her middle twenties she was divorced by Webster, whereupon Lord Holland, paying the injured husband £6,000 damages, married her and was soon to add her family name of Vassall to his own.* (The Vassalls were wealthy plantation-owners in the West Indies.) Fox never learned to like this newly acquired niece. Of looks and manners equally striking, she was eventually to become 'the sovereign lady' of Whig politico-literary society, the celebrated and formidable hostess of the Holland House circle during the 1820s–30s.

Over a period of four years Fox moved many resolutions in the Commons advocating a settlement with France. There were two views of the war, he maintained. It was either being fought against France as a pariah among the nations, a 'monster' (this was broadly Burke's view and was of course absolutely rejected by Fox) in which case nothing but 'unconditional submission' would satisfy. Alternatively, if 'we were at war on account of a specific aggression' – such as the invasion of the Netherlands – 'for that aggression atonement might be made, and the object being attained, peace might be concluded'.[12] Above all, there must be no question of fighting to restore 'Bourbon despotism'. Unfortunately for Fox, however, majority public opinion declined to see this war in the old time-honoured terms, to be contrived to a conclusion by diplomatic accommodation or colonial give-and-take. The French military aggression (the reality of which Fox readily conceded) had a novel 'democratical' ideology flying from its banners. The invaders bore with them the torch of republican virtue and the flag of liberty. The French Revolution, and the ideals it professed through all the bloodshed and terror, were emphatically for export; and no British government could afford to ignore the influence of revolutionary republican doctrines on its domestic situation. It may well be true, and probably is, that Pitt exaggerated that influence, since only a handful of the many associations of radical reformers in the 1790s were either revolutionary or republican. Fox indeed was convinced that the government deliberately cried up the danger in order to suppress legitimate opposition voiced from platform or press.

Fox and the Foxites went out of their way to speak of themselves as the 'patriotic opposition'; but charges of defeatism and of sympathetic

---

*The hugely best-selling Victorian novelist Mrs Humphry Ward used 'Young One' Holland's romance with Lady Webster as the basis for the late (1915) novel *Eltham House*.

indulgence of French villainy were bound to strike home – and painfully. Nor was Fox's patriotism without strict limits. In 1795 for instance, when 4,000 British troops were dispatched to stiffen French counter-revolutionary forces in western France, he was sufficiently outraged to express sentiments which, sixty years afterwards, the editor of his *Memorials and Correspondence* still thought it prudent to suppress:

> Violent as the wish may sound, I would much rather hear that they were all cut to pieces than that they gained any considerable success, for in the latter case the war may be prolonged to the utter destruction of both countries and to the total extinction of all principles of liberty and humanity in Europe.[13]

Towards the end of 1796, after the defeats inflicted on the continental allies and the collapse of the coalition, Pitt sent Lord Malmesbury to Paris to try to secure a negotiated peace. The attempt failed (as an earlier one had in the spring), since France proved as unready to withdraw from the Austrian Netherlands as Britain was to surrender the Cape of Good Hope and Ceylon. The collapse of these negotiations was much to the relief of Burke, who was passionately opposed to what he protested would have been a 'regicide peace', and who rejoiced to see Malmesbury 'whipped back to his kennel with his tail between his legs';[14] but to Fox it offered a glimmer, however brief and flickering, of an opportunity. Pitt's ministry, his continental diplomacy, and his own stock as war leader had all endured a succession of rebuffs. The domestic situation was unhappy, with a great shortage of victories to be celebrated and an extremely poor 1795 harvest which brought dearth, unrest, and some rioting for bread. (There was even a demonstration against the King as he drove to open parliament. A stone broke the window of his carriage, and there were shouts of 'Peace and Bread! No war! No King!') Fox, though he always insisted that he would never serve *under* Pitt, had already by mid-1795 arrived at a tactical understanding with his old *bête noire* Shelburne, now Marquis of Lansdowne. Although he 'never had a good opinion' of the man, as he admitted to his nephew, nor would 'give him credit for sincerity', and although Pitt's ministry still enjoyed an apparently impregnable Commons majority, in politics situations could change quickly. If therefore 'an opening' were to come to either of them, the two old rivals had agreed 'to communicate and consult mutually'. It had, after all, been failure in war which had eventually brought North down in 1782, and let the Whigs in. Might not Pitt's failures now perform a like service?

In the debate following Malmesbury's abortive mission, Fox's attack was once again renewed:

> I am certainly not one of those who despair of the country ... I very well know that we are not at the end of our resources ... but if the war is to continue any length of time, God only knows what may be the dreadful consequences. Certain, however, it is that peace cannot be obtained by a perseverance in the present system [i.e. under the present government]. It must be changed. I am not one of those who wish to alter the constitution; I wish only to reform it; to restore the voice of the people to that rank in it which it is entitled to hold; to make the opinion of the [prime] minister nothing; to see that of the people everything ...

But Pitt, 'the pilot who weathered the storm', would weather it for a time yet; and Fox's hope of any 'opening' coming from the King for a change of 'system' were faint indeed. With every month he grew more tired of politics, more frustrated, more anxious to get away to St Anne's and his books.

Although the defection of the Portland Whigs to Pitt had drastically reduced the numbers of the parliamentary opposition, it had the paradoxical effect of actually enhancing Fox's authority as party leader. After July 1794 he no longer needed to measure his every word to avert or postpone a schism. Henceforth he was unfettered and unchallengeable as the opposition's mouthpiece; and around him were forty or fifty devoted members, greatly under his personal spell, and at least *almost* all of them unambiguously committed to follow his lead. There were only forty of them, said Lord Thurlow, but 'every one of them was ready to be hanged for Fox'.

Two issues predominated. In foreign affairs – war or peace? At home, how real was the danger posed by revolutionary doctrines imported from France? A threat grossly exaggerated, was the Foxite answer; played up by the government and a majority of the propertied classes in order to encourage 'war patriotism' and to justify a succession of repressive measures aimed at silencing radical anti-governmental criticism. Three measures in particular were attacked by the Foxites: the suspension of Habeas Corpus for a year during 1794–5,* and the Treasonable Practices Act and Seditious Meetings Act of 1795–6. Under these, the net was spread so wide and loose that almost any outspoken criticism of the King or the government

---

* It was suspended again later, for 3 years between 1798 and 1801.

might be considered actionable for treason, while magistrates were given powers to ban any public meeting which they feared to be tending to sedition. (In fact, not one radical reformer was ever prosecuted under the terms of the Treasonable Practices Act.)[15]

There were certainly many radical associations springing up all over Britain during the 1790s. The London Corresponding Society was one of the oldest and most important. Then there were 'Constitutional Societies' in Sheffield and Manchester, and active radical groups in many other towns, including Leeds, Derby, Nottingham, Stockport, Leicester, Birmingham, Newcastle, Edinburgh, Stirling, and Dundee. Most of their members were artisans and tradesmen, with leavening and sometimes leadership from the better-off. Their central demands were usually reform of parliament and manhood suffrage, and although among them there was much talk of 'the rights of man', few followed Tom Paine into outright republicanism. The claim most commonly asserted was, as the Sheffield reformers put it, 'equality of rights, in which is included equality of representation' – but what those same Sheffield men went on to say is sharply to the point and underlines the very *un*revolutionary egalitarianism of most of the radical groups of this decade. 'We are not speaking', they declared, 'of that visionary equality of property ... which would desolate the world and replunge it into the darkest and wildest barbarism.'[16] Even some of those men regarded by the government as highly dangerous, like John Thelwall, argued that any attack on private property would only produce anarchy. It was Thelwall, together with three other prominent radicals, Hardy of the London Corresponding Society, Thomas Holcroft, and (the ex-Rev.) John Horne Tooke, who in 1794 provided British justice with one of its most significant victories. Arraigned for high treason, they were triumphantly acquitted by their London jury, to the discomfiture of Pitt's ministers, to loud rejoicing in the streets of London and Westminster, and to the considerable pleasure both of Fox and of one of his ablest and most eloquent followers, Thomas Erskine, who had been counsel for the defence.

Fox was painfully aware that to oppose *in parliament alone* the two bills outlawing 'seditious' meetings and 'treasonable' practices was bound to be inadequate. He wrote to his nephew:

> We have opposed as strenuously as we are able, though with very small numbers ... I am convinced that in a very few years this government will become completely absolute ... We are to have a meeting in Westminster Hall tomorrow, where the Duke of Bedford is to move a petition; I hope and believe, we shall avoid riot. Do not be angry with me for saying, Why

is not Henry here? Can he deceive himself to such a degree as not to know that he ought not to be a *spectator* of the struggles that are likely to ensue?

The meeting was held, not in Westminster Hall, but in nearby Palace Yard, and it is a touch ironical that the minister responsible for policing and ensuring good order was Fox's admirer and former ally – now Home Secretary – the Duke of Portland. His routine report to the King was able to say that 'an appearance of good humour prevailed generally', and that after an hour had passed without disturbance, he had thought it well to send his military detachment, on hand as a precaution, home to barracks.

Fox expressed satisfaction, and perhaps relief, that at least in Westminster, and perhaps 'universally among the lower classes' he seemed to have kept his popularity; and this feeling was confirmed when in the general election a few months later he comfortably headed the Westminster poll. In the time-honoured ritual, he was then 'chaired' aloft to Devonshire House in Piccadilly. The amount of dissent and rowdiness on the occasion hardly exceeded the normal, only a few windows and the triumphal chair suffering damage, and Fox begged his supporters, 'for his sake and their honour', to disperse in peace, which it seems they did.[17]

Regularly during consecutive Februaries in the 1790s, Wilberforce introduced resolutions in the Commons for banning the trade in black slaves, either completely or within prescribed limitation, and on each occasion Fox spoke strongly in support.[18] The 1793 and 1794 proposals were both defeated, but the 1795 measure for prohibiting the sale of slaves to *foreign* countries managed to pass the Commons only to be rejected by the Lords. Then in 1796, to Fox's surprise, the House again passed Wilberforce's annual resolution, this time in a bill proposing complete abolition, though 'at a time to be limited'. In the summary of all Fox's Commons speeches published after his death, both he and Pitt are described as on this occasion supporting Wilberforce 'with much eloquence and ardour', but in Fox's own version of the day's proceedings it is noticeable that the rare good word he spares for Pitt has to be qualified, if not indeed quite outweighed, by a couple of accompanying ungenerous ones. He writes:

> I was yesterday in an unexpected majority upon the Slave Trade, 93 to 67 for bringing the Bill, but I fear we shall do no good, for though Pitt spoke very well, I cannot think him in earnest, as Dundas took so eager a part on the other side. What a rogue Pitt is! It is quite unpleasant to think that a man with such parts should be so totally devoid, as he seems to me, of right feelings.[19]

Although the campaign to ban the slave trade was here enjoying a momentary glimpse of reward, full success had still to wait for another ten years, and the eventual abolition of slavery itself (within the British Empire) another quarter-century after that.

In terms of Commons votes or, in general, of public opinion (away from such havens of Foxite loyalty as the constituency of Westminster), the political outlook of the Whig parliamentary opposition appeared by the beginning of 1797 to be without hope, either immediately or even in the medium term. As Fox had already admitted to Holland, 'We, as a party, I fear, can do nothing'. He saw himself and his group of friends caught between the Scylla of what he insisted on calling 'the Court' (that is, the ministry) and the Charybdis of the radicals. The contest, he wrote,

> must be between the Court and the Democrats. These last, without our assistance, will be either too weak to resist the Court ... or, if they are strong enough, being wholly unmixed with any aristocratic leaven, and full of resentment against us for not joining them, will go probably to greater excesses, and bring on the only state of things which can make a man doubt whether the despotism of monarchy is the worst of all evils.[20]

These pessimistic reflections led him once again to consider a parliamentary tactic with which he had toyed twice before, first in 1793 and then in 1795 – non-attendance. In 1795 he had eventually rejected this, as 'the measure a shabby fellow would take in our circumstances'. But now, although his close associates Fitzpatrick and Guilford were still opposed to secession, others such as Bedford, Lauderdale, Erskine, and Whitbread advocated it, and Fox, with the consolations of his Surrey garden and his study beckoning, did not find it too hard to go along with them. What the Whig leaders agreed between them was that in the Lords the Duke of Bedford should move 'On the State of the Nation', while in the Commons Grey should table a motion for parliamentary reform. During each debate the Whigs were to announce their withdrawal.

This decision to secede came, as it happened, at a time of serious national crisis. Bonaparte, after his triumphant Italian campaign of 1796–7, had turned his energies towards England and Ireland; and although the immense difficulties in the way of a successful invasion caused him eventually to postpone the project and to undertake instead the conquest of Egypt, the hour was emphatically not propitious for politicians to be absent from parliament, and to be seen as guilty of a lack of patriotism. In 1797, not only were there naval mutinies at the Nore and Spithead, but in Ireland too the chronically and violently disturbed situation was sliding into turmoil and confusion, towards what was shortly to become open and bloody rebellion. Fox's enemies in the press were quick to attack him now with very damaging charges alleging anti-patriotism and revolutionary leanings. The *Times* for instance, during May, while it conceded both brilliance and reasonableness to his speech supporting Grey's motion for parliamentary reform (in which he foreshadowed secession) flatly accused him of inciting rebellion in Ireland and mutiny in the navy. If he persisted, the paper said, he would 'lead a revolution'; if he desisted, he would be paying tacit homage to a ministry he constantly reviled.

One of Fox's last major speeches before he retired self-rusticated to St Anne's Hill was addressed to the looming dangers of the Irish situation. In March 1797 he had introduced a motion in the House asking his Majesty to 'be graciously pleased ... to adopt such healing and lenient measures ... best calculated to restore tranquillity, and to conciliate the affections of all descriptions of his Majesty's subjects'. Fifteen years before, under the Rockingham administration, it was Fox who had been responsible for piloting through the Commons the measure giving legislative independence to the Dublin parliament. He had hoped – indeed, had assumed altogether too easily – that the 'healing' effect of that move would have done enough permanently to appease the Irish. It had not. It had left the Protestant establishment still ruling the executive roost in Dublin Castle, and the Protestant minority still in control of parliament. Many of the old discriminatory laws had gone, and Pitt had enfranchised some of the Catholics; but no Catholic yet had the right to sit in parliament or hold major office in the country.

Fox's friend Fitzwilliam (he still regarded him very much as a friend despite his defection to Pitt) had in 1795 been sent as Lord Lieutenant to Ireland; when there he had indicated a clear intention to advance further Catholic emancipation; but had then been disowned and summarily recalled by Pitt in March of that year. 'See what has happened', said Fox in his speech of 1797; 'the hopes of the people have been disappointed, the cup ... having been dashed from their lips'. What then ought to be done? he asked. 'I would concede', he said, quoting at some length the parallel of Burke's great speech of 1775 on conciliating the Americans; 'and if I found I had not conceded enough, I would concede more':

I know no way of governing mankind but by conciliating them ... I will

therefore adopt the Irish expression, and say that you can only govern
Ireland by letting her have her own way ... What is she now? Little more
than a diversion for the enemy. If you keep Ireland by force now, what must
you do in all future wars? You must in the first place secure her from
insurrection ... The consequences of a war with Ireland are dreadful to
contemplate; public horrors would be so increased by the laceration of private
feelings as to spread universal misery through both countries. My wish is
that the whole people of Ireland should have the same principles, the same
system, the same operation of government and, though it may be a
subordinate consideration, that all classes should have an equal chance of
emolument; in other words, I would have the whole Irish government
regulated by Irish notions and Irish prejudices. [Only thus] will she be bound
to English interests ...[21]

When, in 1798 Ireland became submerged under all manner of evil —
hardship, murder, rebellion, atrocity, counter-atrocity — Fox was already
an absentee from parliament. The 'laceration of private feelings' which he
had warned of, though it did not deeply affect him personally, did however
bring grief and tragedy to the Lennox-Richmond side of his family. Emily
(*née* Lennox), Duchess of Leinster, was one of his mother's younger sisters,
and it was one of her sons, Lord Edward Fitzgerald, Fox's cousin, who
joined the 'United Irishmen' and became one of the leaders of the rebellion.
He was wounded while resisting arrest and made prisoner. While he was
awaiting trial, his distraught family, aghast at the prospect of his being
hanged as a traitor, understandably explored every available avenue of
influence, at least to ensure him a fair trial. To that end his uncle the Duke
of Richmond even secured an audience with the King. The Prince of Wales
was among those approached and, naturally, Fox also. Both Fox and the
Prince, however, felt bound to offer a similar response, suggesting that
their intervention, given their political stance, might militate against rather
than in favour of the prisoner. Despite this, said Fox, he stood ready to
come over to Dublin for the trial.

Edward Fitzgerald, handsome, romantic, idealistic, and rash, had been
one of the republican patriots who in 1796 had gone secretly abroad to
concert plans for a French invasion of Ireland — which was indeed undertaken that December, and then aborted by the 'Protestant wind' blowing
in Bantry Bay. Although after his capture in 1798 Fitzgerald was well
treated in prison, he died there (wounded, with fever supervening) before
his trial could begin. Another Irishman who sought Fox's help that year
was Arthur O'Connor, also a United Irishman. He had been arrested, with
others, at Margate, on the way to France; and at his trial he succeeded in

summoning the principal Whig leaders, including Erskine, Norfolk, Sheridan, Whitbread, and Fox, to testify to his character. 'I earnestly hope ... they have got nothing against him', Fox wrote to Fitzpatrick; and the Maidstone jury (Fox had wished it could be a London one) did acquit him, though one of his fellow prisoners, a priest, was hanged. O'Connor, re-arrested on a fresh charge, was in the end freed on condition that he lived in future abroad. It was generally thought that he had been lucky to escape, and the ministerial press made much of the way in which Fox and his colleagues, as they said, had been duped.

Although party tactics now called for secession, Fox did very occasionally attend the House over the next, nearly three, years. He was there at the turn of the year 1797–8 and spoke at length against Pitt's unpopular Assessed Taxes Bill (on inhabited houses, windows, male servants, horses, and carriages). We are told that in the debate on this measure on 14 December, 'when Mr Fox passed through the lobby of the House, which was full of strangers, there was a great burst of applause and clapping of hands ... Every one on the gallery rose as with one impulse'.[22] Then again he was as usual present when in April Wilberforce once more moved his yearly resolution concerning the slave trade. But he did not attend at all during 1799, and was to take no further part in the affairs of the House until February 1800.

Self-exiled from the Commons and happy to lead the life of a man of letters, scholar, and country gentleman, nevertheless he could hardly be altogether an absentee from Westminster and the world of politics. He would sometimes attend meetings of the Whig Club. Moreover he now enjoyed the privilege, as a national institution, of having his birthday celebrated in the finest possible style at a grand public dinner; and it was the 1798 occasion of this which produced some complicated consequences not bargained for by its organizers. On 24 January, at the Crown and Anchor Tavern, before a very large company, he was present to hear the ninth Duke of Norfolk, 'jockey Norfolk', give the chief toast of the evening:

> We are met in a moment of most serious difficulty to celebrate the birth of a man dear to the friends of freedom. I shall only recall to your memory that not twenty years ago the illustrious George Washington had not more than two thousand men to rally round him when his country was attacked. America is now free. This day full two thousand men are assembled in this place. I leave to you to make the application ...[23]

Unluckily for him, the Duke did not stop there. Replying later to a toast offered to *him*, he said, 'Give me leave, before I sit down, to call on you to drink our sovereign's health, *the Majesty of the People'*. During that same evening, the strongly radical Horne Tooke, with whom the more moderate Fox had often differed and whom he personally disliked, seized the occasion to declare that he and Fox were as one. Upon these birthday sentiments and junketings Pitt's private comments were that Norfolk's speech was 'not much short of treason', while Horne Tooke's public profession of 'reconciliation and coalition' with Fox gave excellent grounds for, he thought, ministerial satisfaction.[24] But officially also, as prime minister, he wrote to the King, taking

> the liberty of submitting humbly to your Majesty the expediency at the present moment of marking the sense entertained of the Duke of Norfolk's conduct ... by dismissing him from the Lieutenancy of the West Riding of Yorkshire, and [Mr Pitt] has no doubt that such a measure is expected by all the zealous friends of the Constitution, and would give general satisfaction.

Norfolk was immediately removed, both from the Lord Lieutenancy* and from the colonelcy of the West Riding militia, whereupon his friend Fox wrote him a letter of warm and indignant sympathy:

> ... The ministers call for unanimity, for suspension of party disputes for the purpose of repelling a foreign enemy, and then they dismiss your Grace from not only a Lieutenancy, but a Regiment, for an opinion ... which to have controverted in the times of the first two Georges would have been deemed a symptom of disaffection.

Then Fox too went a step further, as Norfolk had on the festive evening. At a Whig Club dinner he made a point of repeating the Duke's offence: after a speech containing praises of the Glorious Revolution of 1688 he proposed the toast, *'Our Sovereign the People'*. So, for a second time, Pitt 'and such of your Majesty's servants as Mr Pitt has as yet had an opportunity of consulting' requested the King to take some suitable punitive step. Various possible ideas for such a move had been going through Pitt's mind – ordering Fox to attend parliament; 'if he disavows, prosecuting the printer; if he avows, ordering him to be reprimanded'; if he offered 'a fresh insult', sending him to the Tower for the remainder of

---

*Three times during the reign of George III, the West Riding Lord Lieutenant was made to pay for uttering not-to-be-forgiven indiscretions. In 1762 Lord Rockingham was dismissed for his hostility to the peace preliminaries of that year. In 1798 it was the turn of the Duke of Norfolk, who was replaced by Earl Fitzwilliam. Then in 1819 Fitzwilliam himself suffered removal, for his condemnation of the 'Peterloo massacre' and his support for a Yorkshire protest meeting.

the session. Prosecuting him in the courts would probably backfire, since a London jury would acquit him. In the end therefore Mr Pitt humbly submitted to the King 'the propriety of directing tomorrow that Mr Fox's name should be erased from the list of Privy Counsellors'. With this suggestion from his prime minister the King 'entirely coincided', and proceeded himself to draw a line through Fox's name, not perhaps without quiet satisfaction.[25]

Only exceptional circumstances over these years were able to draw Fox back from St Anne's Hill to the House of Commons. Throughout 1799 he contented himself, apart from sometimes attending the Whig Club, with acting as political mentor to the 'Young One', Lord Holland, now returned from his long European tour and beginning to take part in House of Lords debates. Thus Fox's opinions, which were critically hostile, on Pitt's radical innovation of a wartime tax on incomes or his proposal for an Irish Union (which meant effectively bribing or bludgeoning the Dublin parliament to commit suicide) were neither to be heard in the House of Commons nor to be read in the public prints. They may be found chiefly as occasional paragraphs among his letters to his nephew, interspersed with disquisitions on Pope's *Essay on Criticism* and *Rape of the Lock*, on Chaucer's *Clerk's Tale* (he had been reading it to his wife – 'what a genius Chaucer was!'), on various of the tragedies of Euripides (*Medea*, *Heraclidae*, and *Alcestis*, yes, and indeed almost any of his plays rather than *Hippolytus*), on *Don Quixote*, on the *Conquista di Granada* by Graziani, on *The History of Scotland*, by Laing, et cetera, et cetera – and of course there was always Homer, especially the *Odyssey*, 'the most charming reading of all'.

Some years after this, when 'Young One' had almost reached the mature age of 30, we still find Fox writing to him in his best avuncular-tutorial vein: 'What can you mean by saying there is little good of the new poetry in Cowper? What, not the triplets to Mary, not the "Shipwreck" or "Outcast"?* Pray read them over again, and repeat your former judgement if you dare.'

But in February 1800 the re-emerging issue of peace or war did drag Fox back to the House; just how very reluctantly, Lord Holland indicates in a passage of his memoirs which surely says something, trivial perhaps

---

* This must refer to the verses now known as *The Castaway*, nearly the last, probably the finest, and certainly the most tragically moving of Cowper's poems:

We perish'd, each alone,
But I beneath a rougher sea
And whelm'd in deeper gulphs than he.

but eye-opening, about his uncle's character and nature. Stressing how loath Fox had been to leave St Anne's Hill, Holland writes that his uncle

> stipulated for remaining at Holland House only two nights, and, when he heard that the debate was postponed in consequence of Mr Pitt's indisposition, sat silent and overcome, as if the intelligence of some great calamity had reached his ears. I saw tears steal down his cheeks, so vexed was he at being detained from his garden, his books, and his cheerful life in the country.[26]

The subject of the debate was the immediate British rejection of a sudden peace offer which in January had arrived from France in the form of a 'personal' overture to George III from Bonaparte, who had recently become First Consul, following the Brumaire *coup d'état*. Peace at that moment would have suited his book well, before Pitt could complete diplomatic negotiations for a second anti-French coalition. After Bonaparte's early triumphs, French military fortunes had recently slumped. French armies had been defeated in North Italy. Bonaparte's Egyptian and Syrian campaigns, again after brilliant success, had been left stranded when Nelson shattered the French fleet and thus the victorious army's lines of communication. The invasion of Ireland had been judged altogether too risky. It was a time for both the French and the British to pause for breath. It was just this idea of a mere *pause* in the fighting (Dundas had so referred to it) which Fox was to pounce on, and make such bitter play with towards the end of his speech.

When on 3 February 1800 he rose in the House, he first apologized for subjecting members of the House, 'at so late an hour of the night', to what they must have known was to be a speech of some weight. Although beginning so late, it nevertheless occupies thirty-eight pages in the published version; and it also happens to be, of all Fox's speeches, one of the most realistically reported. The printed text, for once, gives a good impression of what is generally agreed to have been Fox's characteristic style – all spontaneity and impetuosity, without the studied and ordered periods of, for instance, Chatham or Burke or the younger Pitt. He had been speaking for several hours before he arrived at his peroration:

> Where then, Sir, is this war, which on every side is pregnant with such horrors, to be carried? Where is it to stop? Not till you establish the house of Bourbon! And this you cherish the hope of doing because you have had a successful campaign. Why, Sir, before this you have had a successful campaign ... One campaign is successful to you – another to them; and in this way ... you may go on for ever ... And all this because you may gain a better peace a year or two hence ... We must keep Bonaparte for some time longer at war, as a

state of probation. Gracious God, Sir, is war a state of probation? is peace a
rash system? Is it dangerous for nations to live in amity with each other? ...
'But we must *pause*'. What! must the bowels of Great Britain be torn out –
her best blood be spilt,– her treasure wasted – that you may make an
experiment? Put yourselves – oh! that you would put yourselves – in the
field of battle, and learn to judge of the sort of horrors that you excite. In
former wars a man might, a least, have some feeling, some interest, that
served to balance in his mind the impressions which a scene of carnage and
of death must inflict. If a man had been present at the battle of Blenheim, for
instance, and had inquired the motive of the battle, there was not a soldier
engaged who could not have satisfied his curiosity, and even, perhaps,
allayed his feelings – they were fighting to repress the uncontrolled ambition
of the *grand monarque*. But, if a man were present now at a field of slaughter,
and were to inquire for what they were fighting – 'Fighting!' would be the
answer; 'they are not fighting, they are pausing.' 'Why is that man expiring?
Why is that other writhing in agony? What means this implacable fury?' The
answer must be, 'You are quite wrong, Sir, you deceive yourself – They are
not fighting – Do not disturb them – they are merely *pausing*! – this man is
not expiring with agony – that man is not dead – he is only pausing! Lord
help you Sir! they are not angry with one another; they have now no cause
of quarrel – but their country thinks that there should be a pause. All that you
see, Sir, is nothing like fighting – there is no harm, nor cruelty, nor bloodshed
in it whatever – it is nothing more than *a political pause*! It is merely to try
an experiment – to see whether Bonaparte will not behave himself better than
heretofore; and in the mean time we have agreed to a pause, in pure
friendship!' And is this the way, Sir, that you are to shew yourselves the
advocates of order? You take up a system calculated to uncivilize the world,
to destroy order, to trample on religion, to stifle in the heart, not merely the
generosity of noble sentiment, but the affections of social nature; and in the
prosecution of this system, you spread terror and devastation all around
you ...[27]

He sat down at 3.30 a.m., and wryly declared at a Whig Club meeting
next day, that perhaps as many as *three* members might have changed
their voting intentions as a result of his speech. The division had been 104
to 265 – yet, he felt sure, he had 'spoken the sense of the country'. It was
to be regretted that 'the active power of the constitution was gone', since
parliament no longer 'responded to public opinion'. He therefore claimed
to see no purpose in attending further debates, and proposed to continue
secession for as long as Pitt's position seemed so impregnable.

14

PEACE OF AMIENS,
FRENCH VISIT,
WAR AGAIN

There were other things to do. For example, he had recently revived a project he had played with earlier, a history of the reign of his great-great-uncle James II and of the events leading to and following the Glorious Revolution. But he soon ran up against the prime difficulty of the honest amateur historian. How was he to avoid merely repeating earlier authors without first checking their sources? There were family memories too at the back of his mind which needed looking into, for instance something which his great-grandmother the Duchess of Portsmouth was said to have said about the political intentions of Charles II just before his death. Where was he to find the truth about that? And then, earlier authors had quoted from a journal kept by the Duke of Monmouth – but where could he find the journal itself? And how could he trust the published histories of Hume and Rapin until he could find where these writers drew their facts from, 'in regard to the Popish and Ryehouse plots particularly'? Could Lauderdale help him, even perhaps in some matters act as research assistant? Perhaps also direct him eventually to a suitable publisher?

He made only slow progress. First, he said, it was 'the speaking season', and then in the autumn the shooting season – again with Coke and the company at Holkham – which interrupted the flow of the work. He did manage in that year 1800 to complete an Introduction; but, he lamented, 'I am the slowest writer that ever took pen in hand'. He persisted however, and would be occupied with his project for a long time yet.

He had been working on his *Reign of James the Second* for about a year when he was obliged to confess, 'Whether my attempt will ever come to anything, I know not; but, whether it does or not, I shall grudge very much the time it takes away from my attention to poetry and ancient literature, which are studies far more suitable to my taste'.[1] This was written to a distinguished classical scholar, the Rev. Gilbert Wakefield, then serving a term of two years imprisonment in Dorchester Jail for writing what had been judged a seditious pamphlet. Wakefield had dedicated his 'magnificent and beautiful' new edition of Lucretius to Fox, 'one whom I love and reverence' – and there ensued a long and remarkable exchange of letters, not quite completely preserved but still occupying nearly 150 pages of the Fox *Memorials and Correspondence.*[2] The discussion between the two men was not on Lucretius alone, but covered a host of authors both Greek and Roman, some well known (for instance, Ovid, Cicero, Seneca, Pindar, Homer, Sophocles, Euripides), some to the modern world deeply obscure (Lycophron, Apollonius Rhodius, Diogenes Laertius, Tryphiodorus, Nicander, etc., etc.).

Wakefield and Fox expound and exchange their enthusiasms, dislikes, and pedantries at great length. Sometimes Fox appears to be content to stay *in statu pupillari*, but often jumps eagerly into the academic argument. Each clearly had the utmost respect for the other. When in September 1799 Wakefield, only half-way through his prison sentence, learned that Fox had suffered a shooting accident – his gun had burst in his hand – the Reverend jailbird, who disapproved of killing animals for pleasure, judged it proper to read the sportsman-politician-scholar a 'respectful', learned, mildly censorious lecture, complete naturally with an eight-line quotation from Cicero:

> Am I, Sir, indecently presumptuous and free, am I guilty of a too dictatorial officiousness, in pronouncing *those pleasures to misbecome a man of letters* [translating here from the Cicero quotation] which consist in mangling, maiming, and depriving of ... its existence, an inoffensive pensioner on the universal bounties of the Common Feeder and Protector of all his offspring?

Fox replied that if one was allowed without offence to kill *tame* animals such as domestic fowl or oxen, surely to kill *wild* animals ought to be permissible.

> But then to make a *pastime* of it – I am aware there is someting to be said on this point. On the other hand ... there is nothing in which all mankind, civilised or savage, have more agreed, than in making some form of chace (for fishing is of the same nature) part of their business or amusement. However, I admit it to be a very questionable subject; at all events, it is a

very pleasant and healthful exercise. My wound goes on, I believe, very well ...[3]

It was in 1798, about a year after the Whigs had first determined to absent themselves from parliament, that Fox took on as private secretary the nephew of the Bishop of Down, a certain John Trotter, who was still to be in his service eight years later, at the time of Fox's death. Trotter soon acquired an intense admiration, indeed a degree of lyrical adulation, for his employer, which was so thoroughly to impregnate his political and personal judgements, as well as his prose style, that it does not always do to take him too literally or seriously. But the recorded first impressions of St Anne's Hill upon this 'mind of sensibility' fall pleasantly enough upon the ear:

> When I first visited St Anne's Hill, the summer was yet young, and all the freshness of nature was on that beautiful spot: its sloping glades were unparched by autumnal suns – the flowers and shrubs were redolent with sweets, and the choir full of birds, which burst from every tree and shady recess, filled the heart with gladness, and with that reviving sentiment of pleasure which at that period is felt by minds of sensibility. The rich expanse of cultivated country; the meadows, corn, woods, and villages, till the sight caught the far distant smoke of London; the graceful Thames, winding below that hill ... gave a magical, but not delusive, effect to all I saw ...
> The house is embowered in trees, resting on the side of a hill; its grounds declining gracefully to a road, which bounds them at bottom. Some fine trees are grouped round the house, and three remarkably beautiful ones stand on the lawn ... The simplicity and benignity of [Mr Fox's] manners, speaking with the integrity and grandeur of his character, soon dispelled the feelings of awe which one naturally experiences ...[4]

In these *Memoirs* of John Trotter there is much of this *Et ego in Arcadia*, but his is not an isolated voice, and there is plenty of evidence, both from visitors to St Anne's Hill and from Fox himself, that the place was for him indeed a little private piece of Arcadia. It is Trotter who gives us an idea of the St Anne's Hill regime. Mr Fox, he writes, in summer

> rose between six and seven; in winter before eight. After breakfast he usually read some Italian author with Mrs Fox, and then spent the time preceding dinner at his literary studies, in which the Greek poets bore a principal part. A frugal but plentiful dinner took place at three, or at half past two in summer, and four in winter; and a few glasses of wine were followed by coffee. The evening was dedicated to walking and conversation till tea-time, when reading aloud, in history, commenced, and continued till near ten. A light supper of fruit, pastry, or something very trifling finished the day; and at half past ten the family were gone to rest.[5]

It was a world away from Newmarket—The House of Commons—Brooks's and £5,000 won or lost, all within the twenty-four hours.

Pitt's Act of Union became operative from 1 January 1801. He had always intended, and all but promised the Irish Catholics, that it would be closely followed by a further measure to complete the remaining stages of emancipation. However, when the King saw that this was now seriously intended, his alarm was intense. He begged Mr Speaker Addington to try his powers of dissuasion, and then wrote to Pitt offering, if only he would 'stave off' the Catholic question, to 'be silent' on the subject, 'from affection to Mr Pitt'. But further than this he would not go, for that would mean the betrayal of the coronation oath by which he had sworn to safeguard the Protestant religion. Pitt's situation was thus rendered untenable. Putting up no resistance on behalf of the Catholics, he resigned, and strongly advised Addington to accept the premiership when the King offered it to him. Warmly embracing his new prime minister on 10 February, George declared 'My dear Addington, you have saved your country'.

Less than a week later, George III, now in his sixty-third year and having been for the past twelve years in good health, was struck down by a recurrence of his old affliction, porphyria. As in the early stages of the 1788 attack, it was thought very possible that he might be on the brink of death. There were all the old symptoms: uncontrollable hurry in speech, intolerable nervous tension, intestinal attacks, wandering wits, periods of high fever and delirium, with intermissions of complete lucidity when it was the *fear* of returning madness which tormented him. The duration of the acutest danger was shorter now than in 1788–9, although for many weeks into the spring and early summer George remained weak, irritable, occasionally feverish and unaccountable in behaviour; his nerves still taut; prone to bursts of sudden tears.

All Fox's information concerning the King's condition arrived at St Anne's Hill at second or third hand, most of it faulty or garbled, but he was content to remain, physically at least, aloof from the centre of events. He would not repeat his mistakes of 1788–9, and was relieved to learn that there was no question of a second regency crisis. The Prince of Wales was, for once, behaving impeccably, accepting without demur the arrangements proposed in Pitt's bill of 1789, complete with its restrictions. But the sudden change of ministry in February 1801 had certainly put Fox in a quandary. That Pitt was *out* was in itself satisfactory enough. As he wrote to Grey, 'Pitt was a bad minister; he is out – I am glad'. However, he would not go to town while Addington's ministry was in the process of being put together, for, he said, 'I am sure my going at such a time would be subject to imputations and sneers'. He had never before felt so strongly that he needed counsel. He therefore consulted his oldest ally, Fitzpatrick, and then Grey, and Bedford, and Lauderdale, and – of course in a somewhat different sense – Mrs A., as he was still calling her in letters even to his closest friends. ('Mrs A. makes me write this', he tells Fitzpatrick, 'because she knows how very helpless I am in difficult circumstances without advice.')[6]

The trouble was, he could get little hard news. What was coming to him was rumour. The King was mad, but *how* mad? 'There is every reason to think', he wrote, 'that if he is not again violent, he will sink into perfect imbecility ... But this is all guess.' However, once the King's life was no longer in danger and Addington's administration was solidly in place, it was more than ever certain that there was not the slightest chance of Fox being involved in any new 'arrangement'. 'You may be sure,' he had said when Addington was first called on, 'the new ministry is quite one to [the King's] heart's content.' He told his friends now that only if 'the Catholic question' was brought forward would he feel bound to attend the Commons; but in fact that particular matter had just been emphatically shelved, after Pitt (being told that the King had charged him with responsibility for bringing on his illness) sent to the convalescing invalid his famous message, promising never again to 'agitate the Catholic question', whether in or out of office. On the whole, Fox considered and advised that the Whigs should continue to lie low. His instinct, he said, was 'very strong indeed for forbearance; I shall by no means urge any one to action'. All the same, once and once only he put in an appearance at Westminster, making a lengthy and weighty speech in support of Grey's 'state of the nation' motion on 25 March.[7] But, as he wrote to Grey a little later, did it all much matter? 'According to my notion the constitution of the country is declining so rapidly that the House of Commons ... will shortly entirely cease to be a place of much importance.'[8]

Fox's intervention in the 25 March debate concentrated naturally enough on the government's war policy. Although Nelson had won another spectacular success, shattering, off Copenhagen, the fleet of the Armed Neutrality of the North, the general European picture was now gloomy. French armies under Moreau and Bonaparte had won great triumphs, and Austria had been humbled by the Treaty of Lunéville. Bonaparte's own share in these achievements was certainly large, though hardly as all-important as his propaganda had trumpeted abroad. Moreau's decisive victory at Hohenlinden had been somewhat put in the shade by the First Consul's own massive success at Marengo. This had followed his crossing of the Alps to relieve Masséna, who had become dangerously hemmed in at Genoa, and was in fact made possible largely by the skill and resource of his subordinate commanders Desaix and Kellermann, who on that day in June 1800 rescued him from disaster. Even Bonaparte's much glorified crossing of the Alps to reach Marengo was, in sober fact, made on muleback three days behind his main forces, not at all in the romantically heroic style of David's famous painting. However, the great French victories *were* won, and the European anti-French coalition *was* effectively destroyed. Fox in 1801 showed himself as ready to credit a larger-than-life portrayal of Bonaparte the military magician, as he had been in 1789 to accept the deluge of revolutionary publicity (again, inventive, romanticized, and largely mendacious) which followed the storming of the Bastille.[9] In the debate of 25 March a government speaker had made the point that the entire European situation would have appeared crucially different if Bonaparte had *lost* the battle of Marengo. '*If* the battle of Marengo had been lost', Fox taunted:

> '*But*' – '*If*' – Why, Sir, I do not know what degree of fortune there may be in this battle or that; but I believe the right honourable gentleman never was more mistaken than he would find himself, even in the event of Bonaparte's defeat at Marengo. Such were the precautions of that fruitful mind; so well did he arrange his measures; so little did he, in truth, trust to mere fortune, that if, against all probability, Marengo had been lost, that mighty genius had so disposed his resources that many a bloody battle must have been gained by his enemies before they could have made much impression upon the incomparable system of his operations in Italy last summer.[10]

Now that there was again a chance of serious peace negotiations being started, Fox wrote, 'Bonaparte's triumph is now complete indeed; and since there is to be no political liberty in the world, I really believe he is the fittest person to be the master'.[11]

What was to prove only a temporary end to the war, indeed little more than the 'pause' Fox had recently derided, came within reach by December 1801, when the preliminaries of what was to become the Treaty of Amiens were agreed. Fox continued to keep his distance from Westminster, but he did consult fairly regularly with, in particular, his colleagues Grey and Lauderdale. But in May 1802 we find him writing to his chief lieutenant, Grey, rather more as personal friend and fellow-gardener-countryman than as committed politician. (Grey, like Fox, was often away from the centre of political activities, in his case up at his Northumbrian seat.)

> The frost here [Fox writes] has done, I am afraid, a great deal of mischief. It was very well I did not go to town for the debate, as I should exceedingly have disliked to have been kept the two days. I hear Sheridan did very well; perhaps it was rather shabby in me to be absent, but I do not care ... All opposition seems to be out of the question, perhaps for ever; and we may boast, I expect, that we were the last of the Romans.

Then, a little later:

> I shall be in town on Tuesday, for the Whig Club, and stay for Belgrave's motion ... Though rather cold out of the sun, it is a delightful day here: nightingales singing merrily, etc. Pray when all this nonsensical [parliamentary] business is over, give me a day or two here.

It was to Grey that he had written the previous spring: 'Mrs A's cold is still bad. She sends you a violet of a size which I much doubt if you can equal; and its sweetness is in proportion to its size.'[12]

The Treaty of Amiens was signed in March 1802, and peace – precarious, but still peace – was to reign for the next fourteen months. A number of the British aristocracy, starved of foreign travel during the preceding decade, now grasped the opportunity of visiting the land of their late and future enemy, and Fox was eager to be among them. When it was suggested that eyebrows would be raised at so eminent a public man travelling abroad in the company of his mistress, he now at last allowed the world to learn that she was in fact no longer his mistress, but that they had been man and wife for the past seven years. All Fox's friends were angry with him, if we are to credit Lady Bessborough (who had previously been herself the mistress of that other leading Whig, Sheridan): 'I cannot see anything but what I always knew of him', she wrote, '– that he is kindness and weakness itself to everything that he loves ... The odd thing is that people who were shock'd at the immorality of his having a mistress are still more so at that mistress having been his wife so long.'

Mr and Mrs Fox, with secretary Trotter, left St Anne's Hill for Dover on 29 July, made the three-hour crossing to Calais by packet, and then for the next month undertook a leisurely tour through Flanders and the Netherlands (all of it territory then under French control) before going south through Brussels to France proper – what Trotter calls 'old France'. Though observant of the exterior scene – town buildings, the condition of local farming, and so forth – the tourists still had long hours confined in their carriage, when Trotter, to keep their minds wakeful and lively, would read aloud from Fielding's *Joseph Andrews* and *Tom Jones*, and also drink in Fox's views on that excellent author. He would even occasionally venture an opinion of his own, though always as pupil to tutor, disciple to sage, ready to be instructed or corrected. Apart from Fielding, there were the *Aeneid*, the *Iliad*, the *Odyssey*, and, inevitably, Ariosto (*Orlando Furioso*), all of which came under discussion *en route*, Trotter proving always a willing listener, athirst for improvement. *Tom Jones* is a long book, but Trotter tells us that they managed to finish it just before arriving at Paris towards the end of August. Fox had not only been an enthralling conversationalist; throughout their travels, he had been 'easy, affable, and cheerful'; adept at surmounting all 'the little obstacles, disappointments, and unpleasantnesses'; always moreover consulting in everything Mrs Fox's comfort and convenience.

In Paris they lodged at the Hotel Richelieu, and the Foxes were soon exchanging gossip and travellers' tales with friends and relations, who like them had been released from years of imposed insularity. If the French had failed to invade England, the English had clearly succeeded in occupying Paris. Among the visitors were Richard Fitzpatrick, James Hare, Robert Spencer, Thomas Erskine, Robert Adair, and 'Young One' Holland, now (like his uncle) married to his former mistress. Soon after their arrival Fox and his party visited the theatre for two of Racine's tragedies, *Andromaque*, and *Phèdre*, for the second of which Trotter tells us he prepared not only himself but Mrs Fox too, by reading aloud to her Euripides' drama on the same subject. It was at the performance of *Phèdre* that the audience recognized their English visitor and, again in Trotter's words:

> Every eye was fixed on him, and every tongue resounded Fox! Fox! The whole audience stood up, and the applause was universal. He alone ... was embarrassed ... So unwilling was Mr Fox to receive the applause as personal, that he could not be prevailed upon to stand forward ... No man had ever less vanity.

There is corroboration from James Hare for this reticence in acknowledging applause or praise. Fox, says Hare, was 'reckon'd very proud [in France] from not being delighted with the fine speeches made him, and only answering them by his little short bows, which look more like nods of approbation than anything else'. It is only when Trotter proceeds to tell us that Bonaparte was present also, but received an ovation 'much inferior to that bestowed on Mr Fox', that one remembers to allow just a little for the estimable author's hero-worship.

They visited the Louvre – Fox himself several times – with its 'fruits of conquest ... the choicest paintings of Italy, Germany, Flanders, and Holland ... a magnificent sight'. ('Of the pictures which Mr Fox most admired, his greatest favourite was the St Jerome of Domenichino.') Naturally the 'cumbrous pile' of Versailles, that 'pride of despotism ... seemed little to suit Mr Fox's taste'. There was rather more to like among 'the gardens in the English manner' at the Petit Trianon, with its ruined cottage and grass-grown walk, and its mournful memories of Marie-Antoinette, a shepherdess among her rustics, playing out her romantic make-believe in that already distant age of *sensibilité*, a world later submerged under so much blood and savagery. The Petit Trianon itself, Trotter reports, had become a tavern.

There was of course much seeing of notables and being entertained by them. The Abbé Sieyès, for instance, political theorist and by then out-of-fashion revolutionary; 'Mr Fox seemed to consider him in a respectable light but to entertain no very high opinion of him'. There was Talleyrand, an old acquaintance, back from his exiled wanderings and now foreign minister. The Foxes dined with him and his wife and a company of some forty guests at, to an Englishman at least, the absurdly late hour of eight – but then Talleyrand had that afternoon been closeted with Bonaparte. Everything at the Talleyrands seemed to be in 'a profuse and elegant style'. Rather more excitingly, there was Lafayette, 'the virtuous and unshaken friend of liberty'. He and Fox, embracing, were both much affected by the emotion of meeting again, as indeed was Trotter also in observing them: 'Destined from their youth to be, in their respective countries, the protectors of the sacred cause of liberty, they had followed different paths, but each led to the same temple ... Their hearts were united, and the people's cause was to both like a polar star'.

There were many more of the great and the good and the not quite so good to pay respects to or be entertained by: Josephine Bonaparte ('Mr Fox seemed to think extremely well of her' and exchanged agreeable, largely botanical, conversation); Eugène Beauharnais, soon to be Viceroy of Italy; Kosciuszko, the exiled Polish patriot; Madame Récamier, the most admired beauty of the day (*déjeuner* at three o'clock); Madame Tallien, lovely and fascinating, Trotter considered, though 'on a large scale' – she was currently somewhat in disgrace, her extra-marital favours having been on a scale similarly large; the wealthy banker Périgaux; and a whole assembly of leading generals and marshals-to-be, including Masséna, the 'venerable circumnavigator' Bougainville, and Berthier, with whom he spent a day shooting. And then, of course, there was Bonaparte himself, on two occasions, the first at a rather over-formal reception, when Bonaparte delivered himself of a few apparently well-prepared compliments (he had learned them by heart, Lady Holland thought), the second altogether more *tête-à-tête*, with some serious exchange of political views: '*Il me combattait avec chaleur en son mauvais français*', Bonaparte said afterwards — though there were Frenchmen who considered his own Corsican accent *assez mauvais*. On his side Fox declined to allow Bonaparte to go unchallenged when he asserted that Windham and Pitt had promoted attempts to assassinate him. In home territory, Fox rarely showed magnanimity towards his great rival, but abroad he refused to hear him slandered. Madame Junot described another occasion when someone maligned Pitt, and suddenly Fox, 'changing colour', was transformed; no longer '*le chef de l'opposition*', but '*le frère de M. Pitt, le secourant au milieu d'un cercle de ses ennemis*'.[13]

Fox had gone to France for business as well as pleasure. He had been given permission to research among the diplomatic archives at the Quai d'Orsay and elsewhere for his history of the reign of James II. Hence, most days between eleven and three o'clock he worked through the relevant records, especially those relating to the financial negotiations transacted between James and Louis XIV's minister Barillon, and so discovered how 'the abject and narrow-minded James, thus degraded through his hatred to liberty, feared to involve himself too far, without ample funds in his possession' from the French treasury.[14] The foreign archivist was help-fulness itself, and Trotter was of course readily available too. We have at least *his* word for it that 'a mind such as that of Mr Fox' became 'wearied and disgusted by the examination of these papers', although 'the detestation of the mistakes and falsehoods of historians' did afford him some 'consolation for his labours'.[15] These were to be continued in future months, though only spasmodically, and the book was never completed. It is his history of the *early part* of James II's reign which was to be eventually published after his death, 'just as my angel would have done and as I wished', wrote Mrs Fox to Lord Holland, wistfully then recalling 'the dear angelic looks I used to get while employed in copying it'. In view of the author's 'disgust' at James II's conduct and the implied glorification of the revolution which dethroned him, Fox the historian may safely be seen as one of the early father-figures of the much debated 'Whig interpretation of history'.

Already, before the Foxes left Paris, there was a rumour current — 'but I cannot believe it', Fox wrote — that the fragile peace was in danger. He finished work on the archives by early October, and Trotter then went home. Fox and his wife remained for a further six weeks, returning via Calais and Dover – a crossing of four and a half hours. The last stage of the journey proved most troublesome, their carriage breaking down three miles out of Dover – 'a sad scrape indeed'. Finally on 17 November they reached 'dear dear home where we arrived about six, very very glad to be here and happy that my Liz bore all the fatigues of the journey so well'.[16]

The next day Fox wrote to Lauderdale. The war, he assured him, would not be resumed. '1st, I am sure that Bonaparte will do everything that he can to avoid it. 2nd, that low as my opinion is of our Ministry I can not believe them quite so foolish as to force him to it.' He was of course wrong, but the peace did have another six months to run; and perhaps in any case he was hardly as optimistic for peace prospects as such casual top-of-the-head remarks suggest. He knew that he would be accused in the ministerial press (as indeed he was) of being pro-French; caricatured too, as when Gillray pictured him as Citizen Volpone bowing and scraping before Bonaparte. But perhaps pro-governmental opinion was not altogether at fault here, for whereas Fox seemed sometimes rather easily to find extenuating circumstances for Bonaparte's offences and aggressions, or at least to play down their hostile significance to *British* interests, he was contemptuously merciless towards the incapacity, as he saw it, of the Addington government. This appears even more strongly in his private than his public remarks, and particularly in his correspondence with Grey, Holland and Lauderdale. 'I am more than ever convinced', he wrote to Grey, 'that, if it is war, it is entirely the fault of ministers, and not of Bonaparte.'[18] Again to Grey: 'You will see that we shall go to war, and be wrong in the opinion of all Europe.'[19] And he remained, in his own words, 'obstinate' in the opinion 'that Bonaparte's wish is peace – nay, that he is afraid of war to the last degree'. Admittedly, French aggression against Switzerland was 'odious', but why should it be regarded as 'insulting to *us*'? – still less as providing a *casus belli*. And in what way did the French incursion into north Italy affect *British* interests? Probably the clearest statement of Fox's position at this time comes in a letter to Grey written only about a month after his return from France:

> ... If we are driven to war, why then I say that if we are driven to it by the enemy, we must support, and support it in earnest; but if, which is far more likely, we are driven into it by the folly of our own government, we must support it also, but with a constant advice of negotiation and peace.[20]

Meanwhile, ministers should be 'holding language more decidedly pacific', and should evacuate Malta and Alexandria as they had undertaken to, by the terms of the Peace of Amiens. Since the signature of that treaty Bonaparte had declared himself President of the 'Cisalpine Republic', strengthened his position in Switzerland and western Germany, sent troops to San Domingo (Haiti), retained an army in the Netherlands, promoted an ambitious programme of naval construction, and demanded both the extradition from England of the Bourbon princes and the silencing of British newspaper libels upon him. The reply of the Addington ministry was to delay the promised evacuation of Malta.

There was no longer any talk from Fox of secession. He seemed to have returned from his working holiday reinvigorated, ready again for the political fray. Grey wrote to Mrs Grey: 'Fox seems in the highest spirits and is in the best looks. He is like a young man in the prime of life who has just married a girl of sixteen. Is it not a fine thing to grow young at fifty?' Thomas Creevey professed himself at this time 'perfectly astonished at the vigour of body, the energy of mind, the innocent playfulness and happiness of Fox', while some others of the old Whig 'gang' had 'the air of shattered debauchees', and Pitt, yellow-faced, looked *'done'*. Pitt had indeed been ill, at Bath with 'the gout' – though we need to remember that that expression in Georgian England is medically almost meaningless, providing a convenient umbrella description for any disease not otherwise diagnosable in its own right. Leigh Hunt, then in his childhood, later recalled seeing Fox at this time, 'fat and jovial, looking somewhat quaker-like as to dress, with plain-coloured clothes, a broad round hat, white waistcoat and, if I am not mistaken, white stockings', as he stood in Parliament Street 'making two young gentlemen laugh heartily at something which he seemed to be relating'.[21]

During the spring of 1803, France and Britain drifted towards war, and it became inevitable by the middle of May. Within a month, the French had occupied Hanover and the British St Lucia and Tobago. On 23 May, when the Commons debated the royal address upon the war's renewal, Pitt (taking up a position in the third row behind the government front bench)* decisively demonstrated how wrong Creevey had been in writing

---

*To divide Commons members sharply between 'Whigs' and 'Tories', or even between 'government' and 'opposition', is at this time – or indeed at most other times in Georgian Britain – simplistic and misleading. In 1803 Fox himself reckoned the state of the parties as follows: Foxites 69, Pittites 58, Grenvillites 36, the remainder ministerialist – or as Fox preferred to call them, the Court party.

him off, by delivering a speech of great force, ('one of the most brilliant and magnificent pieces of declamation', said Sheridan, 'that ever fell from that rascal Pitt's lips'),[22] supporting the need for the war's 'vigorous prosecution'. 'Pitt's speech ... was admired very much, and very justly', Fox wrote to his nephew. 'I dare say you have heard puffs enough of my speech ... so that I need not add my mite; but the truth is, that it was my best.'[23] And Mr Speaker Abbot's diary for 24 May reads: 'Mr Fox ... delivered a speech of more art, eloquence, wit, and mischief, than I ever remember to have heard from him'. It had been made in support of an amendment moved by Grey, concurring in pursuit of the war, but asking for 'every facility' to be afforded 'to any just arrangement' by which peace might be restored. It covered, at formidable length, the whole range of issues, military, colonial and diplomatic, territorial and moral, involved in the current Anglo-French quarrel, in language sober, measured, occasionally humorous, more often earnest, rarely (*pace* Abbot) mischievous. It distinguished carefully and extensively between areas of dispute which could reasonably justify war and those, much more numerous, which could not. As for possession of Malta,

> [A previous speaker, he said] had vindicated the expediency of the war, as it was for Malta; as it was not for Malta alone, but for Egypt; as it was not for Egypt alone, but for India; as it was not for India alone, but for the vital interests of Great Britain. Every one of these four propositions Mr Fox denied; he denied that Malta was worth a war by itself; he denied that Malta was worth it as essential to the security of Egypt; he denied that Egypt was essential to the security of India; he denied that our Indian possessions ... were essential to the vital interests of Great Britain.[24]

There had been a proposal that the Tsar should be asked to mediate on the Malta issue. Fox endorsed it enthusiastically: 'Which would you prefer', he asked, 'Malta or the friendship of Russia? I have no hesitation in answering – the friendship of Russia ... Justice, believe me, is a very powerful weapon for you, and if you accept the mediation of Russia, the justice of your object will be palpable to the world.' Considerations of morality, too, dictated his very forthright rejection of Bonaparte's demand for the extradition of the Bourbon princes:

> No one, perhaps, politically speaking, has less respect than I have for the House of Bourbon; yet I am ready to declare that for that family, nay, for the worst prince of that family if among them there should be a bad one, I should be ready to draw my sword and go to war, rather than to comply with a demand to withdraw from him the hospitality to which he had trusted.

Grey's amendment was defeated by 398 votes to 67, and neither he nor Fox chose to divide the House on the main motion supporting the war. But there was no doubting that the fundamental drift of Fox's speech had been *against* it:

> Switzerland and Holland are, in my opinion ... the countries the liberation of which from the yoke of France would be most desirable. But have you any chance of accomplishing such an object? ... No man has more earnest wishes than I have to see the power of France reduced. Much, certainly, in one way, may be done towards this object. You may seize her islands – you may take her colonies and destroy her trade ... and, for aught I know you may distress her even more. Even then, what will you ultimately gain? On the other hand, what may you ultimately lose? You may be driven to the brink of bankruptcy yourselves. But France, we are told, will have been destroyed first. France may indeed be made a beggar, but will that make her a better neighbour to you? ...

However, three days later, Fox declared in the Commons that the country being now 'actually at war' he would give it 'the best support in his power'. Nevertheless, on that same day he formally moved that the Tsar's mediation should be sought. Hawkesbury (Charles Jenkinson), for the government, accepting the motion, Fox then withdrew it.[25] Nothing, of course, came of this idea of mediation, and the war had another twelve years to run, outlasting both Pitt and Fox by nearly a decade.

Although systematic secession was ended, Fox had come to feel himself too often handicapped by the frequent and sometimes prolonged absences from Westminster of his closest political friends – Grey, for instance, for long periods hundreds of miles away on his Howick estate in Northumberland, or Lauderdale, further away still in Scotland, and busy writing a book on political economy which was rather far from gaining Fox's unstinted admiration. Fox was repeatedly crying out for the presence and support of these two especially, and of Fitzpatrick too, wanting to consult them upon issues and to discuss tactics. No one doubted that Fox was leader of the Foxites, but he was a long way from being, or wishing to be, sole arbiter of policy. He was surprisingly prone to hesitation and uncertainty, and was sometimes quite desperate for advice from those he trusted. Once for instance (this was in 1805, when crucial negotiations were pending) he confessed to feeling 'frightened, particularly in the absence of you [Grey] and Lauderdale and Fitzpatrick';[26] and several times in his letters to these three men especially there are *cris de coeur* for guidance. 'Pray come as soon as you can', he begs Fitzpatrick in January 1804. 'Mrs F. says I should say nothing but *come, come, come*, and she would say it down on her knees. You know she thinks there is no adviser but you. Pray by return of post say when you come exactly.' Then, a few months later, with the Addington ministry *in extremis*, he begs Grey* to realize how *very material* it was that he should come to London: 'You must brave the expence and inconvenience, and bring Mrs Grey for a month or two. Make Lauderdale come too if you can. Sheridan has been here ... but you will easily believe my dependence on him is not very firm.'[27] Again to Grey, in December 1804: 'Do, for God's sake, make up your mind to one unpleasant effort, and come for the first two months at least of the session. I understand you have a governess with whom Mrs Grey can leave the younger children.' Hang the expense and the trouble, he urged; 'come *en famille*'. Surely this was a time to make some sacrifices, even though he admitted that 'Burke was right, idleness is the best of all earthly blessings ... I love idleness so much, and so dearly, that I have hardly the heart to say a word against it; but something is due to one's station in life, something to friendship, something to the country'.[28]

'Without coalition, *nothing* can be done against the Crown', wrote Fox; 'with them, God knows how little!'[29] But to put together a coalition capable of commanding a parliamentary majority required some unifying cause. For a time towards the end of 1803, any hope having disappeared of mustering a majority for negotiating peace, Fox thought that perhaps the endless troubles of Ireland, with its associated and no less perennial 'Catholic question', might provide the cause he was looking for. There had been another republican insurrection, after whose speedy failure its leader, Robert Emmet, had been captured and hanged. (At that time, Fox's younger brother Harry was commander in chief in Ireland.) On 17 December, Fox wrote to Grey:

> I have deferred writing till I had an answer from Ireland. I had one from Grattan some days ago, and I have one from G. Ponsonby today. They are both against bringing on the question at present, and so of course I must give it up, but with more regret I must confess than I ever felt upon any political subject in my life. It is the only question that can be started to make what can be called a *cause* against the Court. We missed the opportunity very

---

* Grey was always pleading domestic responsibilities, as subsequent generations of his parliamentary colleagues were also to discover. He had been the lover of the Duchess of Devonshire and had a child by her; but his family life was to prove particularly felicitous, and (like George III) he had fifteen children.

unwisely in 1801; the insurrection of last summer gave us another, and when we shall have lost that, it is not easy to foresee when we shall have another. If the French land there, *tout est dit* ...[30]

To make a coalition out of the various groups opposed to Addington and, as Fox would add, to the Court, allies were necessary. Among these, potentially at least, were some old friends for whom Fox by this time had much distrust. There was, for instance, Sheridan. Ever since the King's first attack of madness in 1788, when Sheridan seized the opportunity while Fox was still abroad to set himself up as spokesman for the Whigs and adviser-in-chief to the Prince of Wales, relations between the two men (and also between Sheridan and Grey) had become cool. In recent years, too, Sheridan, both in the Commons and in his successful Drury Lane 'spectacular', *Pizarro*, had been loudly banging the patriotic drum. By this time, 1803, he was really not a Foxite at all, but rather co-leader with Lord Moira of the political group sometimes known as 'the Prince of Wales's friends'. Worst of all, in Fox's eyes, Sheridan seemed to be altogether too well disposed towards Addington and his ministry. When in November 1803 the Prince 'summoned' Fox to town actually to discuss a 'junction' between the Foxites, the 'Prince's friends', and Addington, Fox naturally obeyed the call and, as he related to Grey, met the Prince and Sheridan at Moira's. Sheridan having then been commissioned to test the prevailing temperature of the political water, 'it has ended', wrote Fox, 'as you may suppose, in *nothing* ... The Prince, if he can be undeceived, must be so now'. Fox's worst fears of Sheridan were being confirmed. There he was, 'courting the ministers more and more every day', getting drunk *tête-à-tête* with the Prince, 'mad with vanity and folly'.[31]

To *join* with Addington Fox judged to be neither practical nor desirable. They must somehow get rid of him. Fox despised Addington, whom he thought feeble, foolish, and, above all, dull. 'The insipidity of the House of Commons during the Addington ministry', he told Grey (who as usual was preferring Northumbrian family pleasures), 'is beyond conception, and I think it is catching, for the few times I have felt myself obliged to speak I felt some way as if I was speaking like Addington, and I really believe I was.'

It increasingly appeared that the most hopeful direction in which to look for allies was towards the Grenvilles – the three cousins of Pitt and their 'appendages' (as Fox described them), and also those members of parliament by now loosely associated with them, such as Windham, Fox's old friend Fitzwilliam, and his even older friend and sometime Northite, Carlisle. These men together made up a total of perhaps forty or so. At the core of 'the Grenvilles' were the three sons of that George Grenville who had set American hostility alight with his Stamp Tax in 1765. The eldest of the brothers, also George, had been the Lord Temple who in 1783 had been instrumental in helping the King to defeat Fox's India Bill in the House of Lords. He was now Marquis of Buckingham, lord of the great house of Stowe with all the political clout that went with it. The second son, diplomat and bibliophile, was Fox's old friend Tom Grenville. The youngest, William, the future prime minister (1806–7) – 'a very direct man', Fox noted – after being created Baron Grenville had been Pitt's foreign minister from 1791 to 1801. These men shared at least some of their cousin Pitt's views and of Fox's own, notably on 'the Catholic question'. Fox was clearly delighted when in January 1804 he received a proposal from them, 'to join with us in a systematic opposition for the purpose of removing the ministry and substituting one on the broadest possible basis ... There was an openness and appearance of cordiality in the manner of making the proposal that much pleases me'.[32] That Pitt had intimated to his cousin William his determination not to join any such 'systematic opposition', despite his growing hostility towards Addington, did not surprise Fox. Indeed his comments on Pitt's behaviour at this time make a fair match with those he was making about Sheridan: Pitt was 'a mean, low-minded dog'. 'What a man!' 'Oh, he is a sad stick!'[33]

The working alliance with the Grenvilles stood; but suddenly in February 1804 the political lie of the land changed; party alignments had to be reconsidered, and stances adjusted. The King was ill again – *as* ill, Fox insisted, as in 1788. He might die. He might recover physically, but stay permanently deranged. Once again, for the third time, the role and tactics of the Prince of Wales became important. Would there perhaps be a regency, with Lord Moira at the head of affairs? As it turned out, the acute phase of George's malady (as in 1801) did not last long, though for the remainder of the year his health was erratic and his behaviour sometimes strange. Sixty-six now, he would never be entirely well again, although for a further five years he was to stay fully sane, and he continued to transact business with his usual thoroughness.

The upsets of January to April 1804 saw the end of the Addington government, Pitt having at last turned decisively against it. After the King, however unwillingly, accepted Addington's resignation, he turned again towards Pitt, treating with him through Lord Chancellor Eldon. Pitt now wanted both Fox and Lord Grenville to be in his new administration — Fox as Secretary of State — to which the King, while accepting Grenville, professed astonishment that Pitt could 'one moment harbour the thought' of bringing before his notice a man who had been expelled from the Privy Council. This 'decided negative' Fox had fully expected, and he urged his friends and associates to ignore it and accept any government post offered them. Grey was invited to become Secretary at War, but declared that 'no earthly consideration' would persuade him to accept office without Fox, and Grenville similarly declined to join a government formed 'on a principle of exclusion'. Such refusals weakened Pitt's new ministry from the start. Even Addington, newly created Lord Sidmouth, who was briefly included in it, soon departed. But it was Grenville's non-cooperation which most angered Pitt. 'I will teach that proud man', he said, 'that in the service and with the confidence of the King, I can do without him, though I think my health such that it may cost me my life.' Pitt was only 45 but, unlike Fox, he had never been able to take good health for granted, and now he began to *look* an ageing man, or as Fox had said, intending a rather different sense, 'a sad stick'.

There seemed no hope now of a quick end to hostilities; as Fox lamented 'people seem to be making up their minds to perpetual war'. The greater part of domestic political controversy was therefore for a time inevitably concerned with the threat of invasion posed by the Grand Army and its troop-carrying transports being assembled along the Channel coast by Bonaparte — or rather by the newly self-proclaimed Emperor Napoleon, envisaging now his supreme triumph and ultimate dream: 'Let us be masters of the Channel for six hours and we are masters of the world'. Fox found difficulty in taking this threat of invasion seriously, and was inclined to dismiss too easily 'the nonsense of the Volunteers' and Pitt's 'ridiculous defence Bill'; but he had to go some way towards modifying his scepticism when he admitted, some two months before Nelson's victory at Trafalgar, indeed just after Nelson's ships had returned from their wild-goose-chase to the West Indies and back in search of the elusive French fleet: 'The alarm of invasion here was most certainly a groundless one ... but whether there may not be on the cards a possibility of some naval events which may render the alarm a most serious one is another question'. These were the months when British representatives in Vienna, Petersburg, Stockholm, Naples, and Berlin were busy trying to piece together another European alliance against the power of France — 'Pitt's Third Coalition' — the assembling of which came in time to oblige Napoleon to abandon his plans for the invasion of England, some time *before* Nelson finally succeeded in contacting the by now combined Franco-Spanish fleet and destroying it. Yes, Trafalgar was 'a great event' said Fox, bringing satisfaction solid enough to outweigh the regrettable succour it would undoubtedly bring to Pitt! 'I am very sorry for poor Nelson', he added, 'for though his conduct at Naples was atrocious, I believe he was at bottom a good man, and it is hard he should not enjoy (and no man would have enjoyed it more) the popularity and glory of this last business.'[34]

15

LAST DAYS OF PITT
AND FOX

1804–1806

Fox the politician, though operating under the handicap of an apparently permanent and unsurmountable royal veto against his ministerial employment, remained as busy as ever, exhorting his supporters to 'fall on Pitt without mercy'[1] – all the more confidently after the continental coalition began to look very shaky, Napoleon having outgeneralled and defeated the Austrian army at Ulm. But there were several other Foxes, all continuing well and lively: Fox the scholar, the lover of books, and (when the demands of 'idleness' allowed) the persisting if struggling historian; Fox the minor landed proprietor, occupied just now in putting up a small marble 'temple' in his grounds, in the fashion of the times; Fox the gardener, where his interests and those of his 'dearest Liz' conjoined; Fox the small gentleman-farmer. As to the *History of James II*, he was currently dealing with the execution of Monmouth, and hoped to make a better job of it than the hangman did on the day. 'Monmouth would have been dead yesterday', he writes, 'if the fine weather had not saved him; and though ... I dare not quite say that I will not dine before his head be off, I have hopes.' In December 1804 the amateur gardener was writing to Grey, "If you chance to see Lauderdale, pray tell him that I wrote him, near a fortnight since, a letter which I desired he would answer by return of post, about some vine cuttings, etc.' Similarly to Grey, the same year: 'Inclosed is some seed of the Anemone Pulsatilla [the pasque-flower], which Mrs Fox sends Mrs Grey. It should be put in light bog-earth as soon as possible.' Again to Grey, 'I have been making a very bad job of fattening two oxen. If you, upon your large scale, were to do as ill, it would be sad work'. Earlier, in

1803: 'My potato oats are coming up very thin in most parts of my field, owing as they say to a damned worm of some sort ... My Swedish turnips come up well, but ... there are abundance of weeds ... which unskilful hoers cannot distinguish from the turnips themselves while they are young ... However, we are doing our best.'

The house at St Anne's Hill stood in well-coppiced country much favoured by the nightingale, and a recurring theme in the Fox correspondence during the nesting season of April–May is the song of that nonpareil of summer visitors. Sometimes the commentary expands into a miniature essay, with literary references and classical allusions, particularly on the centuries-old debate – was that thrilling song essentially 'melancholy' or 'merry'? In April 1804 Fox was writing to his nephew, who was then in Spain:

> P.S. Nightingales not come yet, and it will be well if I do not quite miss hearing them this spring [because of the demands of politics] ... Pray remember to inquire at what time nightingales usually appear and sing where you are. Here, you know, it is about the 12th of this month; and do the Spanish poets count them lively or melancholy?

Napoleon's crushing victory over the Austrian and Russian armies at Austerlitz in December 1805 left Pitt's European coalition in ruins. His own health was in hardly better shape, and when he returned that month from Bath, his friends were speaking of his face bearing its 'Austerlitz look'. Others, in the accepted pseudo-medical lingo of the day, spoke darkly of his 'gout in the stomach'. Hester Stanhope, his niece-secretary-housekeeper, afterwards offered a simpler diagnosis; it had been, she said, a case of murder – he was literally working himself to death. At the turn of the year there was speculation that he would resign, and on 2 February 1806 Fox wrote to Lord Holland:

> If there *be* any truth in the report of his going out, for God's sake do all you can to prevent our friends from being eager to come in, until they are sure of being quite and entirely masters. The taking of anything short of complete power would be worse than anything that has yet happened, and most especially for the Prince.[2]

In this same letter there occurs a passage which Lord John Russell, editing the *Memorials and Correspondence* in the 1850s, suppressed, presumably since he judged it to detract from Fox's character. 'Even if Pitt is dying', the lines omitted read, 'the ruling passion will prevail, And in those moments as in all the past, "O let me keep my place" will be his last'.[3] A week or two later Fox talked privately of his great rival's grave illness in words rather kindlier. A lady present had shocked him by being openly glad that Pitt might be dying. No, said Fox, death was 'a poor way of getting rid of one's enemy'; future debates in the Commons would be flat and uninteresting; he would 'hate going to the House. I think I shall pair off with Pitt'.[4]

Three days later, still only 46, Pitt died – as it happens on the day before Fox's fifty-seventh birthday. The motion which came before the House on 27 January for a public funeral and a Westminster Abbey memorial to Pitt, '*that excellent statesman*', put Fox in a painful dilemma. He had faults, but hypocrisy was not among them. He was ready to speak, and did speak, of Pitt's integrity, moderation, disinterestedness, and other 'great personal qualities', but praise for the excellence of his statesmanship would have stuck in Fox's throat. 'Public duty', therefore, 'in the most imperious and irresistible manner', demanded that he should oppose the motion, which in the company of eighty-eight others he did.[5] A week later, however, when it was proposed that Pitt's debts should be defrayed from the public purse, he was able unhesitatingly to agree with the majority: 'never in my life', he said, 'did I give a vote with more satisfaction'.

When it became plain that the surviving members of the Pitt government would be unable to continue in office under a new leader, the King sent for Lord Grenville, whose response was that a collaboration between him and Fox would be essential to the formation of a Grenville ministry. The King, it was said, had only recently been declaring that he would 'risk a civil war' rather than employ Fox – a remark which, if indeed it was ever made, may or may not have been intended quite literally. In either case, when Grenville insisted that his government must embrace Fox and his party, George's attitude proved altogether different. He is reported as accepting Fox's inclusion in words which at any time over the previous twenty years and more would have been scarcely believable: 'I thought so, and I meant it so ... I will come to town and stay till it is done. There are to be no exclusions'.

Thus, once again Fox was Foreign Secretary and Leader of the House. Among the new ministers, Grey was first Lord of the Admiralty, Erskine Lord Chancellor, Fitzwilliam Lord President, Windham Colonial Secretary, Spencer Home Secretary, Fitzpatrick Secretary at War, and Sheridan Navy Treasurer. These last two were not cabinet posts, but to the scorn of many and the disgust of some, room was found in the cabinet for the *ci-devant* Addington, now Lord Sidmouth. *Why?* railed Lady Bessborough; 'Is he grown wiser and better? Oh no, but it will conciliate the K[ing], and he commands 40 votes'. Canning preferred to affect philosophical amusement: Sidmouth was like the measles – everybody had to have him once.

There was the customary soliciting for the freshly available loaves and fishes, and in this dispensing of favours and junior appointments Fox found himself obliged to disappoint some old friends. 'It is a damned thing', he told Lauderdale, 'but I saw it would not do, and one must not be impatient.' To the Duchess of Devonshire (a sad figure now, and near to her death) he wrote: 'Your note has distressed me to the greatest degree ... Indeed, indeed, my friends are hard upon me'. But his aunt Sarah Napier with her clutch of military sons for whom she was seeking favours, although she too was among the disappointed, would suffer nothing to be said against her ever-admirable Charles:

> I dare say [she wrote] it will be the old story again, for I hear that C. Fox is so thoroughly occupied with the *essential* business of England, viz. with Bonaparte, that he lets Lord Grenville take a much larger share of the loaves than belong to him. It is very much like Charles to be above the 2dary business. I admire him very much for it ... and I love C. the better for being duped to the end of the chapter.

It was true that Fox had set his sights above the '2dary'. He gave himself two grand objectives, to abolish the slave trade and to negotiate peace with France. Then he would retire. And indeed when he became ill, as very soon happened, he was approached by Grey speaking as cabinet mouthpiece, with the suggestion that he might care to reduce his burden of work by hastening that retirement – resigning the foreign ministry, continuing in the cabinet as minister without portfolio and, *if he wished*, accepting a peerage. The following narration by Lord Holland has some added interest from our knowledge of his own ambition (unstated here, but widely known, and admitted elsewhere) to *succeed* his uncle in the Foreign Office:[6]

> Mrs Fox was in the room when this suggestion was made. At the mention of the peerage, he looked at her significantly ... and after a short pause, he said: 'No, not yet, I think not yet'. On the same evening, as I sat by his bedside, he said to me: 'If this illness continues, I must have more quiet than with my place I ought to have, and put the plan I spoke to you about [for Holland to succeed him?] sooner in execution than I intended. But don't think me selfish, young one. The slave trade and peace are two such glorious things, I can't give them up, even to you. If I can manage *them*, I will then retire ...

The peerage, to be sure, seems the natural way, but ... I have an oath in Heaven against it; I will not close my politicks in that foolish way ...[7]

In the three months before his illness took a serious turn in May, Fox laboured, though with growing pessimism, to work out a peace settlement with Napoleon. The talks – conducted by Talleyrand for the French and by Yarmouth (and later Lauderdale also) for the British – were always to a degree complicated by the fact that Franco-Russian peace negotiations were simultaneously in progress. But a more fundamental obstacle to progress was Napoleon's well-justified confidence, all the stronger since Austerlitz, that on land he was as indisputably master as the British were on the seas. Far from making concessions, therefore, he more than once lodged additional claims, some of them substantial – for instance that he should be permitted to take over Sicily. 'The manner in which the French fly from their word disheartens me', Fox wrote: 'they are playing a false game.' Even before his illness compelled him to hand over to Grenville, he had become convinced that he was chasing rainbows.

His last important speech in the Commons was made on 10 June. Fittingly it was on a subject dear to him, on which he had spoken many times before. The difference now was that he voted with the majority – a surprisingly decisive one, 114–15 – for the motion that the House should 'with all practicable expedition proceed to take effectual measures for abolishing the African slave trade'. One at least of his two 'glorious things' had been set in train.

Nobody expected George III to show any *liking* for his new Foreign Secretary, but their brief mutual relationship during the period February to May 1806 was conducted on terms of the strictest propriety. According to a memorandum from the King's daughter Princess Augusta, later published in the *Quarterly Review*,

> When Mr Fox, came into the Closet for the first time, his Majesty purposely made a short pause and then said, 'Mr Fox, I little thought you and I should ever meet again in this place. But I have no desire to look back on old grievances, and you may rest assured I shall never remind you of them'. Mr Fox replied, 'My deeds, and not my words, shall commend me to your Majesty'.[8]

The King by this time was completely blind in one eye and nearly so in the other. Hence all his letters had now to be dictated, but he is reported to have *said* that Fox treated him 'frankly and respectfully'; that Fox's manner towards him contrasted favourably with that of 'another of his

Whig ministers who, when he came into office, walked up to him in the way he should have expected from Buonaparte after the battle of Austerlitz';[9] moreover that Foreign Office business was transacted with dispatch and efficiency. When in fact George came eventually to be told of Fox's death, his daughter Mary Duchess of Gloucester was in the room with him, and she afterwards recounted to Lord John Russell her father's reaction to the news. The country could ill afford to lose such a man, said the King: 'I never thought I should have regretted the loss of Mr Fox as much as I do'. None of this accords well with the assertion in Lord Holland's *Memoirs of the Whig Party*,[10] unsupported elsewhere, that George 'could hardly suppress his indecent exultation' when Fox died. Holland was to inherit little of either the character or ability of the uncle-father he idolised, but he did succeed to a generous share of Foxite antipathy to the monarch. Perhaps his slur upon the 'decency' of the King is best attributed to inventive malice.

The first stage of Fox's illness was marked by pain and swelling of the legs, with extreme fatigue after the slightest exertion, which then became rapid physical decline during June. For a while he had attempted to continue work by dictating his correspondence, but soon he was too ill to permit this. Dropsy was diagnosed. During the daytime his niece Caroline, Mrs Fox, Lord Holland or John Trotter would occupy his mind with readings aloud. Holland mentions especially the eighth book of the *Aeneid* and 'the whole of Crabbe's *Parish Register* ... in Ms; some parts he made me read twice'. Fox moreover suggested some emendations, which Crabbe's published version later adopted. He knew of course that he was seriously ill, but 'I don't mean to die, young one', he said, or 'give the thing up, as my father did'.

Fluid was drawn off on several occasions – each one a painful ordeal – and after one of them, when *four gallons* had been extracted, he felt sufficiently better to propose being moved from his house in London (it was in Stable Yard) to St Anne's Hill. However, this journey of perhaps as much as three hours was judged too severe for one in his condition, and the Duke of Devonshire therefore offered him the use of Chiswick House as intermediate staging post. Without mishap, but hardly without difficulty, this part of the homeward journey was successfully accomplished towards the end of July. More fluid was then drained, and during August, he was able sometimes to sit in the Chiswick House gardens and even undertake little rides, in the the carriage. 'He kept my hand in his all the time we were out', wrote his wife, 'made me kiss him several times and admired the Thames that we saw in the road back from Kew Bridge.'

His room was close by the one in which his friend, Duchess Georgiana, had died two or three months before, and many of his old friends now visited him there, Fitzpatrick, Fitzwilliam, John Townshend, and Robert Spencer quite frequently. In the evenings it would be mostly Trotter reading aloud to him:

> Palamon and Arcite, improved by Dryden – Johnson's Lives of the poets – the Aeneid – and Swift's poetry. He found, also, great pleasure in shewing me the pictures ... which adorn the delightful villa at Chiswick, and also the garden and grounds ... As I drew him round Chiswick garden alternately with a servant, his conversation was ... chiefly directed to objects of natural beauty, botany etc ... At times Mrs Fox or Miss Fox walked beside the chair.[11]

On Monday, 8 September, as Lady Holland's journal tells, while Fox was being 'led about the rooms at Chiswick to look at the pictures, a *gush* of water burst from the wounds; he fell into a state of alarming weakness'. She and Lord Holland were sent for. 'On Wednesday, about four, he began to revive, and, during the night, whilst Lord H. was sitting up with him, carried on a conversation in French, that his servant who was present might not understand it, as it concerned Mrs Fox, etc.' ('*Je crains pour elle*', was the substance of this. He expressed his worry more than once: what would become of her?) 'In the course of the morning he was wheeled into an adjoining room, and put on his spectacles to look at a caricature which Ld L[auderdale] had sent from Paris. I went into the room, kissed his hand, and he spoke kindly to me ...' (Lady Holland was well aware that she was no favourite with him. Earlier, in July – at least according to Creevey – he had refused to allow her in to see him, whereupon she took up position 'in one of the rooms below stairs under pretence of waiting for Lord Holland' and prevented 'his admitting any other women'.)

Mrs Fox, who 'had a strong sense of religion', wished prayers to be read by the bedside, at which Holland, who like his uncle had no such strong sense, took some alarm, 'lest any clergyman called in might think it a good opportunity for displaying his religious zeal, and acquiring celebrity by some exhibition to which Mr Fox's principles and taste would have been equally averse. When, however, Mr Bouverie, a young man of excellent character, without pretension or hypocrisy, was in the house, I seconded her request.' Hence, Mr Bouverie stood behind the bed-curtain and read the service. Fox remaining quiet throughout, towards the end his wife knelt on the bed and joined his hands.

When John Trotter's memoirs were published in 1811, Lord Holland (in *his* memoirs, published just afterwards) criticized the account Trotter gave of the episode, with his over-fervent, misleading conjectures concerning 'the religious tenets and principles of Mr Fox'. At the same time he sought to correct Trotter's 'insinuations against the family' and the false impression given 'with respect to the persons present' round or very near Fox's deathbed.[13] Apart from 'the family' are included in Holland's list, Fitzpatrick, Trotter, the surgeon Hawkins, and one (or on occasions all) of the three physicians in attendance. It is interesting to notice among the obvious 'family' names that of a Miss Willoughby. This was Harriet Willoughby, then probably 21 or 22, who is presumed to have been a natural daughter of Fox. The diarist Farington had written some thirteen years earlier of this 'little girl' of whom Mrs Armistead was 'very fond ... though not her daughter'.[14*]

During the last two hours before Fox died on 13 September 'without a struggle or groan', his articulation became indistinct. However, quite clearly to be heard were the words 'I die happy', and 'Liz', and also (to his wife) according to Lady Holland, 'Bless you, I pity you'. Alternative further versions of his last words come from Trotter, who, when Fox's speech became too mumbled for those present to understand, claimed to hear him say 'Trotter will tell you', and from Mrs Fox herself, who managed finally to distinguish her 'angel' saying, 'It don't signify, my dearest Liz'.[15]

So died, as Holland wrote, 'the best and greatest man of our time'. Coke went one better: he mourned him as 'the greatest man in Europe'. Many years later, Lauderdale, an old man by then, told John Cam Hobhouse, 'Charles Fox was not only the most extraordinary man I have ever seen, but also the best man'. And when that other close friend of his, Lord John Townshend, devised an epitaph for his own tomb, it was to read: 'The friend and companion of Mr Fox, a distinction which was the pride of his life and the only one he was desirous might be recorded after his death'.[16]

Fox's will named his wife as executrix and inheritor of the bulk of his estate. Among the lesser beneficiaries, receiving bequests or pictures were those his will described as his 'oldest connexions'; these included

---

*It is usually assumed – and probably correctly – that the union of Charles and Elizabeth Armistead/Fox produced no children. On the other hand, John Drinkwater, preparing his Fox biography in the 1920s, interviewed a Rev. E. V. R. Powys, Fox's great-grand-nephew. Mr Powys, writes Drinkwater, 'tells me that he remembers two old ladies who were the daughters of Charles and Elizabeth Fox' (p. 281, 287). Elizabeth Fox did not die until 1842, when she was nearly 92. She is buried in Chertsey Parish Church, close to her 'dear home' St Anne's Hill.

Fitzpatrick, Fitzwilliam, and John Townshend. Harriet Willoughby was given a reversionary interest in a small annuity, and a 500-guinea legacy was divided equally between the son of his younger brother General Henry Fox and a certain Robert Stephen, 'a youth now living with Viscount Bolingbroke in America' (a natural son? – we do not know). The unfinished history of the reign of James II came naturally into the hands of Lord Holland, who two years later published it in its uncompleted state.

The funeral could be nowhere but in Westminster Abbey, though briefly the claim of Foxley, in ancestral Wiltshire, was considered. Fox's father had chosen it for his bitterly-fought-for title, Baron Holland of Foxley. But Charles Fox and the constituency of Westminster had been inseparable for more than a quarter-century, and in fact his funeral was now delayed for a week or two to coincide with the anniversary of his first election to that least undemocratic of British boroughs. Its citizens turned out in strength to line the route of their late member's journey from Stable Yard to the Abbey, and to view the carriage procession of noblemen, gentlemen, and dignitaries, Volunteer Cavalry at the head, marching bands playing funeral music, banners carried by gentlemen on horseback – all the tributary *comme-il-faut* of a Georgian public funeral, and if it cost less than a quarter of Nelson's (at St Paul's, so recently) and only half of Pitt's (whose tomb and Fox's were now to be not many inches away from one another),* it was still impressive enough. 'My angel', wrote Mrs Fox, 'was carried to his last worldly home ... attended by so many proofs ... of love and esteem for his memory and deep-felt regret for his loss that I cannot but feel gratified that so much goodness was not thrown away upon an ungrateful world.'

---

* From Scott's *Marmion*:
   Genius and taste and talent gone,
   For ever tombed beneath the stone ...
   Drop upon Fox's grave the tear,
   'Twill trickle to his rival's bier.

16

LEGACY
AND LEGEND

The peculiar and enviable position among statesmen of the past which Fox came to hold for a century and more after his death arose from a happy combination of two elements: one, that he was remembered as an example of that rare phenomenon, a leading politician both intellectually outstanding and personally attractive, even lovable; and the other and more important, that he was viewed as representing a set of principles which came by wide consent to be considered progressive and estimable. Just what these were perceived to be is well shown in the report of a rousing speech made in Edinburgh by Sir James Mackintosh, some seventeen years after Fox's death. Mackintosh, like Fox, had been a champion of the French Revolution at least in its early stages, and although his opinions afterwards approximated more closely to Burke's, he remained a liberal-minded reformer. To his 500-strong audience in 1823 he was offering some 'vehemently' received rhetoric in praise of Fox's memory:

> Will those who think the principles of Mr Fox were pertinaciously maintained assert that we have had too few wars? (*cheers*) Too light burdens? (*cheers*) Too few suspensions of the constitution [i.e. of Habeas Corpus]? (*cheers*) Too many checks to undue power? (*cheers*) Too few violations of personal liberty? (*cheers*) Too many extensions of the liberty of the press? (*cheers*) Too great a control upon the prerogative of the Crown? (*cheers*) Too little restraint upon the assembling of the people? ... But it is said, those who hold the opinions of Mr Fox are the advocates of Catholic emancipation and parliamentary reform. *We are* the advocates of Catholic emancipation and parliamentary reform (*Vehement cheering*)[1]

Mackintosh's catalogue of issues presented here does not omit many major aspects of Fox's record or Foxite policy. Certainly American Independence is not mentioned, but that was a dead issue by 1823. In any case, although 'Fox the champion of America' has looked well in many subsequent tributes to him, it must be admitted that it was political opportunism rather than a love of freedom which first shaped his attitude in that matter, America having provided a convenient weapon with which to belabour Lord North. Perhaps purer considerations came later. Perhaps, too, Mackintosh missed the chance of including slavery and the slave trade in his catalogue, for in 1823 slavery within the British Empire was still legal, and in this area of humanitarian reform Fox's record stood above criticism. As for parliamentary reform, his advocacy of which had never been either consistent or enthusiastic – less so than Grey's – the shaping hand of Fox was still being seen behind the reform act of 1832 nearly a century later by G. M Trevelyan, Macaulay's great-nephew and the last of the great 'Whig historians', who in 1922 was writing:

> The persistence of the Foxite tradition in one section of the governing class made it possible for Grey, at the end of his long career ... to pass the Bill that abolished the rotten boroughs. Nothing else could have ultimately averted civil war ... If the whole of the privileged class had joined Pitt's anti-Jacobin bloc ... the constitution could not have been altered by legal means, and change could only have come in nineteenth century Britain along the same violent and blood-stained path by which it has come in continental countries. It is 1832 that justifies the action taken by Fox forty years before.[2]

Similarly, at the repeal of the Test Act and the passage of the last major measure of Catholic emancipation during 1828–9, Fox's honourable support for earlier attempts to liberalize the religious laws was not forgotten. Indeed, during the debates Peel himself, a Tory and a late convert to emancipation but now the chief architect of it, paid Fox the handsomest of tributes. He recalled how, during the interval between leaving Harrow and proceeding to Oxford, he had listened, a boy of 17, to Fox speaking on Catholic emancipation in May 1805. 'He never heard', Peel admitted, 'a speech which made a greater impression on his mind than that delivered by Mr Fox'.[3] The verdict from Holland House in 1829 was more predictable, if less impartial, Lady Holland awarding almost all the merit to Fox and the successor Foxite Whigs. 'The world are very just', she wrote to her son Henry,

> and ascribe the merit entirely to Fox and Grattan and those worthies who first agitated the matter. Those at the eleventh hour [like Peel], and Canning

even, have not the glory. The old Whigs have acted admirably, and are much respected for their high, disinterested and zealous conduct.[4]

The tenth of October, 1780, when Fox was first elected for Westminster, 'became a date that was to be celebrated for generations as a milestone in the history of man's quest for freedom'. So writes an American biographer of Fox.[5] Fox as apostle of liberty, as exemplar of the quest for freedom, was a concept powerful enough, and containing moreover a sufficient proportion of truth, to last (if not always or altogether unchallenged) for well over a century. And as freedom's champion, Fox the leader of the Whigs came inevitably to be seen, when the Whig chrysalis developed into the Liberal butterfly and spread its Victorian wings, as the chief of the proto-Liberals, the grandfather of Liberalism. As the poet-playwright-biographer John Drinkwater wrote sixty-odd years ago, summing up Fox's place in history, however extravagantly:

> It was Fox more than any other man who in English public life transfigured the Whig into the Liberal ... To stake everything for a cause, to lose everything, to fight the House of Commons, the nation, the world, single-handed if need be in vindication of belief, to be unsubduable and unsilenced in defeat, and to be prepared in all extremities to accept the consequences of liberty – we see Fox detaching himself from the great figures of the time, and going out alone to take up these advance positions in the field of political thought and action.[6]

Fox the warrior for liberty, the champion of good causes, was seen by the nineteenth century, and particularly by Victorian Liberals, as the man above all others (even above Burke) who had consistently challenged the political influence of the Crown. In this view, George III had encroached upon hard-won parliamentary liberties and privileges, while Fox had 'constitutionally' campaigned against an abuse of royal prerogative. It is indeed a fact that for George III the phrase 'the King's ministers' meant to a considerable degree what it said, the *King's* ministers, while what Fox maintained – indeed had specifically asserted in the debates during the crisis-year 1783–4 – was that the Crown, being 'endowed with no faculty whatever of a private nature',[7] ought always to bow to the wishes and decisions of a parliamentary majority. The King's powers were properly exercised only through the King's ministers, who must be men enjoying the support of a majority in the House of Commons, and thus by implication of 'the people'. If in this regard Fox certainly had the future on his side of the argument, whether that fact made him *in the 1780s* constitutionally correct and the King incorrect is another matter. Ever since 'the Whig interpretation of history' began to fall out of favour some sixty years ago, political and constitutional historians have been rather less dogmatic in this matter than their predecessors. And in respect of another of Fox's claims, made in 1782 upon the death of prime minister Rockingham, that a cabinet in office (rather than the monarch) had the right by majority vote to choose its own leader as prime minister, even the most devoted Foxites felt bound to admit that this undoubtedly innovative constitutional theory (accepted neither then nor since) stemmed almost entirely from Fox's personal animus against Shelburne, who was the King's choice for the new premiership.

The process of sanctifying the memory of the flesh-and-blood Charles Fox, of elevating and transforming him into the legendary statesman, freedom's champion, the all-but-canonized Charles James Fox,* began very soon after his death. It was Holland House (shortly to enter its most famous era, with the imperiously outrageous Lady Holland presiding over its distinguished politico-literary salon) which was to become the chief centre and spiritual home of the new Foxolatry – a shrine almost – with 'Young One' Holland, from the very moment of his uncle's death, guardian of his sacred flame. Holland moreover could become astonishingly alarmed when he thought he saw this unique situation of his threatened by the incursion of a rival, some heretic corrupting the purity of the faith. When he heard that John Trotter, who as secretary had been close to Fox over several of his latter years, was publishing his memoirs, Holland took fright. On publication, he read the book immediately. Alas, not only had Trotter presented a religiously tendentious and inaccurate account of Fox's last days, but – worse – he had completely missed the major point of Fox's career, the sacrifice he had made in a manly struggle against those malign forces represented by Crown influence and those ministers who had benefited from it to exercise political power. In considerable agitation he wrote again to Jeffrey, editor of that premier Whig journal, the *Edinburgh Review,* suggesting who ought to be chosen to review Trotter's book, and the line of criticism which should be taken.[8] Although Trotter's published memories of Fox could hardly have been more profusely adulatory – Trotter looked upon him almost as a demigod – nevertheless they irritated

---

* The inclusion of the second forename carries a small point of its own. Very rarely, indeed almost never, was he called Charles *James* Fox in his lifetime, but subsequently – ever since the obituary tributes and the first biographies – he became, when not simply Fox, compulsorily the bearer of the full resonance of all three names. Moreover, the fashion of christening male children Charles James became suddenly widespread.

Holland sufficiently for him to begin jotting down his own version of the events in question, later incorporated and expanded in his two sets of *Memoirs of the Whig Party*.

Holland never became leader of the party. When that seemed a future possibility, one commentator dismissed the idea out of hand: no one so completely under the thumb of his wife could be acceptable; and on a later occasion Lord John Russell (who enjoyed much favour at Holland House) explained to Lady Holland herself that her husband could never become Foreign Secretary while she opened all his letters.[9]* That did remain his ambition however. It was never achieved, but by dint of being Fox's political heir and being 'the Repository of his great Mind', he remained until his death in 1840 a most influential figure within the Whig leadership.

It was particularly in matters affecting France that the voice of Fox speaking through Holland is constantly to be heard. Fox in 1789–91 had seen events in France as mirroring, from one direction, the Whig revolution of 1688 and, from another, his own failed 'revolution', the contest with George III in 1782–4. He never quite managed to disavow that famous accolade he had repeatedly given to the storming of the Bastille, never quite accepted that it was a very long way indeed from being the greatest and best thing that had ever happened in the history of the world. He had taken his stand, and no revolutionary fanaticisms or horrors or hypocrisies, no internecine slaughter or reign of terror, even when he came genuinely to deplore and detest them, could ever shift him. Revolutionary France came to stand for 'liberty', Britain for the abuse of executive power. The excesses and extremes of the French Revolution could be, if not condoned, always *explained* by their being provoked by the follies and trickeries of Louis XVI and Marie Antoinette. Robespierre was evil, but 'Bourbon despotism' more so. However bad the conduct of the French had been after 1792, that of Prussia, of Austria, of Pittite Britain was always represented as worse. And all this became as much Holland's system of political belief as his uncle's. As Fox would assuredly have been, he was horrified at the restoration of the Bourbon monarchy in 1814. Typically, he spoke of it in terms of Fox's convictions and, specifically, of the uncompleted *History of*

---

*Lady Holland's domineering ways were notorious. She forbade Holland to dine with (among others) Coke of Holkham, because Coke was known to have cast aspersions on her scandalous early amours. And Macaulay relates how once, Lady Holland having consented after the intercession of Grey to let her husband (then about 60) have a second slice of melon, Holland gathered courage to say, 'Ah, Lord Grey, I wish you were always here. It is a fine thing to be Prime Minister' (L. Mitchell, *Holland House*, p. 30).

the Reign of James II. 'Read the last sentence of my Uncle's introduction', he advised his sister Caroline in August 1814, 'speculating on events which were probable at James's accession, and substitute Church lands and confiscated property for Church establishment and religion, and it will be as applicable to Lewis 18th's as to James 2nd's accession'.[10] For Holland House the Bourbon restorations of 1814 and 1815 were foredoomed to failure, since they denied the validity of 1789; it would have been precisely Fox's own verdict.

Moreover, Fox had honestly admired Bonaparte and at least flirted with approbation of the Bonapartist system. Unsurprisingly therefore we find Holland – and in this instance even more emphatically his wife, to the alarm of some fellow Whigs – torn between their feelings of British patriotism and their fascinated respect (with Lady Holland, adoration) for the enemy leader. Tom Grenville disgustedly reported to his brother in February 1814 that 'Lady Holland was fool enough ... to say before ten people that she hoped Bonaparte would let but few of the Allies get back to Frankfurt. Even in a woman of such an irregular mind' [this did] 'a mischief and discredit beyond belief' to respectable Grenvillian Whiggery. Yet it was really quite close to the sort of thing Fox had been saying about the Austrians and Prussians allied to Britain in 1793.

Although Gibbon among others had lamented that Fox's 'inmost soul' was 'deeply tinged with Democracy',[11] he was in fact untouched by it. 'You know', he wrote to Holland in 1794, 'I am one of those who think both property and rank of great importance in this country.' Democracy, either in the usual modern meaning of the word or as understood in his day (almost always pejoratively) was alien to him. When Fox was toasted as 'the man of the people', or when Grey founded 'The Friends of the People' (towards which in any case Fox was very cautious), the *people* in their mind represented a quite small proportion of the total population – essentially the owners of property. As for the practicality of universal (male) suffrage, the idea was hardly less preposterous to Fox than to his nephew, who in the House of Lords in February 1817 committed himself to the view that universal suffrage was 'the wildest fancy that could possibly enter into the conception of any human being'. Fox undoubtedly had been by temperament a rebel, but a *radical* he never was. That, however, did not prevent some people long after his death revering him as one, or for instance stop Thackeray's *Vanity Fair* from presenting Miss Crawley, that 'dreadful Radical', as having 'pictures of Fox in every room in the house'.[12] Fox and all his circle at Brooks's and the great Whig houses were inescapably members of a wealthy and privileged aristocracy, nor had they any intention of escaping from that comfortable condition. But it is fair to point out their virtues – and again it is Trevelyan who insists, in his life of Grey:

> It is easy to sneer at the Whigs for being aristocrats, but it is lucky that in an aristocratic age a few aristocrats were Liberals ... The fifty M.P.'s and half a dozen peers who stood, disarmed and apparently helpless [after 1793] beneath Fox's tattered banner were constituting the party destined to reform England and govern her during the best half of the coming century.[13]

The last fifteen years of the life of this 'kind, grand, human creature', Trevelyan wrote, 'though apparently the most complete in their failure, were in fact the best, the greatest, and in the end the most useful: he stood up for liberty in evil days, when without such a Titan to bestride them the friends of liberty would have ceased to exist in Parliament'.[14]

Miss Crawley was not unusual or eccentric in her day for having a houseful of Fox pictures. There were many others somewhat like her – Mrs Siddons, for one, used to keep his portrait in her parlour. And in the grander Whig houses, or in their gardens, Fox as an icon was often to be discovered, his bust sometimes in sole place of honour, sometimes as one among a pantheon of heroes and worthies. At Thomas Coke's Norfolk mansion, Holkham, Fox stood alongside Demosthenes, Alexander the Great, the fifth Duke of Bedford – and eventually Coke himself. At the Duke of Bedford's own Woburn the pantheon had Fox at its centre, and round him ranged an impressive circle of Whig notables. Inevitably, at Holland House, the visitor confronted Westmacott's statue of Fox immediately on entering the lobby.

Fox Clubs began as early as 1790. It was at the Club dinner in 1798, with 2,000 present celebrating their hero's birthday, that the Duke of Norfolk, having drunk perhaps rather too much, proposed the famous toast to the *sovereign people* and thereby eventually cost Fox his membership of the Privy Council. These birthday dinners, in London and in many other towns throughout the country, flourished, particularly during the Regency and beyond, until the Whigs' return to office in 1830. They were more than mere exercises in nostalgia, combining a political with a social function, and sharing some of the uses served by a modern opposition party's conference, reassuring and encouraging the faithful, preserving from extinction the party traditions and legends. For the party leader's 'standing ovation' of to-day may easily be substituted the routine toasts of those years, 'Mr Fox and Parliamentary Reform!' 'Mr Fox and an end to Slavery!' — even at the Norwich dinner fifteen years after Fox's death, 'Mr Fox and Liberalism in Spain and Naples!'[15]

'Mr Fox and Liberalism!' was not quite obsolete as a rallying call a decade later. When the restored Bourbon line was overthrown by Louis Philippe in the July Revolution of 1830, Holland's joyous response came close to being a replay of his master's voice in 1789. He even for a time contemplated going across to Paris to congratulate Louis Philippe in person, and in fact throughout the 1830s his insistent Francophilism, his reluctance to face the realities of French expansionism (towards the Netherlands, for instance, or towards Spain and Portugal), and his resolute championing of European liberalism against the so-called Holy Alliance powers quite often came into conflict with official British foreign policy. Indeed, within the cabinet something approaching civil war was at times being waged between Lord Privy Seal Holland and Foreign Secretary Palmerston, who was much less deeply imbued with Foxite principles.

During the 1920s and '30s historical opinion tended to move away from what had been the conventional view of the political and constitutional history of George III's reign. In 1929 came Lewis Namier's work on the *Structure of Politics in 1760*, and two years later Herbert Butterfield's influential essay, *The Whig Interpretation of History*. In Butterfield's admittedly 'extended sense', the term 'whig' appears sometimes to embrace Martin Luther almost as easily as Charles Fox — indeed, much of the essay concerns the Reformation — but what in general terms Butterfield criticized and found 'astonishing' was the extent to which, 'the historian has been Protestant, progressive, and whig, and the very model of the ninetenth century gentleman'. Historians, the essay argued, had generally written 'on the side of Protestants and Whigs, to praise revolutions provided they have been successful, to emphasize certain principles of progress in the past and to produce a story which is the ratification if not the glorification of the present':

> Whether we take the contest of Luther with the popes, or that of Philip II and Elizabeth ... whether we take Charles I versus his parliaments or the younger Pitt versus Charles James Fox, it appears that the historian tends in the first place to adopt the whig or Protestant view of the subject, and very quickly busies himelf with dividing the world into the friends and enemies of progress ... For this reason it has been easy to believe that Clio herself is on the side of the whigs.[16]

Events seen thus, wrote Butterfield, will enable the historian

> to decide irrevocably and in advance, before historical research has said
> anything and in the face of anything it might say, that Fox, whatever his
> sins, was fighting to save liberty from Pitt, while Pitt, whatever his virtues,
> cannot be regarded as fighting to save liberty from Fox.[17]

Butterfield's central objection was to what he called 'the historian's
"pathetic fallacy" ... the result of abstracting things from their historical context and judging them ... by a system of direct reference to the present'.[18]

The reputation of George III had become peculiarly the victim of such
a system of judgement. In his conflict with Fox during the years 1782–4,
he saw himself as acting properly within his rights under what he himself
considered 'our excellent constitution'. The point was arguable, and in one
major respect Fox's contrary attitude would come to be borne out by
the trend of history, for in the long run it would certainly become
unconstitutional and impermissible for a monarch to sustain in office a
ministry clearly lacking a Commons majority, as George III did during the
early months of 1784. The historians and biographers of the Victorian era
and afterwards, 'abstracting things from their historical context' and
judging by the standards not of 1784 but of their own day, had no
difficulty in finding Fox in the right and the King in the wrong. They
hailed Fox as the champion of popular constitutional government and
condemned the King for being unconstitutional and reactionary and even
(as Trevelyan was writing as late as 1920), for wielding throughout his
reign a 'malign presiding influence'.[19] In the general judgement, George III's
reputation took a long time to make at least some partial recovery from
the depths to which Fox's nephew had already consigned it at the time of
George's death in 1820: 'The lavish and unmerited praise bestowed on the
late King', he then lamented in a letter to his son, 'make me sick and almost
angry ... There was nothing good done in his reign that was not done
against his will, and some of the worst things, the Royal Marriage Act,
the American war, were peculiarly his own measures'.

The advantages of distance now allow a more even-handed judgement
upon the clash of personalities and the conflict of mutual resentments
between Fox and the King. In that other long-lasting conflict, between
Fox and Pitt, it is perhaps no longer necessary to take sides. Fox, while
being constantly worsted in the political battle, remained frequently in a
position to take the moral high ground and shine as the defender of civil
liberty and the champion of peace and reform. At the personal level,

however, his unrelenting bitterness towards Pitt and his constant depreciation of him contrast sharply with his usual magnanimity and generosity of spirit. Politically, it is generally easier for those out of office to display idealism and high-mindedness than for those who are in, burdened as these are with the necessity of choosing, seldom between good and bad, but more usually between competing goods or competing evils, or most often between complicated mixtures of both – and it has been pertinently observed that, had Fox been *in office* in 1789, 'he would in all probability have followed the same policy as Pitt: neutrality. And like Pitt ... 'he would have found himself inevitably dragged into the conflict, at the expense of his desire for peace and reform'.[20]

The decline into disfavour of 'whig' history and a proliferation of modern detailed research – what Butterfield liked to call 'technical history' – have combined to take some of the lustre from Fox's previously shining reputation. It might seem startling, or even seriously wrong-headed, if a historian today were to hail him (as Trevelyan did seventy years ago) as a 'Titan'. A commoner line of conclusion in recent decades would be that 'his great gifts were vitiated by grave mistakes at decisive moments' (1782, for instance, when he rashly and perhaps peevishly resigned, or 1788–9, when he mishandled the regency crisis); that 'his private qualities could not compensate for the disastrous eruption of immaturity at times of crisis and tension'; that there remains 'a sense of greatness dissipated and tremendous potentialities unrealized', which reflect his 'deficiencies of character'; that he paid 'a high price for folly and misjudgement', and 'no amount of posthumous adulation can compensate for frustration and failure'.[21] These are hard words, even though a strong argument can be made for all of them. Yet the picture they present may perhaps remind us of one of those trick sketch-portraits where the lines of the face are so artfully contrived that, holding it one way up, we see a scowling visage of sinister aspect, but, if we turn it upside down, all is smiling and benign.

In this smiling picture we see the Charles Fox whom his political enemies learned to respect, admire, even (like Selwyn, say, or Gibbon) love, and for whom friends did not always remain on the prudent side of idolatry. We see the man who, when he was on his feet in the Commons and as North put it 'in full feather', could fill the House as quickly as Burke sometimes managed to empty it; whose exuberant vitality outlasted the careless wastrel years of his youth and ripened into the sobriety of his uxorious maturity; who, although in many ways a typical eighteenth-century Whig aristocrat happy to 'play the system', nevertheless did have principles, of which a love of liberty was one; who was a good linguist and a classical scholar of sufficient standing to meet the academics on their own terms; who loved Renaissance painting and the literature both of past times and his own; who possessed a talent for happiness and something close to genius for friendship. Perhaps with such a man we ought not to dwell too unforgivingly on his shortcomings and misjudgements.

That there was a good deal to forgive, personally and politically, is hardly deniable. The blue hair powder and red-heeled shoes of the very young macaroni may be passed by with a smile; but the reckless gambler in his twenties, heedless of his mother's reproaches, spunging on his father's wealth and his friends' generosity, presents an unflattering spectacle. 'Never let Charles know', his father had begged, 'how excessively he afflicts me.' The jocular flippancy with which Fox brushed off the financial disaster of 1773, and the apparent absence of repentance or remorse for the wounds he was inflicting on his, as it proved, dying parents show the grown-up-spoiled-child at his unsavoury worst. From his infancy onwards he had undoubtedly been spoiled, and not only by his father. He had grown up to be wondered at — 'the phenomenon of the age' even to such a critical observer as Horace Walpole. He was always the most brilliant of the aristocratic set in whose company much of his youth was spent: the liveliest intellectually, the quickest-witted, the most adept at charming the others, high-spirited, irrepressible and apparently tireless, always at the centre of the circle.

Outstanding as he was acknowledged to be, and the son moreover of an important and wealthy politician who had once actually turned down an offer of the premiership, he had been brought up (as was his main rival and eventual vanquisher, Pitt) to see it in the nature of things that he would reach the highest rungs of the political ladder; and why should it not be to the topmost? But whereas Pitt, from his boyhood on, never let his eyes stray from the goal and neglected no preliminary necessary to achieve it, Fox, with his wider horizons and more versatile interests, was always liable to be drawn away to the excitements of the horse-race or the card-table, to his beloved Ariosto or the Italian painters, to learning another language (he started Spanish), to his mistresses, to Virgil, to Homer, or in his latter years to his country retreat. Even so, during his necessarily short spells of major office, it was generally agreed that no minister could have worked harder or more efficiently.

Where he did fail to win acceptance with his accustomed charm, he might well, like his father before him, bear lasting grudges, one or two of them severely damaging to the prosperity of his career. If we set aside the obvious instance of Pitt, the two most clearly influential in this damaging of his fortunes were Lord Shelburne and the King. Fox's detestation of Shelburne came in part probably as an inheritance from his father; but whatever its origin, it was certainly a factor in the internal divisions of the short-lived second Rockingham administration, and became the decisive factor in Fox's apparently peevish refusal to serve in the Shelburne ministry which followed. His impetuous resignation then was widely considered to have been a serious tactical mistake. Moreover, it naturally reinforced the King's antipathy to him, already strong enough.

Fox's public criticism of the King had always been prudently de-personalized — it was always *the Crown* or *the Court*, rather than King George, that was represented as the fount of corruption and sustainer of misrule — but his frequent outspoken condemnation, privately expressed, could hardly hope to remain private. In any case the King had always found this 'professed gamester''s conduct 'odious'. When in the spring of 1783 Fox judged that he had within his grasp the worsting of his royal enemy, his over-confidence helped to destroy him. If the game was to turn rough, the King was found to flex the stronger muscle, and Fox's political fortunes were not to recover till within a few months of his death. His impetuosity was to be blamed also for his next misjudgement — the word haunts his middle years — when his incautious debating speech during the regency crisis led him to be 'unwhigged' and outmanoeuvred by Pitt. Then a few months later his notoriously laudatory outburst upon the storming of the Bastille certainly ought to have been made in language less excited, more considered and statesmanlike. Characteristically he chose to stand by his first snap judgement and repeat it; but the damage was done, and perhaps it would have been done anyway. Although he tried for a year or two to guide his followers down a more cautiously moderate course, the French Revolution proved too much either for him or for his party to handle, and the Whig debacle was complete.

Still, the mature Fox of those remaining dozen years, years of continuing political defeat, emerges very honourably and estimably: refusing to abandon the long campaign against the slave trade; tireless in defence of religious freedom, of liberty of opinion and expression; passionate in stressing the imperative desirability of peace rather than war. The old cocksure self-confidence faded; the readiness to try the gambler's throw vanished; we even find him frustratedly, sometimes distractedly, seeking the advice of friends and associates, and always the support and counsel of his wife. Perhaps the happiness of his marriage is an essential key to those years, often perforce of semi-retirement though never of idleness. He had begun his political life as a brilliant careerist and sharp-eyed opportunist, ready to gamble away minor office on the way to major power. During the American rebellion and under the tutelage of Burke, his political *principles* began to emerge, though undoubtedly opportunism remained the dominant force. Increasingly, however, in his latter years as elder statesman – generally esteemed and by many revered – the humanity and indeed benignity of his character and personality were beginning to outshine the record of past errors and failures, and he was on his way to becoming the Victorian icon, the stuff of liberal legend.

CHRONOLOGY

1627	(Sir) Stephen Fox born at Farley, Wiltshire; later (1640–1702) serves under five successive British monarchs
1688	The 'Glorious Revolution'
1705	Henry Fox born
1716	Sir Stephen Fox dies
1744	Henry Fox marries Lady Caroline Lennox secretly
1745	Stephen ('Ste') Fox born
1746	Henry Fox Secretary at War
1748	Henry Fox rents Holland House, eventually buying it in 1767
1749	Charles Fox born
1753	Hardwicke's Marriage Act
1755	Henry Fox Secretary of State and Leader of the Commons
1755–68	Fox educated at Wandsworth, Eton, and Oxford, and in foreign travel
1756–63	Seven Years War
1757–65	Henry Fox, as Paymaster of the Forces, amasses a large fortune
1762–3	Henry Fox, again Leader of the Commons, manoeuvres Treaty of Paris through the House; created Baron Holland
1764	Wilkes is expelled from the Commons
1765	George Grenville's Stamp Act
1766	Rockingham ministry repeals Stamp Act, but 'declares' British right to tax colonies
1767	Townshend Duties
1768	Charles Fox M.P. for pocket borough of Midhurst. Middlesex elections. Wilkes riots
1770	Lord North prime minister. Fox a junior minister

1772	(February) Fox resigns ministerial post. George III's Royal Marriages Act. Fox's bill to repeal Hardwicke's Marriage Act defeated. (December) Fox returns as a junior minister
1773	Henry Edward Fox born, eventual heir to the Fox fortunes, and while still a baby becomes 3rd Lord Holland. Boston Tea Party
1773–4	Ruinous gambling debts of Charles and Stephen Fox are met by their father. (January 1774) Winterslow House destroyed by fire. (February) Fox is dismissed from ministry after 'humiliating' North. (July) Deaths of 1st Lord Holland and Lady Holland. (November) Death of Stephen, 2nd Lord Holland
1774–80	Fox M.P. for Malmesbury, Wiltshire
1775–82	Fox repeatedly attacks Lord North and his ministers, Germain and Sandwich, on American policy
1776	American Declaration of Independence
1778	War, first with France, and then with Spain and Holland
1779	Invasion danger. Keppel court martial and riots. Crisis in Ireland. Fox's duel with Adam
1780	The petitioning (association) movement. 'Dunning's motion' passed in the Commons. Gordon Riots. Fox elected for Westminster
1781	Fox and his friends run a faro bank at Brooks's
1782	(March) North's government resigns. Rockingham prime minister, Shelburne and Fox mutually hostile Secretaries of State. (July) Death of Rockingham. Shelburne succeeds as prime minister, Pitt Chancellor of the Exchequer. Fox resigns
1782–3	Fox lives, first, with 'Perdita' Robinson, then with Mrs Armistead
1783	Fox and North form coalition to defeat Shelburne, and become joint Secretaries of State despite King's opposition. India Bill passes Commons but the King contrives its defeat in the Lords
1784	Pitt, constantly outvoted in the Commons, is however sustained in office until his decisive victory in the spring general election. Fox wins personal triumph in the Westminster poll
1784–9	Fox votes with Pitt on parliamentary reform, proposals to abolish slave trade, and the Netherlands crisis of 1787, but opposes Pitt's Irish Propositions and trade treaty with France, and unsuccessfully attempts repeal of Test and Corporation Acts
1785	The Prince of Wales, misleading and embarrassing Fox, marries Mrs Fitzherbert illegally. Fox gives support over settlement of the Prince's debts
1788–9	Fox's foreign holiday curtailed by news of George III's acute illness and madness. Pitt 'unwhigs' Fox in debates on the Regency Bill
1789	Fox enthusiastically hails storming of the Bastille
1790	Burke's *Reflections on the Revolution in France*

1791	Burke breaks with Fox
1792	Fox stays apart from 'The Friends of the People'
1793	War between France and Britain. Fox's finances rescued by friends
1794	Portland, Fitzwilliam, and other leading Whigs join Pitt's ministry
1792–5	Fox opposes Aliens Act, Seditious Meetings Act, Treasonable Practices Act, and suspension of Habeas Corpus
1795	Fox marries Mrs Armistead
1797–1801	Except on rare occasions, the Whigs absent themselves from parliament
1798	Fox expelled from Privy Council. Rebellion in Ireland
1801	Following the Act of Union, Pitt resigns over the Catholic question. Addington prime minister
1802	Peace of Amiens. Fox and his wife holiday in France; he works there on his history of the reign of James II
1803	War again; Fox opposes its renewal
1804–5	Fox moves towards coalition with the Grenvilles
1805	Battles of Trafalgar and Austerlitz
1806	(January) Death of Pitt. Lord Grenville prime minister; Fox, Foreign Secretary, fails to achieve peace but initiates moves to end slave trade. (September) Death of Fox
1808	Lord Holland publishes Fox's uncompleted history of James II's reign
1828	Repeal of Test and Corporation Acts
1829	Catholic Emancipation
1832	Grey's Whig government abolishes the rotten boroughs
1840	Death of Lord Holland
1842	Death of Elizabeth Fox

NOTES

1. ORIGINS AND BEGINNINGS (pp. 1–12)

1. Clay, 2.
2. *Ibid.*, 15.
3. Evelyn, *Diary* (1827 edn., iii. 58).
4. Clay, 263–5.
5. Ilchester Papers, quoted Clay, 137–8.
6. Clay, 319.
7. Ilchester, HFLH, i. 47–61.
8. *Ibid.*, 106.
9. *Ibid.*, 108.
10. Leinster, i. 227–8.
11. Walpole, GII, ii. 148.
12. Namier, S.P., 228.
13. Leinster, i. 300; Ilchester, HFLH, ii. 61–2.
14. H. Fox, *Memoir*, in Ilchester and Stavordale, i. 72.
15. Leinster, i. 310.
16. *A Tour Through England*, quoted Ilchester, HFLH i. 42.
17. *Ibid.*, 43n.
18. Bedford Corr., ii. 126.
19. Leinster, i. 191.
20. *Ibid.*, 205, 207.

2. A LIBERTARIAN EDUCATION (pp. 13–28)

1. Leinster, i. 194.
2. G. O. Trevelyan, 46.
3. Leinster, i. 336, 343.
4. G. O. Trevelyan, 47.
5. Leinster, i. 166.
6. Quoted Drinkwater, 335–6.
7. Russell, LTCJF, i. 8.
8. Ilchester and Stavordale, i. 114, 119.
9. *Ibid.*, 114.
10. *Ibid.*, 151.
11. *Ibid.*, 151, 155, 163, 190–1.
12. Leinster, i. 235–6.
13. *Ibid.*, 233, 251.
14. Fox, M. and C., i. 136.
15. Leinster, i. 364.
16. *Ibid.*, 384, 386.
17. *Ibid.*, 386.
18. Fox, M. and C., i. 22.
19. *Ibid.*, 23.
20. Ilchester and Stavordale, i. 193–4.
21. G. O. Trevelyan, 63.
22. Fox to Uvedale Price, 24 February 1768.
23. H. M. C., Carlisle.
24. Fox, M. and C., i. 44.
25. *Ibid.*, 41.
26. *Ibid.*, 47.
27. Leinster, i. 538, 542.
28. Namier and Brooke, i. 395–6.
29. Ilchester, HFLH, ii. 313–14.

3. WESTMINSTER AND ALMACK'S (pp. 29–51)

1. Ilchester, HFLH, ii. 327.
2. Fox, Speeches, i. 4–6.
3. *London Magazine*, quoted Ilchester, HFLH, i. 89.
4. Walpole, GIII, iii. 359; Fox, M. and C., i. 51–4.
5. Namier and Brooke, ii. 456.
6. Fox, Speeches, i. 10–14.
7. Russell, LTCJF, i. 33.
8. Jesse, MLRG, ii. 2.

9. Walpole, *Last Journals*, i. 70.
10. *Ibid.*, 81–2.
11. Lascelles, 32.
12. Ilchester, HFLH, ii. 353.
13. *Ibid.*, 354.
14. Namier and Brooke, ii. 466.
15. Jesse, *Selwyn*, i. 5.
16. *Ibid.*, iii. 49.
17. Ilchester, HFLH, ii. 355.
18. Malmesbury, i. 277.
19. Ilchester and Stavordale, i. 269–70.
20. H.M.C., Carlisle, 264–5.
21. *Ibid.*
22. *Ibid.*
23. Jesse, *Selwyn*, i. 21.
24. Transl. Hobhouse, 54–5.
25. Fox, Speeches, i. 18.
26. *Ibid.*, 15.
27. Walpole, *Last Journals*, i. 12.
28. Fortescue, iii. 1398.
29. Fox, Speeches, i. 18.
30. Leinster, ii. 204, 214.
31. H.M.C., Carlisle, 273, 294.
32. *Ibid.*, 280, 288.
33. *Ibid.*, 285.
34. Hampshire Records, quoted Namier and Brooke, ii. 456–7.
35. H.M.C., Carlisle, 506.
36. Bessborough, *Georgiana*, 32.

4. AMERICA, FRANCE, AND IRELAND, 1773–1779 (pp. 52–74)

1. Namier and Brooke, ii. 457.
2. I. R. Christie, *History Today* (1958, 110–18).
3. Fox, Speeches, i. 29.
4. Burke, *Corr.*, iii. 390.
5. *Ibid.*, 384.
6. Fox, M. and C., i. 169–70.
7. Fox, Speeches, i. 37.
8. *Ibid.*, 39, 44.
9. Fox, M. and C., i. 140–1.
10. *Ibid.*, 143.
11. Fox, Speeches, i. 61.

12. Burke, *Corr.*, iii. 380–8.
13. Bessborough, *Georgiana*, 32.
14. Fox, Speeches, i. 99–100.
15. Walpole to Mason, 4 February 1778.
16. Fortescue, iv. 34.
17. *Ibid.*, 2847.
18. Quoted Butterfield, GLNP, 68.
19. Fox, M. and C., i. 182.
20. Parl. Hist., xix. 1322–30.
21. Fortescue, iv. 2223–30.
22. *Ibid.*, 2686, 2756.
23. Parl. Hist., xx. 1120.
24. Fitzpatrick to Ossory, 19 June 1779.
25. Fox, M. and C., i. 228.
26. *Ibid.*, 230–4.
27. Parl. Hist., xx. 1116–28.
28. Ilchester and Stavordale, i. 303n.
29. Butterfield, GLNP, 113.
30. Fox MSS, quoted *ibid.*, 169.
31. Parl. Hist., xx. 1123–8.
32. Butterfield, GLNP, 177 and n.

5. THE PEOPLE AND THE CROWN (pp. 75–85)

1. Butterfield, GLNP, 201.
2. *Ibid.*, 223.
3. *Proceedings*, Wiltshire County Meetings; Butterfield, GLNP, 225.
4. Butterfield, GLNP, 192–3.
5. *General Evening Post*, 10–12 February 1780.
6. Butterfield, GLNP, 275.
7. *Morning Chronicle*, 7 April 1780.
8. Butterfield, GLNP, 322–3.
9. Walpole to Mann, 8 April 1780.
10. Butterfield, GLNP, 328.
11. *Ibid.*, 331.
12. *Ibid.*, 332; Fox, Speeches, i. 258–73.
13. Butterfield, GLNP, 375.
14. Fortescue, v. 95–7.
15. H.M.C., Abergavenny, 33; Burke, *Corr.*, iv. 282–3.

6. BROOKS'S (pp. 86–94)

1. Walpole, *Last Journals*, ii. 349–54.
2. H.M.C., Carlisle, 463.
3. *Ibid.*, 475–86.
4. *Ibid.*, 484.
5. *Ibid.*, 488.
6. *Ibid.*, 488, 496.
7. *Ibid.*, 502, 505.
8. *Ibid.*, 507.
9. *Ibid.*, 511, 567.
10. *Ibid.*, 554.
11. *Ibid.*, 555.
12. *Ibid.*, 554–5.
13. *Ibid.*, 562, 593.
14. Wraxall, ii. 1–3.
15. H.M.C., Carlisle, 537.
16. Walpole to Mann, 13 July 1773.
17. Christie, ENM, 217.
18. Fox, Speeches, i. 398–421.

7. SHELBURNE, FOX, AND NORTH, 1782–1783 (pp. 95–115)

1. Windsor MSS, quoted Christie, ENM, 274.
2. Christie ENM, 283–98.
3. H.M.C., Carlisle, 580.
4. *Ibid.*, 586–608.
5. Walpole, *Last Journals*, ii. 443.
6. Grafton, *Autobiography*, 323; Reid, 146.
7. Fox, Speeches, ii. 75.
8. Fox, M. and C., i. 460–1.
9. Elliot to Lady Elliot, 3 July 1782.
10. Leeds, 66.
11. H.M.C., Carlisle, 555.
12. Ilchester and Stavordale, ii. 20, 25–6.
13. Hobhouse, 165.
14. H.M.C., Carlisle, 450; Ilchester and Stavordale, ii. 23.
15. Quoted Hobhouse, 165.
16. Derry, CJF, 122.
17. Fitzmaurice, ii. 104.
18. Cannon, FNC, 29.
19. Buckingham, i. 76.

20. Fortescue, vi. 3872.
21. Buckingham, i. 148–9; Cannon, FNC, 48n.
22. Fox, Speeches, ii. 122–3.
23. Brooke, 238.
24. Fortescue, vi. 4272.
25. *Ibid.*
26. Fox, M. and C., ii. 28.
27. Cannon, FNC, 82.
28. *Ibid.*, 83.
29. Portland MSS; quoted, Cannon, FNC, 100.
30. Walpole, *Last Journals*, ii. 613–14.
31. Fortescue, vi. 4308.
32. *Ibid.*, 4336.
33. Aspinall, CGPW, i. 116–7.
34. *Ibid.*, 123.
35. Fox, M. and C., ii. 57.
36. Aspinall, CGPW, i. 125–6.
37. *Ibid.*, 127.

8. THE KING FIGHTS BACK (pp. 116–32)

1. Sutherland, 391.
2. Parl. Register, xii. 291.
3. *Ibid.*, 29–55, 122–203.
4. Minto MSS, Cannon, FNC, 112.
5. Fox, M. and C., ii. 219–20.
6. Buckingham, i. 285.
7. Quoted Cannon, FNC, 138.
8. Fortescue, vi. 4546.
9. Fox, M. and C., ii, 224.
10. *Ibid.*
11. Wraxall, iii. 199; Cannon, FNC, 149–151; Ehrman, YP, i. 130.
12. Fox, Speeches, ii. 379.
13. Cannon, FNC, 165.
14. Connell, 148.
15. Aspinall, LCG, i. 26–7; Stanhope, i. Appendix, iv–v.
16. Leeds, 95–7.
17. Stanhope, i. Appendix, vi–viii.
18. Cannon, FNC, 193.
19. Bessborough, 78–9.
20. Chatham to Tomline, 4 February 1821.
21. Brooke, 259.

22. Cannon, FNC, 186.
23. *Ibid.*, 188.
24. Fox, Speeches, ii. 434.
25. Stanhope, i. 198; Appendix, x.
26. Cannon, FNC, 208.

9. THE WESTMINSTER ELECTION OF 1784 (pp. 133–8)

1. H.M.C., Rutland, iii. 134.
2. Cornwallis *Corr.*, i. 106; H.M.C., Rutland, iii. 88.
3. Bessborough, 79.
4. Fox, M. and C., ii. 267–8.
5. Stanhope, i. 213–14.

10. PITT AND FOX, 1784–89 (pp. 139–51)

1. Hobhouse, chap. 15, 2.
2. Lascelles, 174.
3. Quoted Derry, C.J.F., 215.
4. Fox, Speeches, iii. 145–52.
5. Fox, M. and C., ii. 162–97.
6. Fox, Speeches, iii. 54–145.
7. Grattan, iii. 252.
8. Parl. Hist., xxv. 777–8.
9. Quoted Derry, CJF, 232.
10. Fox, Speeches, iii. 273.
11. *Ibid.*, 331–8.
12. *Ibid.*, iv. 89–90.
13. Stanhope, i. 301.
14. Fox, Speeches, iii. 310–17; iv. 3–7.
15. Pitt to Eden, 7 January 1788.

11. FOX AND THE PRINCE OF WALES (pp. 152–65)

1. Aspinall, CGPW, i. 167.
2. *Ibid.*, 155–7.
3. Fox, M. and C., ii. 278–83.
4. *Ibid.*, 284–5.
5. Parl. Hist., xxvi. 1070.
6. Gibbon, *Letters*, iii. 132.
7. Buckingham, i. 433–6; ii. 3.
8. Wraxall, v. 203.

9. Parl. Hist., xxvii. 707.
10. Buckingham, ii. 53–4.
11. Parl. Hist., xxvii. 718–19.
12. Quoted Derry, CJF, 269–70; Fox, M. and C., ii. 299–300.
13. Fox, M. and C., ii. 302.
14. Aspinall, CGPW, i. 490.
15. Derry, RCW, 191.

12. HOW MUCH THE GREATEST EVENT (pp. 166–84)

1. Fox, M. and C., ii. 361.
2. Burke, *Corr.*, vi. 25, 30.
3. Parl. Hist., xxix. 248–9.
4. Portland to Fitzwilliam, 26 April 1791.
5. Fox Papers, quoted O'Gorman, WPFR, 62.
6. Fox, Speeches, iv. 210–36; Parl. Hist., xxix. 364–401.
7. Fox, M. and C., ii. 363.
8. Burke, *Works*, iii. 82–7.
9. Holland, MWP, i. 11.
10. Fox to Fitzwilliam, 16 March 1792.
11. O'Gorman, WPFR, 84 and n.
12. Fox, Speeches, iv. 407–12.
13. O'Gorman, WPFR, 87–90.
14. Malmesbury, ii. 459.
15. Burke, *Corr.*, vii. 191, 218.
16. Fox, M. and C., ii. 368.
17. *Ibid.*, 369.
18. *Ibid.*
19. Gibbon, *Letters*, iii. 308.
20. Fox, M. and C., ii. 374.
21. *Ibid.*, 379–81.
22. Fox, M. and C., iv. 291–2.
23. Fox, Speeches, iv. 446, 451–2.
24. Parl. Hist., xxx. 301–14.
25. O'Gorman, WPFR, 114.
26. *Ibid.*, 135.
27. Fox, M. and C., iii. 57–62.
28. *Ibid.*, 79–80.
29. *Ibid.*, 65–6.
30. *Ibid.*, 71–2.

13. FROM SCHISM TO SECESSION (pp. 185–203)

1. Mackintosh, i. 325.
2. Gibbon, *Letters*, iii. 313, 321.
3. Mitchell, DWP, 259–60.
4. Blair-Adam MSS, quoted O'Gorman, WPFR, 162.
5. Jesse, *Selwyn*, i. 21.
6. Fox, M. and C., ii. 364–5.
7. *Ibid.*, iii. 83–93.
8. *Ibid.*, iii. *passim*.
9. *Ibid.*, 78–9.
10. *Ibid.*, 53, 57, 98.
11. Fox Papers, quoted Reid, 313.
12. Fox, Speeches, iv. 221.
13. Fox Papers, quoted Reid, 314.
14. Burke, *Corr.*, ix. 203, 205, 211.
15. Dickinson, BRFR, 40–1.
16. Dickinson, LP, 255.
17. Fox, M. and C., iii. 123–6; Aspinall, LCG, ii. 419–20, 425–6.
18. Fox, Speeches, iv. 55, 193, 384; v. 116.
19. Fox, M. and C., iii. 131.
20. *Ibid.*, 135–6.
21. Fox, Speeches, vi. 305–19.
22. *Ibid.*, 370; Parl. Hist., xxxiii. 1100.
23. *Annual Register*, 1798; Stanhope, iii. 91.
24. Aspinall, LCG, iii. 18n.
25. *Ibid.*, iii. 59.
26. Holland, MWP, i. 156–7.
27. Fox, Speeches, vi. 420–1.

14. PEACE OF AMIENS, FRENCH VISIT, WAR AGAIN (pp. 204–22)

1. Fox, M. and C., iv. 401.
2. *Ibid.*, 296–440.
3. *Ibid.*, 344–6.
4. Trotter, 9–12.
5. *Ibid.*, 15–16.
6. Fox, M. and C., iii. 324–40.
7. Fox, Speeches, vi. 422–55.
8. Fox, M. and C., iii. 341.
9. Schama, 369–425.
10. Fox, Speeches, vi. 438.

11. Fox, M. and C., iii. 345.
12. *Ibid.*, 329, 367–70.
13. Quoted Lascelles, 297n.
14. Trotter 223.
15. *Ibid.*, 220–5.
16. Quoted Reid, 386.
17. Fox, M. and C., iii. 372.
18. *Ibid.*, 404.
19. *Ibid.*, 407.
20. *Ibid.*, 387.
21. Lascelles, 302.
22. Sheridan, *Letters*, ii. 196.
23. Fox, M. and C., iii. 223.
24. Fox, Speeches, vi. 508.
25. *Ibid.*, 530–8.
26. Fox, M. and C., iv. 84.
27. *Ibid.*, iii. 460.
28. *Ibid.*, iv. 69–74.
29. *Ibid.*, 102.
30. *Ibid.*, iii. 102.
31. Fox, M. and C., ii. 419, 421, 427; iv. 11.
32. *Ibid.*, iii, 449–50.
33. *Ibid.*, 452, 455, 464.
34. *Ibid.*, iv. 121.

15. LAST DAYS OF PITT AND FOX (pp. 223–31)

1. Fox, M. and C., iv. 122.
2. *Ibid.*, 430.
3. Quoted Reid, 409.
4. Stuart, 133–4.
5. Fox, Speeches, vi. 626–31.
6. Mitchell, HH, 56 and n.; Holland, MWP, ii. 53.
7. Holland, MWP, i. 249–50.
8. Jesse, MLRG, iii. 473–4.
9. Twiss, ii. 435.
10. Holland, MWP, ii. 49.
11. Trotter, 425–6.
12. Holland, MWP, i. 268–9.
13. *Ibid.*, 271–3.
14. Farington, i. 12, 72.

15. Lady Holland, ii. 179–81; Holland, MWP, i. 265–73; Trotter, 465–6.
16. Drinkwater, 368–9.

16. LEGACY AND LEGEND (pp. 232–44)

1. *Edinburgh Star*, 14 January 1823.
2. Trevelyan, BH19C, 69.
3. Gash, *Mr Secretary Peel*, 47–8.
4. Ilchester, LHS, 101.
5. Reid, 118.
6. Drinkwater, 162.
7. Parl. Hist., xxiv. 460.
8. Mitchell, HH. 57.
9. Keppel, 256–7.
10. Mitchell, HH, 250.
11. Gibbon to Sheffield, January 1793.
12. Quoted Mitchell, DWP, 261.
13. Trevelyan, LGRB, 29, 107.
14. *Ibid.*, 148.
15. Mitchell, HH, 52–3.
16. Butterfield, WIH, 3–8.
17. *Ibid.*, 29.
18. *Ibid.*, 30–1.
19. Trevelyan, LGRB, 117.
20. Derry, CJF, 438.
21. *Ibid.*

BIBLIOGRAPHY

Albemarle, Duke of, *Memoirs of the Marquis of Rockingham* (2 vols., 1852).

Aspinall, A. (ed.), *Correspondence of George, Prince of Wales* (8 vols, 1963–71) (CGPW).

—— *Later Correspondence of George III* (vols. 1–4, from 1961) (LCG).

Auckland, Lord, *Journal and Correspondence* (4 vols., 1861–2).

Ayling, S., *George the Third* (1972).

—— *Edmund Burke, his Life and Opinions* (1988).

—— *A Portrait of Sheridan* (1985).

Bessborough, Earl of, *Georgiana, Extracts from the Correspondence of the Duchess of Devonshire* (1955).

Brooke, J., *King George III* (1972). See also Namier.

Buckingham, Duke of, *Memoirs of the Courts and Cabinets of George III* (4 vols., 1853–5).

Burke, E., *Correspondence* (gen. ed. T. W. Copeland, 10 vols., 1958–78),

—— *Works* (Bohn edn., 6 vols., 1855–6).

Butterfield, Sir H., *George III, Lord North, and the People* (1949) (GLNP).

—— *George III and the Historians* (1957).

—— *The Whig Interpretation of History* (1931) (WIH).

—— *Charles James Fox and the Whig Opposition, 1792* Hist. Journal (1949).

—— *Charles James Fox and Napoleon: the Peace Negotiations of 1806* (1962).

Cannon, J. A., *Parliamentary Reform, 1640–1832* (1973).

—— *The Fox-North Coalition* (1969) (FNC).

—— *Aristocratic Century: the Peerage of Eighteenth-Century England* (1984).

Christie, I. R., *The End of North's Ministry* (1958) (ENM).

—— *Wilkes, Wyvill, and Reform* (1962).

—— *Myth and Reality in late Eighteenth-Century England* (1970).

—— *Stress and Stability in late Eighteenth-Century Britain* (1984).

Clark, J. C. D., *English Society, 1688–1832* (1985).

—— *Revolution and Rebellion* (1986).

Clay, C., *Public Finance and Private Wealth, the Career of Sir Stephen Fox* (1978).

Cobban, A., *A History of Modern France* (vol. 1, 1957).

—— (ed.) *The Debate on the French Revolution* (1960).

Colchester, Charles Abbot, Lord, *Diary and Correspondence* (3 vols., 1861).

Connell, B., *Portrait of a Whig Peer* (1957).

Creevey Papers (ed. Maxwell, 2 vols, 1904).

Deffand, Marie, Marquise du, *Lettres . . . à Horace Walpole* (3 vols., 1912).

Derry, J. W., *The Regency Crisis and the Whigs* (1963) (RCW).

—— *Charles James Fox* (1972) (CJF).

Devonshire, Duchess of, *Diary* in W. Sichel's *Sheridan* (1909).

Dickinson, H. F., *Liberty and Property . . . in Eighteenth-Century Britain* (1977) (LP).

—— *British Radicalism and the French Revolution* (1985) (BRFR).

Drinkwater, J., *Charles James Fox* (1928).

Ehrman, J., *The Younger Pitt* (vol. 1, *The Years of Acclaim*, 1969, and vol. 2, *The Reluctant Transition*, 1983).

Eyck, E., *Pitt versus Fox, Father and Son* (1950).

Farington, J., *Diaries* (ed. J. Greig, vols. 1–3, 1922–4).

Fitzmaurice, Lord, *William Earl of Shelburne* (2nd edn. 1912).

Foord, A. S., *His Majesty's Opposition, 1714–1830* (1964).

Fortescue, Sir John (ed.), *Correspondence of King George III from 1760 to 1783* (10 vols., 1927–8).

Fonblanque, E. B. de, *Life and Correspondence of John Burgoyne* (1876).

Fox, C. J., *Speeches in the House of Commons* (ed. J. Wright, 6 vols., 1815) (Speeches).

—— *Memorials and Correspondence* (ed. Lord J. Russell, 4 vols., 1853–7) (M. and C.).

—— *A History of the Early Part of the Reign of James the Second* (1808).

George, E., *Fox's Martyrs, the General Election of 1784* (T.R.H.S., xxi, 1937).

George, M. D., *English Political Caricature to 1792* (1959).

Gibbon, E., *Letters* (ed. J. E. Norton, 3 vols., 1956).

Glenbervie, Lord, *Diaries* (ed. F. Bickley, 2 vols, 1928).

Grafton, Duke of, *Autobiography* (ed. W. R. Anson, 1908).

Grattan, H., *Memoirs* (1849).

Hibbert, C., *George IV* (1972).

Historical Manuscripts Commission, Abergavenny MSS, Bathurst MSS, Carlisle MSS, Rutland MSS, Stopford Sackville MSS.

Hobhouse, C., *Fox* (1934).

Holland, Elizabeth, Lady, *Journal* (ed. Ilchester, 2 vols., 1908).

Holland, 3rd Lord, *Memoirs of the Whig Party* (1852–4) (MWP).

—— *Further Memoirs of the Whig Party* (1905) (FMWP).

Hudson, D., *Holland House in Kensington* (1967).

Ilchester, Countess of, and Stavordale, Lord: *Life and Letters of Lady Sarah Lennox* (2 vols., 1901).

Ilchester, Earl of: *Henry Fox, 1st Lord Holland* (2 vols., 1920) (HFLH).

—— (ed.) *Elizabeth, Lady Holland to her Son, 1821–1845* (1946) (LHS).

—— (ed.) *Letters to Henry Fox* (1915).

Jesse, J. H., *George Selwyn and his Contemporaries* (4 vols., 1843–4).

—— *Memoirs of the Life and Reign of George III* (3 vols., 1867) (MLRG).

Keppel, S., *The Sovereign Lady* (1974).

Langford, P., *A Polite and Commercial People, England, 1727–1783* (1989).

Laprade, W. T. (ed.), *The Parliamentary Papers of John Robinson* (1922).

Lascelles, E., *The Life of Charles James Fox* (1936).

Leeds, Duke of, *Political Memoranda* (ed. O. Browning, 1884).

Leinster, Duchess of, *Correspondence* (ed. B. Fitzgerald, 3 vols., 1949–57).

Mackintosh, R. J. (ed.), *Memoirs of the Life of Sir James Mackintosh* (1835).

Malmesbury, Earl of, *Diary and Correspondence* (4 vols., 1844).

Markham, F., *Napoleon* (1963).

Marshall, P. J., *The Impeachment of Warren Hastings* (1965).

Minto, Countess of, *Life and Letters of Sir Gilbert Elliot* (3 vols., 1874).

Mitchell, A., *The Whigs in Opposition, 1815–1830* (1967).

Mitchell, L., *Charles James Fox and the Disintegration of the Whig Party* (1971) (DWP).

—— *Holland House* (1980) (HH).

Namier, Sir L., *The Structure of Politics at the Accession of George III (1929)* (SP).

Namier, Sir L. and Brooke J., *The Commons, 1754–1790* (3 vols., 1964).

O'Gorman, F., *The Whig Party and the French Revolution* (1967) (WPFR).

Paine, T., *The Rights of Man* (2 vols., 1791–2).

Pares, R., *George III and the Politicians* (1953).

Parliamentary History of England (1806–20, vols 16–36).

Parliamentary Register, 1780–1796 (ed. Debrett).

Pellew, G., *Life and Correspondence of Henry Addington, Viscount Sidmouth* (3 vols., 1847).

Postgate, R., *That Devil Wilkes* (1956 ed.).

Reid, L., *Charles James Fox, a Man for the People* (1969).

Rogers, S., *Reminiscences and Table Talk* (ed. A Dyce, 1856).

Rose, G., *Diaries and Correspondence* (ed. L. V. Harcourt, 2 vols., 1860).

Rose, J. H., *William Pitt and the National Revival* (1911).

Rudé, G. F. E., *Wilkes and Liberty* (1962).

Russell, Lord J., *Life and Times of Charles James Fox* (3 vols., 1859–66) (LTCJF).

—— *Bedford Correspondence* (3 vols., 1842–6).

—— *Recollections and Suggestions* (1875).

Sanders, L., *The Holland House Circle* (1908).

Schama, S., *Citizens, a Chronicle of the French Revolution* (1989).

Sheridan, R. B., *Letters* (ed. C. Price, 3 vols., 1966).

Sichel, W., *Sheridan* (2 vols., 1909).

Smith, E. A., *Whig Principles and Party Politics* (1975).

Stanhope, Earl, *Life of William Pitt* (4 vols., 1861–2).

Stirling, A. M. W., *Coke of Norfolk and his Friends* (1912).

Stuart, D. M., *Dearest Bess* (1935).

Sutherland, L. S., *The East India Company in Eighteenth-Century Politics* (1952).

Thal, H. van (ed.), *The Prime Ministers* (vol. 1, 1974).

Trevelyan, G. M., *British History in the Nineteenth Century* (1922) (BH19C).

—— *Lord Grey of the Reform Bill* (1920) (LGRB).

Trevelyan, Sir. G. O., *The Early History of Charles James Fox* (2nd edn., 2 vols., 1880).

Trotter, J. B., *Memoirs of the Latter Years of … Charles James Fox* (1811).

Turberville, A. S. (ed.), *Johnson's England* (2 vols., 1933).

Twiss, H., *Life of Lord Chancellor Eldon* (3 vols, 1844).

Veitch, G. S., *The Genesis of Parliamentary Reform* (1913, 1965).

Walpole, Horace, *Memoirs of George II* (ed. J. Brooke, 3 vols., 1985) (GII).

—— *Memoirs of the Reign of George III* (ed. G. F. R. Barker, 4 vols., 1894) (GIII).

—— *Letters* (various editions).

—— *Last Journals* (ed. F. Steuart, 2 vols., 1910).

Watson, J. S., *The Reign of George III* (1960).

Wilkins, W. H., *Mrs Fitzherbert and George IV* (2 vols., 1905).

Wraxall, Sir N. W., *Historical and Posthumous Memoirs* (ed. H. B. Wheatley, 5 vols., 1884).

Ziegler, P., *Addington* (1965).

Index